HIT 'EM
WHERE IT HURTS

HIT 'EM WHERE IT HURTS

HOW TO SAVE DEMOCRACY BY BEATING

REPUBLICANS AT THEIR OWN GAME

RACHEL BITECOFER

WITH AARON MURPHY

CROWN
NEW YORK

Published in the United States by Crown,
an imprint of the Crown Publishing Group,
a division of Penguin Random House LLC, New York.

CROWN and the Crown colophon
are registered trademarks of Penguin Random House LLC.

Hardback ISBN 978-0-593-72714-0
Ebook ISBN 978-0-593-72715-7

Printed in the United States of America on acid-free paper

crownpublishing.com

2 4 6 8 9 7 5 3 1

First Edition

This book is dedicated to everyone

working to save American democracy.

Contents

Introduction

The Dirtiest Word in America

The book in your hands is about the dirtiest word in America: "politics."

There, I said it. If you can handle that, you and I are gonna get along just fine. Though this book is full of dirty words, it's also a battle-tested self-help book for America's fragile democracy. And our democracy needs all the help it can get. It's in shambles. Most Americans *do* believe politics is a dirty word. A *hundred million* of them don't even bother to vote. Sharing what I've learned about how Americans really think and act is one of the most important things I've ever done.

I wrote this book for all Americans who feel uneasy or downright terrified about the future of our nation. It's meant for curious politicos and seasoned campaign operatives alike. It's for Democratic candidates, party insiders, party outsiders, voters, and *should-be* voters. In other words, if you care as much as I do about America holding its shit together, then *Hit 'Em Where It Hurts* is exactly for you.

I wrote some of this book *before* November 8, 2022—Election Day. But the story begins two years earlier, on Election Day 2020. That day, America showed Donald Trump the door and gave incredibly slim majorities in Congress to Democrats. Despite those critical victories, however, it was not a great night for Team Blue. Down-ballot Democrats across the country got their asses handed to 'em. *If we're losing races we should be winning under the best conditions possible,* I worried that night, *then we're definitely going to lose when history suggests we should lose.* That was the moment I began dreading the 2022 midterms and the Midterm Effect.

Ah, the Midterm Effect—the consistent tendency of Americans to vote against members of whichever political party controls the presidency, the "in party." In a typical midterm election, the in party loses four seats in the U.S. Senate and twenty-six seats in the House. In 2010, amid the rise of the Tea Party movement, Republicans picked up a staggering sixty-three seats in the House.

There have been only a handful of exceptions to the Midterm Effect—most recently in 2002. That was the first midterm after the Supreme Court installed George W. Bush as president following a stupid controversy over Florida's paper ballots. Bush's questionable ascension to the White House, followed by the dot-com recession, meant Democrats were heavily favored to make gains in the midterms. But then the terrorist attacks of September 11 happened, washing out domestic worries and invoking an extended "rally around the flag" effect for Bush and Republicans in Congress. In 2002 voters weren't concerned with the president's lackluster performance or the lingering controversy surrounding his election. That year, a *national crisis* overshadowed our pattern of punishing the party in power.

Heading into the 2022 election, with Joe Biden as president and Democrats in control, barely, of both chambers of Congress, the Midterm Effect suggested—no, *insisted*—that Democrats would get slaughtered again. Republicans know the Midterm Effect works too, which is why they predicted a "Red Tsunami" that year. Some in the GOP predicted they'd win more seats in the House than they did in 2010.

I wasn't just worried about control of Congress. In the aftermath of 2020, I could not see a clear path to victory for Democratic candidates running to become or stay governors of three key presidential swing states in 2022. Given the shenanigans of Republicans who lied about and refused to accept the results of a free and fair election in 2020, it was essential for Democrats to win the so-called Blue Wall of governorships in Pennsylvania, Wisconsin, and Michigan in order to guarantee a free and fair 2024 presidential election.

We never saw a Red Tsunami in 2022. Not even a Red Wave. What ended up washing ashore was a little red puddle, barely enough to flip control of the House of Representatives to Republicans, even though they needed to net only five seats to do so. Democrats actually gained a seat in the Senate, picked up several governorships, and won all three of the Blue Wall states. We didn't just defeat conventional wisdom; we knocked it on its ass!

So what happened? We lifted a page from the GOP's playbook. *Negative partisanship* happened. And neither by luck nor by accident, it worked.

A NEW NATIONAL CRISIS

For the two years leading up to Election Day 2022, I made it my mission to convince as many Democrats as I could that the Midterm Effect

1. is real and not just a plot invented by analysts to suppress our party's turnout;
2. was coming right at Democrats in 2022, with momentum and without mercy; and
3. demanded that we develop an electoral strategy to directly deal with it head-on to survive Election Day 2022.

I had a hard time getting anyone to listen until late 2021, after the "blue" state of Virginia flipped red. One year after every presidential election, voters in the Old Dominion elect a new governor. As with the midterms, voters in Virginia usually reject the in party by electing a governor from the opposite party. And 2021 was no exception. Virginia voters elected Republican Glenn Youngkin governor.

Without a strategy designed specifically to disrupt the Midterm Effect, 2022 is gonna be the fuckin' Red Wedding for Democrats, I warned. I urged our party to restructure its paid advertising and campaign messaging as a referendum on the Republicans. *Voters need to believe this election is a choice for America as we confront a new national crisis: the Republican Party—the most dangerous threat to our freedom, health, wealth, and safety.*

You will hear me say this again because it's one of the most important things I can say: *The GOP is a threat to your freedom, health, wealth, and safety. If they gain control of the federal government they plan on passing a national abortion ban, gutting Medicare, destroying Obamacare, raising taxes on working families, and stealing a lifetime of YOUR Social Security money.*

This true statement is an example of negative partisanship, a concept that draws on powerful emotions like the fear, threat, and distrust that voters feel for the other political party. When your party doesn't hold political power, these negative emotions run especially hot. Conversely, members of the party in power tend to be less excited and less motivated to spend time, energy, and money on change. Our main challenge for 2022 was to tap into negative partisanship and convince Democrats that despite our status as the in party we could not afford to sit this one out; that we must fear the very real threats from the Republican Party. We didn't exaggerate or hyperbolize anything, by the way. Given the batshit craziness of today's GOP, we didn't need to! Everything I just said about the Republican Party's plans for America is true, and it's not even the worst of their goals.

I knew we had to make sure voters everywhere heard about and talked about how extreme modern Republicans have become. Every day the news cycle spent time on Republican corruption, insurrection, or the extreme agenda of MAGA wackadoos was a day that disrupted the Midterm Effect and helped Democrats in 2022.

Democrats also got a little organic help. The tightly organized, televised January 6 Committee hearings reminded voters over and over that today's Republican Party is willing to resort to violence, lies, and disorder to overturn the will of American voters. Then we learned that the former president took boxes of *our* highly classified state secrets to his unsecured resort in Florida and hid them from the FBI.

But the real game changer happened on May 2, 2022. That evening, *Politico* published a leaked draft of the Supreme Court's *Dobbs v. Jackson Women's Health Organization* decision. The Republican-appointed, conservative Supreme Court was about to overturn *Roe v. Wade*. News of the decision, decades in the making, tore across the country in a matter of minutes. It grabbed the attention of even the most politically tuned out among us and crystallized what I had been arguing all along. Suddenly MAGA wasn't just a logo on silly red hats at NASCAR races; it was tangible evidence that Republicans had successfully taken away freedom of health autonomy for tens of millions of Americans. And they were just getting started.

The evisceration of that fundamental right, which American women had claimed for half a century, went from an abstract threat to a concrete reality in a single moment. It was exactly what I, and other folks loosely working on "Team Reform" inside the Democratic Party, had argued must be the central message of 2022: *Republicanism itself is a national crisis.*

I saw two different campaign strategies play out among Democratic candidates across the country in 2022. The first strategy followed the rules of our old playbook: pretend your candidate isn't really a Democrat by de-emphasizing his party affiliation, elevate his leadership record and his noble biographical traits, and try your damnedest to get Republicans to cross over and vote for him. As we'll discover, this strategy is familiar to old-school Democratic campaign consultants who make piles of money, but it's no longer a winning strategy in our current political climate because of key changes in voter behavior as our politics have become polarized.

But most important, this strategy does nothing to disrupt the Midterm Effect, which is why it met with epic failure in the previous two midterms Democrats had faced as the party in power: 2010 and 2014.

In 2022, Democrats in Ohio, North Carolina, and Florida stuck with old strategy, and now we're living with the consequences: good Democratic candidates lost winnable races to dangerous Republican ones. Many of those Democrats relied on a strategy that distanced themselves from the Democratic Party, the party that built middle-class America, because they were told that their association with the Democratic Party's brand would turn off swing voters.

Let me be clear: Not only is this "apologetic Democrat" model doomed to fail in our hyperpartisan political climate; it actually *harms* our candidates. Following the "apologetic Democrat" model only reaffirms the Republican Party's main argument against us—that there's something wrong with being a Democrat! If Republicans claim Democrats are bad, and if Democrats agree with them, then our message to swing voters is the same as the Republican Party's message about Democrats: *Democrats are a bad product.* We need to be telling voters how and why Democrats are good—*quite* good—especially for America's beleaguered middle class, and contrasting ourselves with the Republican Party's dismal record. In today's two-party system, in which Republicans are barreling toward fascism and authoritarianism, there is *nothing* wrong with being a Democrat. In fact, we're the only sane game left in town.

The second strategy—one I'm advocating all Democrats embrace—abandons our old and familiar playbook. The second strategy, which Democrats in Michigan and Arizona used with stunning effect in 2022, is about being a brand ambassador for freedom, health, wealth, safety, and common sense. In order to do that, you have to make a clear, compelling case about why today's Republican Party is so dangerous. This requires much stronger and smarter political messaging. It demands that we focus less on identity politics and intellectual debates, and more on meeting Republicans on their pitch.

Democrats in this camp leaned hard into the decision to overturn *Roe v. Wade* and built their campaigns around the threat to American democracy. They seized the opportunity to reinforce the message that Election Day must be a referendum on the Republican Party. And they won. Turns out, fighting fire with fire *works.*

A WELL-PLANNED MIRACLE

The lack of enthusiasm that usually plagues the in party in a Midterm Election suddenly evaporated after the Supreme Court's *Dobbs* decision. Democrats, for once, had a powerful *wedge issue* that forced Republicans to play defense. For months, that's exactly what conservatives and Republican candidates had to do. They tried to change the topic.

"This election isn't about ending the right of women to make decisions about their own bodies," they pleaded. "It's about the high cost of your groceries! It's the economy, stupid! It's about rising crime! It's about trick-or-treaters getting candy laced with Mexican fentanyl!" Sure, those are all potent campaign messages, and some of them are even real issues, but voters—many of them, anyway—didn't buy it. For the first time in recent memory, Democratic messaging in 2022 gave voters bigger things to worry about.

Still, the GOP believed the Midterm Effect would deliver huge Republican majorities in Congress and in state capitols across the country. So did plenty of Democratic insiders—let's call them Team Status Quo—who were openly wringing their hands over Team Reform's emphasis on the existential threat to democracy instead of playing defense against the GOP's preferred messaging on inflation and crime.

In the end Democrats beat back the Midterm Effect thanks to negative partisanship, and certainly not by accident. We didn't luck out, dodge a bullet, or stumble our way to victory. No, we were aware of predestined results, and we worked our asses off to beat them back. What Democrats did in 2022 was a well-planned, carefully executed strategic lift, and we pulled off a miracle to give democracy a fighting chance in 2024.

In order to keep saving our democracy, Democrats need to do it again in 2024, and again in 2026. We also have to reinvent the way we communicate with voters—*messaging*—which this book explores at length. We've got to shitcan our erudite explanations and factual proof points and instead *personalize* what it means to live under the control of Republicans.

Today's GOP wants to strip women of their bodily autonomy and empower rapists to force births on their victims. They want to end free and fair elections, ban books, and pass anti-freedom cultural and religious laws better suited for oppressive theocracies like Iran. If you consider yourself middle class, they believe you ought to pay higher taxes. If you rely on Social Security or Medicare, today's Republican leaders want to leave you high and dry. *That's* how we need to frame the stakes.

And as draconian as all this sounds, it's all true! And if you don't believe it's true, it's because the GOP's own messaging works so damn well.

Democrats have to get their heads out of the clouds and go for gut punches the way Republicans do; we've got to make the abstract concrete, as Republicans do. We must show voters that today's GOP has veered far, far off track from the old-fashioned platforms of fiscal conservatism, small government, and strong national security. We must brand Republicans as a bad product, as Republicans do to Democrats.

We also need to accept what we Democrats have utterly failed to understand in the past: that most of the American electorate is neither informed nor engaged when it comes to politics. Most Americans are completely, happily, and intentionally unaware of the Republican Party's MAGA agenda because they don't follow the news. If we want voters to know what Republicans are really up to, it falls on *us* to tell the story. We must connect the dots for voters who don't connect dots on their own. So instead of saying, "This Republican candidate says dumb things, has a history of lying, and he's friends with Donald Trump," we should be saying, "This candidate wants to control your life with crazy beliefs that will rob you of your freedom, give your tax money to billionaires, then force you to work till you die!"

The overturning of *Roe v. Wade* flipped a switch and gave Democrats momentum and clarity, but we can take nothing for granted. Until the Republican Party gets its own shit together, America will always be just one Election Day away from fascism. And that's why I wrote this book.

I call out dummies and their dumb ideas. I don't put up with fascists, racists, liars, or political leaders who advocate for authoritarianism, especially the silent enablers. I tell people what they need to hear, not what they want to hear, even when they don't want to hear it. Over the past decade I've watched America slide from democratic instability into a full-fledged democratic crisis. Even with the electoral successes of 2022 and 2023, America's democracy is out of time for Band-Aids and security blankets. It's on life support, and it needs our full, immediate attention.

My job as a political science professor, data analyst, elections forecaster, pollster, media commentator, and now strategist is to understand the trends, behaviors, and civic culture of the American electorate. I've learned a whole lot about our nation's brilliant and messy system of government, about the voters who shape it, the politicians who lead it, and the millions upon millions of ordinary people who ignore it. I've used political science fundamentals and a new theory about voter behavior to predict election outcomes. I'm the foulmouthed grown-up in the room, here to make you take your medicine. And why do I do this? Because I must if we are going to survive our democratic crisis.

And because you're reading this, you probably think so too.

Or maybe you have no idea what all the fuss is about. Maybe you're wondering why so many people don't give a crap about politics. Maybe you run a political party or a well-intentioned nonprofit organization that seems to be stuck in the mud. Maybe you need a primer on what it's going to take to steer this clunker of a ship around the iceberg ahead.

In football, they say a good offense starts with a good defense. In American-style politics, it's the exact opposite. If you're defending, you're losing. The party with the ball gets to score, and as of the writing of this book that party is usually the Republicans. Why? Why is the Grand Old Party always a step or three ahead of Democrats when it comes to shaping public opinion, crafting effective messages, and driving the narrative? How does a party full of bozos, blowhards, and grifters keep running the ball down the field with an agenda that overtly threatens the freedom, health, wealth, and safety of every person who lives in this country? And most important of all, why the hell do swing voters keep falling for it?

This book is my attempt to provide some illumination and to light the way for a bold new strategy. This strategy has a simple endgame: saving our democracy by winning elections and by beating Republicans at their own game. And it starts by sharing some hard lessons political scientists already know about the American electorate.

PART I

ROUGH CLAY

Democracy is the theory that the common people know

what they want, and deserve to get it good and hard.

—H. L. MENCKEN,

A Little Book in C Major, 1916

1

Democracy on Its Deathbed

How many times have you heard a politician or a political pundit say something to the effect of "the American people are too smart for that"?

If you watch the Sunday news shows, or any cable news for that matter, you've heard it many times. The only problem is, it's not true. Sure, Americans are plenty smart. Like most developed nations, our nation is home to a highly educated population with ample access to the calories and high standards of living that are the hallmarks of modern civilizations. But overall intelligence is not the same as civic intelligence. A space genius can build a rocket that can land upright on its launchpad without knowing a damn thing about how his own government works while your HR manager may well be able to explain the intricacies of presidential primaries around the office coffeepot.

What separates these folks isn't IQ or what they study in school. What marks them distinct from each other is *interest*. To illustrate this, think of something you like a lot. It can be anything: sports, Hollywood, cooking, fashion. Whatever it is, your interests and passions are an important driving force that builds and strengthens your working knowledge, and I bet you know a lot about it. Sports fans can list half the roster of every major-league team in the country. Football fans can still recount the ins and outs of Deflategate. Now think of something that doesn't interest you at all. If you could care less about, say, country music, you probably know very little about it and can't name very many people involved in the country music world.

See the knowledge gap between the things you're interested in and the things you aren't? Now consider America's current political landscape. If you're an average American, politics isn't your jam, which means you don't fill your precious time following, worrying about, or even understanding political events.

Because you're reading this book, you likely have more interest in politics than the average American (*much* more), so it's important to accept this fact right off the top: The average working political knowledge of the average American voter sucks.

Sound harsh? Well, I'm being generous. When behavioral research first emerged in the field of political science in the 1950s, it uncovered some stunning findings. For the first time ever, political scientists quantified that the average American knew next to nothing about politics and government. *But don't worry,* these political scientists asserted, *because in our unique two-party system Americans don't need to know much to adequately fulfill their democratic obligations. They can simply use a candidate's party identification as a heuristic* (a shortcut) *to quickly figure out which candidate to vote for—no mental commitment needed!*

In fact, the American Political Science Association published a report way back in 1950 arguing that it would be really great if America had two "responsible" parties with clearly discernible platforms, programs, and ideologies so that lesser-informed Americans could make even better use of the party heuristic when deciding whom to vote for.

This is why you should always be careful what you wish for.

If we're going to understand why the Democrats' traditional electioneering efforts come up short, which we soon will, look no further than our inability to accept that the American voter is, at best, *rough clay.* Some of the most important works of art started out that way. We can work with rough clay. We can soften it, mold it, change it. Republicans have long understood this and have built an electioneering system that shapes the electorate and meets voters where they actually are.

Much of the Democrats' system does not do this. Many of the Democratic Party's leaders wrongly assume that American voters know their civics and engage in politics, which results in an electioneering strategy aimed at selling a product few want to buy or have interest in. In my line of work as an analyst, I often hear, "But everyone already knows [insert political fact]!" No, no, they don't. And we're gonna spend the next few pages proving it.

First, consider this: The nonpartisan Annenberg Public Policy Center regularly measures what Americans know about politics in its annual Constitution Day Civics Survey. In September 2022, Annenberg researchers found that less than half of the 1,113 Americans they surveyed, only 47 percent, could name (not explain, *name!*) all three branches of the U.S. government. And that's an improvement from the recent past. Back in 2006, only 33 percent could name all three branches. Asked to name any of the five rights guaranteed in the First Amendment of the U.S. Constitution, 37 percent of those surveyed by Annenberg couldn't name a single one.

Another respected nonpartisan research organization, the Pew Research Center, found that not long after John Roberts cast the Supreme Court's deciding vote to uphold Obamacare in 2012, only 39 percent of the thousand-plus Americans surveyed could even identify him as chief justice. And a 2020 survey by New York's Stony Brook University suggests up to 80 percent of Americans follow politics only "casually or not at all."

These are lights-and-sirens warnings about the state of America's democracy. Our political system is sick and barely wheezing by on life support.

Healthy democracies around the world are defined by values like equal treatment under the law, widespread access to voting and fair elections, the acceptance of majority rule, and the tolerance of nonviolent dissenters and opposition parties. Citizens in healthy democracies vote consistently and regularly because they understand the consequences of low participation. They know that if they stop being part of their own democracy, tyranny will fill the void. They understand that *democracy is fragile, a lesson World War II taught Europe well.*

Many Americans, however, don't understand that fragility—or have forgotten it. We take our democracy for granted and have, until recently, been lucky enough to live in a country so stable and well run that most of its citizens can completely ignore the government and the people who run it. You cannot ignore the government in authoritarian regimes like Iran or Russia because it's up your ass every day.

If you do happen to follow the day-to-day work of Congress—if you know the who's who of the political world, its winners and the losers, who's up for reelection—then you may find it difficult to understand the civic behavior and political opinions of average Americans who don't follow politics closely at all. Many Americans wake up, maybe scan some quick headlines, work all day, attend school band concerts or ball games, catch a show on Netflix, chill if they're lucky, then go to bed without a single thought about whatever happened in Congress or at the White House.

So what are normal Americans interested in, if not politics and government? If you really want to understand modern Americans and their interests, turn to their aggregated search data, which is always illuminating. Google's five most searched topics in America in all of 2022 were

1. Wordle;
2. election results, because 2022, after all, was a big election year;
3. Betty White, who died just days before her hundredth birthday;
4. Queen Elizabeth, whose death at ninety-six ended the longest reign of any British monarch; and
5. Bob Saget, the *Full House* star who died unexpectedly.

Well, what about the news? Everyone cares about news, even if it's not political news, right? So let's narrow our focus a bit. Google's five most searched *news stories* in America in all of 2022 were

1. election results;
2. Queen Elizabeth's passing;
3. Ukraine;
4. Powerball numbers; and
5. Hurricane Ian.

Wait, wait, wait. Election results make sense, but what about the Republican Party's historic repeal of *Roe v. Wade* in June 2022, ending *half a century* of constitutionally protected reproductive rights for women? Surely Americans googled *that* news, right? Here's where the repeal of *Roe v. Wade* landed on Google's list of top news searches in 2022:

6. monkeypox;
7. Texas school shooting (the assault-weapon massacre of nineteen children and two teachers in Uvalde);
8. Will Smith Oscars, for his infamous, live-TV slap of Chris Rock;
9. Johnny Depp verdict, in his defamation lawsuit against his ex-wife Amber Heard; and
10. *Roe v. Wade*. Ah, there it is!

Yep, Americans were more interested in the Johnny-and-Amber trial, and their own unlucky Powerball numbers, than millions of women losing their right to autonomy over their own bodies, at least according to Google. Now have I convinced you that ordinary Americans don't really know—and don't care to know—much about politicians and our government? The data don't lie.

Americans have also been cultured to *not give a shit* about our government or our elected leaders. We've somehow made it okay to *loathe* politics in America. Half or more of eligible voters sit out our most consequential elections. Tens of millions of Americans admit they just don't care, or believe that "both parties are corrupt," or, worse, that their participation won't make a difference, even as American politics has become a round-the-clock blood sport.

The toughest nut to crack in restoring the health of our democracy is *to convince voters that our democracy will fail without their active, competent participation.*

A "FUNDAMENTAL LACK OF INTEREST"

You probably have a friend who's ashamed to admit that she skipped her Peloton workout but she has no shame in telling you that she doesn't vote. In fact, for her, not voting is a point of pride. She is among the majority of Americans who don't vote at all. In 2022, 53.4 percent of eligible voters in America—nearly *128 million* qualified citizens—did not vote in the 2022 midterms that decided which party would control each chamber of Congress. This is America's true majority.

You might be tempted to think our low turnout rates are a product of voter suppression laws, but you'd be wrong. The main driver of low turnout is low interest. In the summer of 2019, the nonpartisan John S. and James L. Knight Foundation conducted a massive survey of more than twelve thousand nonvoters from across the nation to better understand why so many Americans just don't vote. Who are they? Why do they refuse to take part in their own government? What's important to them, if not voting or politics? The Knight Foundation's 100 Million Project uncovered some fascinating truths about our civic culture.

"[Nonvoters] come from all walks of life and every strata of society, and are fairly divided in their party, policy and candidate preferences," the research concluded. "Americans with a pattern of chronic nonvoting report lower belief in the efficacy of the election system, lower engagement with news and information about politics, and somewhat lower civic engagement and life satisfaction."

As for why?

"Many non-voters cite a fundamental lack of interest in politics as their rationale for not participating in elections," the Knight Foundation learned. A plurality of respondents, 29 percent, said they just don't care and probably won't care in the future. Fifteen percent said they don't know. Thirteen percent believe their individual votes wouldn't matter even if they did bother to vote. Other less-cited reasons for not voting: too complicated, no time, "I keep forgetting to register," and even "to avoid jury duty"—another civic duty. And then there are even people who don't vote as a matter of protest because they didn't get the presidential candidate they wanted, or because they think it helps legitimize past wrongs, or because they just really love virtue signaling.

Our embarrassingly low voting rate is not due to a lack of access to voting, though that's becoming an increasingly worrisome problem. And it's not just poor, undereducated Americans in underserved communities who don't vote. More than 100 million Americans—roughly equivalent to the populations of the United Kingdom, Ireland, and all of Scandinavia combined—don't ever vote because *they just don't give a shit,* or because they aren't convinced that voting matters. These Americans don't vote because we have failed to establish a healthy civic culture, one that makes democratic maintenance a point of pride, one strong enough to overcome crippling cynicism. And that's why "politics" is the dirtiest word in America.

What about countries that require all eligible citizens to vote? There are twenty such nations (twenty-one if you count North Korea, which claims to be a democracy but isn't). Australia has had compulsory voting since 1924 and enjoys one of the highest voter turnouts in the world—hovering around 90 percent in recent elections. Australia even fines citizens who fail to vote. But democracies with compulsory voting don't have extremely high voting rates because citizens fear fines. Sure, that's a factor. But the main reason voting rates are so high in these countries is that their political systems are designed to make it easy for citizens to fulfill their legal obligation to vote. Australia holds elections on Saturdays and allows voters to cast ballots at any polling location across the country. Australian citizens are small-s socialized to value the importance of voting as a basic component of democratic maintenance.

Even in the American states where it's easiest to cast ballots, it is still infinitely more difficult than our democratic peer countries. Now the infrastructure needed to help Americans fulfill their obligation to vote is either crumbling around us, as in New York, or Republicans are weaponizing that obligation against us, as in states like Arizona, Texas, Florida, and Georgia.

THE WEAPONIZATION OF VOTING ACCESS

Some blue states like Oregon, Washington, California, and Colorado have made voting easier. *Much* easier. In Oregon, voters are automatically registered to vote when they obtain a state ID; then they receive ballots in the mail every subsequent election. All an Oregon voter has to do is fill out that ballot, pop it in the enclosed envelope, and make sure it gets back to the elections office by the Election Day deadline. These institutional innovations have affected both overall turnout and turnout of marginalized voter groups, but not as much as you might expect. Meanwhile, red states are doing just the opposite.

Republican leaders know they can restrict turnout by making institutional access to voting more difficult; they know institutional design and voter turnout rates are highly correlated. You can win elections by being more popular than your opponent, or you can win them by preemptively shaping the voter pool in your favor—by changing the voting system to make it easier for your supporters to vote or more difficult for your opponents' voters. This is why we've seen unprecedented efforts by Republican lawmakers in recent years to restrict voting access.

The Brennan Center for Justice, a nonpartisan law and policy institute within the New York University School of Law, closely tracks all state legislation designed to expand or restrict voting access. In 2021, a year that began with a violent, Republican Party–approved attempt to overthrow the U.S. government, state lawmakers in forty-nine states—most of them Republicans—introduced more than 440 bills that make voting more difficult. The Brennan Center reports at least 34 of those bills, in nineteen states, became law in 2021 and calls the numbers "extraordinary":

State legislatures enacted far more restrictive voting laws in 2021 than in any year since the Brennan Center began tracking voting legislation in 2011. More than a third of all restrictive voting laws enacted since then were passed this year. And in a new trend this year, legislators introduced bills to allow partisan actors [such as secretaries of state and governors] to interfere with election processes or even reject election results entirely.

The Republican Party claims its reasons for making voting more difficult is to preserve the *integrity* of American elections—at least in red states and in swing states they believe *should be* red. But just why are Republicans so keen on manipulating election laws to limit access or ease of voting?

Two reasons. First, there's a party-wide belief among Republicans that more voters in an election hurts them electorally (though the conservative journal *National Affairs* claims "there is no evidence that turnout is correlated with partisan vote choice"). Second, the relationship between state election laws and voter turnout is clear: When the act of voting is made easy and convenient, more people will vote. Conversely, when Republican lawmakers make it more difficult to vote, fewer people will—apparently assuaging the GOP's fear that more voter participation hurts their chances of winning.

In the 2022 general election, the average turnout in the United States was 46.6 percent. However, states on the Brennan Center's "most restrictive voting systems" list fell well below that average. Turnout was just 42.5 percent in Texas, where, prior to Election Day, the Republican-controlled legislature limited access to ballot drop boxes, ended twenty-four-hour drive-through voting, and made it illegal to help voters return their absentee ballots (so-called ballot harvesting). States with the most accessible voting systems, like Oregon and Colorado, both of which use mail voting, significantly exceeded the national turnout average. Oregon saw a 62.4 percent turnout in 2022, and Colorado clocked in at 58.5 percent—and did so without even being on the national "swing state" list. Colorado's turnout has increased by nearly 7 percent in the decade since the Centennial State instituted mail voting.

In states where Republican legislatures make the laws, however, the weaponization of voting access is glaringly obvious. Georgia made it a crime for volunteers to hand out *water* to people waiting in long lines to vote, long lines they devised to suppress Black voter turnout. The Republican Party's war on democracy is especially devastating when it comes to disenfranchising voters of color.

Independent research compiled by the Brennan Center shows us that laws requiring certain IDs to vote disproportionately sideline Black and Latino voters from participating in elections. When Florida, Texas, and Georgia restricted voting on Sundays, Black voters (many of them churchgoers who traditionally took part in church-led get-out-the-vote events following Sunday services) were affected most. Voters of color also regularly face longer lines on Election Day due to factors like the recent consolidation of polling places, which in turn makes transportation and finding childcare more difficult. If you find yourself in a seven-hour line to vote in Georgia, you'd better have brought your own water.

U.S. law may treat voting as a right, but the institutional constraints placed on voters, particularly in red states (and even some blue states like New York, which has been slow to modernize its electoral system), ensure that our right to vote very much remains a *privilege*.

MORE VOTERS . . . AND GROWING PAINS

Speaking of privilege, for most of America's history, our political system was the exclusive domain of white, wealthy, mostly Christian, educated men. The transition of our system in recent decades to a more inclusive, multiracial, pluralistic democracy has come with some growing pains. A *whole hell of a lot* of growing pains, actually, and we can measure them via the resulting expansions of the American electorate.

The end of the Civil War brought the franchise of voting to Black men, at least in spirit. The Nineteenth Amendment added women to the national voter pool starting in 1920. Then came the Voting Rights Act of 1965, which increased Black voter participation dramatically. In Mississippi, turnout among Black voters went from just 6.7 percent in

1964 to nearly 60 percent in the 1968 cycle. A few years later, in July 1971, we adopted the Twenty-sixth Amendment to the Constitution, giving all adult citizens eighteen and older the right to vote.

But counterintuitively, as America's political system opened up to tens of millions more eligible voters, overall turnout rates in our elections went down. Why? A big part of the answer is something political scientists call "political socialization"—the process by which people form their political and civic attitudes. The key source of political socialization is your family, particularly your parents.

The late Christopher Joyner, a political researcher who founded Georgetown University's Institute for International Law and Politics, concluded decades ago that "parents are the most significant factor in determining a child's party affiliation," which "begins early in life, perhaps between the ages of seven or eight." This explains why most children of Democrats mostly stay Democrats as they get older, and most children of Republicans stay Republicans. But the most important socialization these folks received from their parents wasn't loyalty to one of America's two major political parties. No, the most important socialization that occurs is *the act of voting* itself.

If you were lucky enough to learn from your parents at a young age that voting and political participation are key to sustaining the health of our political system, congratulations! You hit the civics jackpot. You probably understand the essential duty to vote and that you shouldn't take it for granted. You probably trust that your vote will be fairly counted. You know your vote is your way of allowing others to represent your best interests by enacting and enforcing laws. And if your candidate loses, unless you voted for Donald Trump or Kari Lake, you probably accept that the collective decision by a majority of your fellow voters outweighs your individual choice.

Whenever I give a lecture or a speech, I always ask, "How many of you had parents who regularly voted?" Just as I expect, every single person in the room—who is voluntarily learning more about civics—raises a hand. "The reason you're sitting in this room today," I tell them, "the reason you have enough interest in politics that you've at least come here to engage with me—is that your parents *socialized* you into civic participation." And if that socialization process doesn't happen from adults to their children, one of the only other things that intervenes is higher education. That's why college-educated voters are disproportionately represented in the American electorate.

Now, understand that many millions of Americans aren't as lucky. For those who weren't exposed at an early age to the importance of civic participation, politics doesn't seem accessible or trustworthy. If your parents never voted, there's a good chance *their* parents never voted—not because they didn't care about politics, but because maybe nobody told them that they should vote, or that they can vote, or that they have a right and an obligation to vote. Though the Fifteenth Amendment technically gave Black Americans the right to vote in 1870, that right wasn't enforced until the passage of the Voting Rights Act nearly a century later. Today, to many eligible voters in America, our political system doesn't seem designed *for* them. After all, it wasn't!

Opening up a political system to everyone is never an easy change. Dudes who once got the whole pie found themselves having to share it with their wives. In terms of its institutional advantages, white male hegemony has been severely challenged by a truly democratic America.

Wah, wah, poor white dudes, I just heard you mutter.

Look, I get it. But this enormous shift in America's power structure—the slow end of white male dominance, which we lived under for centuries—is key to understanding WTF happened to democracy in America (and to other western democracies, like the United Kingdom with Brexit and the 2022 election of a far-right nationalist in Italy).

Of course, vigorous participation is critical to a vigorous democracy, but when it finally started happening in America, the chickens of our inept civic society came home to roost. That's because as our political system was forced to reckon with an ever-widening heterogeneity of views and identities, political decision-making became more complex, combative, and *continuous.*

THE PERMANENT CAMPAIGN

Of course, there are other factors that have contributed to the flatlining health of America's democracy. Over the decades, media corporations have been forced to squeeze every ounce of profit out of their news programming. Social media gave rise to the abundance of online information (and disinformation) that, thanks to a strictly interpreted First Amendment, allows lies and conspiracy theories to flourish. Put all that together and America really is the Wild West of elections.

Not too long ago, those of us who pay attention to politics for a living followed two separate political conditions: (1) election-year electoral politics (when we focused on candidates and their campaigns), and (2) at least one year of governing and policymaking (when we focused more on politicians and their official responsibilities). Those two systems have been replaced by a now inseparable system known among political scientists as the *permanent campaign*. We live in a civic society that no longer differentiates between electioneering and governing and policymaking, and, man, is it exhausting.

Other democracies around the world enjoy robust freedom of speech. But for the most part, those nations balance free speech with community standards in order to maintain healthy and fair political debate. Some of those countries limit elections to a matter of weeks and not months or years. Some (Canada, Poland, and South Korea) limit campaign spending and even publicly finance campaigns. Some (South Africa, Belgium, and France) limit political advertising delivery options, and some (Canada, Mexico, and France) limit the length of time political ads can air. Israel limits ad content, and Italy and Japan even ban "negative" advertising outright. There's no political advertising at all in Switzerland, and both Denmark and Finland have reached voluntary consensus not to use political ads. That these three countries dominate the list of happiest countries in the world can't be coincidental!

The United States has relatively few election system guardrails, and this creates a political environment where nearly anything goes. We Americans celebrate our free speech as absolute. Even *hate speech* is robustly protected. Our nation's highest court has even defined money as free speech. Year-round campaign coverage churns out handsome profits for the news media, and that only incentivizes more spending. All this means our political discourse isn't just jacked up on steroids. It's a heart constantly pumping under so much weight and pressure that it's about to burst.

A political climate so consumed by electioneering that we call it a permanent campaign, where free speech and money are basically un-limited, is exactly the kind of environment where authoritarianism and fascism find purchase because such an environment is conducive to the spread of lies, disinformation, and propaganda. Once that happens, these things dominate our civic discourse. Our current political system allows honest public servants to be castigated over fake, or at least greatly exploited, scandals. It rewards zealots and dingbats seeking fame and fortune, like Marjorie Taylor Greene, who could care less about you or me or the future of America or our noble experiment in democracy—not when there's money, power, and notoriety to be had!

Scariest of all, under these conditions and with enough repetition, ridiculous claims from ridiculous people become truths—at least to those who have been conditioned to believe them. And today, the Re-publican Party is standing over democracy's deathbed, ready to pull the plug. Republicans are already hijacking your freedom so they can turn America into a rogue nation, making you sicker, poorer, and less secure as they do. This will become our permanent future unless we band to-gether to fight it at every level.

Our democracy may be fragile and sick, but the good news is it's fix-able. Its full recovery starts with hard-to-swallow medicine. It requires an honest look at where we are and how we got here. It involves a close examination of how the Republican Party plays the game, and how they win. And it ends with clarity on how we can play a better game, and how we can win democracy back for all of America.

2

Partisanship Is a Helluva Drug

In his famous farewell address, America's first president warned that political parties are the mechanisms "by which cunning, ambitious, and unprincipled men will be enabled to subvert the power of the people and to usurp for themselves the reins of government, destroying afterwards the very engines which have lifted them to unjust dominion." George Washington said this 169 years before Kevin McCarthy was even born.

When researchers first started looking closely at public opinion and political behavior decades ago, they found not only do Americans know virtually nothing about individual political candidates, they also aren't ideologically consistent. Even today, research regularly suggests that when pressed about politics, many Americans express preferences that seem to conflict with each other. I'm sure you know plenty of people, for example, who claim they dislike government regulations, then immediately complain about how the government should have "done more" to keep poisonous trains from exploding on top of their small towns. Or they say they hate socialized medicine while admonishing the government to "stay out of my Medicare!" We humans have a hard time recognizing our own double standards and logical fallacies, especially when it comes to our political opinions.

But data from the Pew Research Center confirm that *ideological consistency* has firmed up in recent decades. Although a majority of Americans continue to hold a mix of liberal and conservative views, over the course of the past decade more Democrats express consistently liberal preferences while more Republicans express consistently conservative views. What happened?

Once upon a time, there were liberal Republicans who dominated northeastern America and conservative Democrats concentrated in the South. Then the civil rights movement produced two game-changing pieces of legislation: the Civil Rights Act of 1964 and the Voting Rights Act of 1965. Together these two laws forced the end of racial segregation in the South and in doing so fueled the Dixiecrat Revolution, a decades-long realignment of conservative whites in the South shifting their allegiance from the Democratic Party to the Republican Party both by party switching and via generational replacement.

This realignment concentrated the Republican Party's power base in the American South and into the Plains states and the Mountain West. As the Republican Party became sharply more conservative both economically and socially, it triggered a *de-alignment* of the liberal Republicans in the Northeast and the West Coast, who were turned off by the party's increasingly hard-line, conservative platform positions.

These regional changes were amplified by another important realignment for Republicans: rural America. Although Democrats dominated rural politics for decades during and after the Great Depression, rural parts of America began to shift swiftly to the Republican Party, vastly outpacing the rate at which urban areas shifted away from Republicans. Today, the Republican Party dominates rural politics, and not just in the South. Over the past twenty years, Republicans have essentially doubled their margins in the presidential vote in rural counties nationwide.

This "party sorting" reshaped the American electorate quite significantly from what it was prior to the 1960s through the 1980s. It's how the Republican Ronald Reagan upset the traditional Electoral College map twice, winning electoral votes from all but six states in 1980 against the incumbent Democrat (and Southerner), Jimmy Carter. Four years later, Reagan captured 525 out of all 538 electoral votes, winning every state except Minnesota (the home state of his opponent, Walter Mondale). That was the greatest Electoral College shellacking in American history.

Given what we know about modern elections, it might seem all but impossible for a presidential candidate today to earn 525 Electoral College votes. That's because it is! Successful as it was, the "Reagan Revolution" benefited primarily from its excellent timing. The 1980s and 1990s were peak realignment periods, with the South and the Northeast fully immersed in forming their new political identities.

With liberal Republicans and conservative Democrats in flux, Reagan and, to a lesser degree, Bill Clinton shaped their presidential campaigns around cross-party appeals that worked because the correlation between party identification and political ideology (liberal or conservative) has more than doubled since 1972. Since the 1980s, more voters have stuck with the candidates who belonged to their political parties. By the 2020 elections, 88 percent of Republicans and Republican-leaning independents voted for their own party's candidates. Ninety-three percent of Democrats and their independent leaners voted for Democratic candidates.

To better understand what this means, let's look at Georgia's 2022 U.S. Senate race between incumbent Democrat Raphael Warnock and former University of Georgia football great Herschel Walker. Over the course of that year's election season, serious scandals dogged the Heisman Trophy winner and undercut his campaign. He was an objectively flawed candidate who faced persistent allegations of domestic abuse and intellectual incompetence. But even worse for Walker were credible accusations that he had paid for abortions for his girlfriends.

Though supporting abortion should be an unforgivable sin among many conservatives in the South, Walker suffered virtually no penalty among Republican voters in Georgia. CNN exit poll data found that 95 percent of voters who identified as Republicans voted for Herschel Walker despite his flawed candidacy, while 98 percent of those voters supported Brian Kemp, the Republican governor. Kemp won his election handily, while Walker lost both the general election and Georgia's runoff election by narrow margins.

How? Well, the answer lies in the voting behavior of Georgia's independent voters—the voters who claim they don't belong to either party. Exit polls say independents supported Kemp over Democratic candidate for governor Stacey Abrams by just a single percentage point, but they favored Warnock over Walker by eleven points—53 percent to 42 percent. Independent voters, not Republicans, determined the outcome of Georgia's U.S. Senate election.

In the eyes of the Republican voters of Georgia, it didn't matter that Herschel Walker was a flawed, morally questionable candidate. For them, he had the only qualification that mattered: He was a Republican—and that, my friends, is what hyper-partisanship is all about.

PARTISAN CIRCUITRY

Over the past two decades, party identification has become such a powerful predictor of vote choice that it has overshadowed other indicators such as the strength of America's economy, which for decades served as the most important factor in predicting the outcome of presidential elections. Partisanship creates a convenient shortcut that low-interest and low-information voters can rely on to make their vote decisions, and it colors our entire perspective of the political world.

That's because partisanship provides a perceptual screen that relies on motivated reasoning to discount information that conflicts with a voter's partisan interests, while simultaneously seizing on information that reinforces and validates those interests. This explains why Republicans overlooked Herschel Walker's flaws and why they dismissed numerous inconvenient black eyes for Donald Trump, like his business failures and scams, divorces, rape allegations, and the *Access Hollywood* tape. Those revelations weren't even believable to many of Trump's supporters; they conflicted too much with Trump's brand as a business-savvy outsider focused on disrupting the entire political system.

This partisan circuitry also provides us with a handy mental shortcut that helps us make political decisions. Here's an example: If someone knocks on my door and introduces herself as a Republican candidate running in my congressional district, I can safely assume that she is antiabortion, pro-gun, and, more recently, antidemocracy. And these days, it doesn't matter if she's a cultural flamethrower like Marjorie Taylor Greene or a more "mainstream" Republican like Mitch McConnell. The attribute that matters to voters is *which team* the candidate plays for: Democrats or Republicans. This political identity by party gives us a whole lot of information about the candidate's positions without our having to do any research. No need to read boring news articles or party platforms, ask questions, or watch candidates duke it out in live debates. The party label performs all the cognitive work for us!

This is why turnout in primary elections, among candidates who belong to the same political party, is often incredibly low. With all candidates representing the same party, our handy cognitive shortcut is no good. Now we have to find other, more costly and time-consuming ways to figure out which candidate to support. Even the Super Bowl of primary elections, New Hampshire's closely watched presidential primary, barely cracked a 40 percent turnout in 2020. This lack of voter enthusiasm helps explain why so many conspiracy-theory-spouting Republicans with pugnacious personalities and extreme policy ideas win their primaries. I'm looking at you, Matt Gaetz, and you, Lauren Boebert.

When Colorado held its primary election in June 2020, the state reported 551,820 total registered voters in its Third Congressional District. Overall turnout in the Third District's primary didn't even crack 40 percent. Though these base voters represented a minority of the voting population, they were fired up and eager to send a partisan firebrand to Congress, and they showed up at the primary to do it. And that meant thirty-three-year-old Boebert, one of America's most controversial, least serious politicians, won the Republican primary in her district with only 58,670 votes (about 55 percent of Republican primary voters). But another way to look at it: Less than 11 percent of the overall electorate voted for her! Still, Boebert's vote share was enough for her to move on to the general election, which she comfortably won to become a member of Congress (she *barely* won her reelection bid in 2022).

By the way, the lack of enthusiasm among voters who'd rather not spend precious time researching candidates they don't know also explains why *name recognition* is so powerful in presidential primaries. Name recognition or familiarity is the second "shortcut" voters turn to once party identification is removed. Trump, after all, was a household name long before he jumped into politics. Arnold Schwarzenegger benefited from damn-near-universal name recognition when he was elected governor of California in 2003. Ronald Reagan was also a famous actor when Californians elected him governor in 1966. Though he was never a Hollywood celebrity, Americans knew Joe Biden for eight years as Barack Obama's vice president, which gave him a huge advantage in the crowded 2020 presidential primary. Usually, the best-known candidates heading into a presidential nomination cycle are the same two or three battling it out at the end.

THE POLARIZED ERA OF POLITICS

America's political and cultural chasm has gotten so wide we are now living in what we call the polarized era of politics. Candidates and their individual strengths are less important than the strength of their loyalty to their party. For Republicans in this polarized era, this loyalty is a blood oath.

That's how we end up electing increasingly extreme Republicans who would have been tossed out of the GOP a decade ago. It no longer matters if a Republican candidate has an actual record of sex crimes. Or that she believes JFK Jr. is going to return from the grave to run QAnon. Or that he wore an assault rifle pin to Congress the day after someone murdered schoolkids with an AR-15. For a majority of Republican voters, those little details don't matter as long as the candidate is a loyal Republican who falls squarely in line with the Republican Party—as long as he'll vote in the Senate to confirm Republican judges who can't even meet the standards of the American Bar Association (Trump nom-

inated ten candidates to federal judgeships who were rated "not qualified" by the nonpartisan organization) and as long as Donald Trump
doesn't hate him.

So when voters discover that their unknown new congressman
from, say, Long Island is not the wealthy businessman who earned two
college degrees and played volleyball for Baruch College as he claimed,
his membership in the Republican tribe becomes a get-out-of-jail-free
card. His reputation can survive flagrant lies *simply because he's a loyal
Republican.* For today's GOP, proven lies, hypocrisy, overt racism, sex-
ism, and xenophobia are small prices to pay when the balance of power
in Congress is at stake.

THE TRUTH ABOUT SWING VOTERS

If you follow election coverage closely on cable TV, you might believe
that in any given competitive election there seems to be a large pool of
independent-minded swing voters who are politically engaged, truly
undecided citizens handwringing over their vote choice and just waiting to be persuaded by the candidate who makes the most convincing
case. If you haven't heard this from a political scientist yet, allow me to
be the first:

THAT'S NOT HOW ANY OF THIS WORKS!

Many swing voters don't make their vote decisions based on policies
or the quality of the candidates, and they certainly aren't as mysterious
or deliberative as the media make them out to be. Most swing voters
included in stump interviews aren't admitting the whole truth, maybe
even to themselves. They too are taking a political shortcut.

If asked, "Do you lean toward the Democratic Party or the Republican Party?" the majority of so-called swing voters will admit they do *lean*
toward one party's candidates over the other party's candidates. This
means the ultimate vote choice of these self-proclaimed swing voters—
about 80 percent of them on average—is actually *very* predictable. They

are "closeted" partisans. Subtract these partisan *leaners* from our pool of independents, and we're left with only about 10 to 15 percent of the electorate who are true independent swing voters, at least in the competitive elections. Political scientists call these folks "pure independents."

Many pure independent voters don't have strong political preferences. In election after election, they tend to break along predictable lines—against whichever political party currently holds the American presidency, or the *in party*. In 2016, with Democrats in power, pure indies broke in favor of Donald Trump. In 2020, when Republicans were the in party, those swing voters broke in favor of Joe Biden.

Pure independents live in the fuzzy nexus between the two political parties. They tend to vote because at some point in their lives someone (say, Mom or Dad) or something (say, the military or a government job) convinced them that voting was a civic duty, but not necessarily a passion. They lack the strong opinions and heightened interest in politics and current affairs that lead other voters to identify with political parties.

Now, can you find passionate, purely independent, truly undecided swing voters who really do know about the candidates and the differences between each party, contemporary events, and nuanced political issues? Sure, you can. I'm related to one! And our news media do a great job of ferreting these folks out for their TV interviews. But ask anyone who runs focus groups for a living and they'll tell you swing voters aren't all they're cracked up to be.

Many purely independent swing voters pay little attention to current events and politics because they don't share the same interest in politics that many partisan voters do. They'll vote, but they usually need a good reason, or a good reminder, and usually both. They're not loyal to either party, but they're also not following the ins and outs of the daily news cycle. Sure, they care about who's making decisions on their behalf, but not enough to pick a team and attend every home and away game. In other words, many swing voters are like most other voters, and most other voters are like Jon Snow: *They know nothing.*

NEGATIVE PARTISANSHIP STRATEGY

In this polarized era of American politics, competitive election outcomes are decided by two things. The first is the strength of each party's *coalitional turnout:* a party's reliable base voters and its "independent" leaners (again, the independent voters who *lean toward* supporting one party's candidates). The second factor is which party outperforms the other among pure independents. These swing voters are also called conversion pool voters because their votes can change from one party to another. And this means modern electoral campaigns have dual goals that often compete against each other:

1. To maximize the turnout of their own coalition by focusing on the usually partisan red-meat issues that excite loyal base voters; and
2. To win over swing voters in the conversion pool by focusing on moderation and bipartisanship. Swing voters like moderation and bipartisanship, right?

Actually, no. These days only Democrats try to convert swing voters by focusing on moderation and bipartisanship. Republicans don't center their strategy on winning over swing voters; instead, the Republican Party's strategy is designed to push swing voters *away* from voting for Democrats—*any* Democrat. For them, maximizing coalitional turnout and swing voter conversion are not competing objectives that often work against each other. Republicans pursue the two in tandem, combined into a single, highly effective tactic that I call *negative partisanship strategy.*

Over the past decade, the GOP has perfected winning by *disqualifying the other option.* Through effective messaging fueled by the breadth and depth of right-wing media (which we'll cover next), the Republican Party has successfully branded modern Democrats as a party of unpatriotic, ultra-woke, godless perverts slipping into socialism in the only western democracy that doesn't even offer paid maternity leave yet.

In terms of both its coalition and its base, the Republican Party fig-

ured out a long time ago the power of negative partisanship—the negative emotions, like fear, anger, and threat, that members of one party
feel about the other party. Those feelings become more pronounced
when the other party holds power. Republicans exploit negative feelings
toward Democrats both to drive up their coalitional turnout and to push
swing voters away from Democrats.

The Daily Show's Desi Lydic accurately summarized my take on negative partisanship strategy this way: "Winning elections isn't about persuading the undecided. It's about motivating your team to show up, and
the biggest motivator is how much you dislike the other side."

MEASURING PUBLIC OPINION: MIND THE MARGIN

So how, exactly, do we know what voters are thinking and feeling about
American politics? How do political dweebs like me understand, with a
good deal of certainty, who's voting for whom, when candidates are winning or losing, and when political parties are booming or busting—all
before we see any actual results on Election Day?

Well, polling companies look for hundreds or thousands of voters—
respondents—willing to spend a few minutes answering political questions, usually over the phone but increasingly online. The questions are
neutral. The polling firms don't even tell the hired hands conducting
the interviews who their clients are. After the calls or online surveys are
completed and all the answers are recorded, a data expert (a "pollster")
crunches the numbers and interprets the results to provide a snapshot
of public opinion. While we commonly call this a poll, it's actually a
scientific survey.

A lot of political surveys are never shared with the public. They're
usually conducted privately by campaigns or political organizations and
used internally to provide guidance, feedback, and direction. Good surveys can help us suss out voter behavior and patterns, and they do tend
to give insiders and operatives a clear picture of the political environment at a specific moment in time.

The results of surveys that are released to the public, however, chronically disappoint us. Why do so many pre–Election Day surveys get it wrong? It's a fair (and common!) question with an answer that all civically literate news consumers should be aware of. The surveys you read about in the news are usually commissioned by media organizations for the intrinsic news value of their results, or they are conducted for the sole purpose of becoming news stories. Political junkies and casual news consumers alike love to know which candidates are winning the horse race, or how popular or unpopular their elected leaders are. But surveys are often *incapable* of telling us who's going to win a political horse race because by their very nature they rely on *sampling*.

A survey, whether meant for private use or public release, will measure the opinions of a few hundred voters in, say, Pennsylvania, then will use those opinions as a proxy for all voters in the broader Pennsylvania electorate. The moment you take a sample out of a broader population, you're stuck with some statistical baggage called the margin of error. You can usually find the statistical margin of error in the fine print at the bottom of most surveys as, for example, "MOE +/− 3."

On October 17, 2022, *The New York Times* published the results of a political survey it conducted with Siena College that found that "49 percent of likely voters said they planned to vote for a Republican to represent them in Congress" in the November midterm election, "compared with 45 percent who planned to vote for a Democrat." A link to a page with more details about the survey indicated, in fine print, that the margin of error was "+/− 4.1 percentage points for the likely electorate." Though the article itself made no mention of this not-insignificant margin of error, its headline was "Republicans Gain Edge as Voters Worry About Economy, Times/Siena Poll Finds." While Republicans did edge out Democrats to recapture control of the House, the story of the 2022 midterms was that Republicans had actually lost their edge, underperforming all expectations.

So what's the rub? Depending on the size of the sample (in this case, 792 respondents nationwide), and because of inescapable polling errors, the results could be off by a few points in either direction, among both candidates (that's why margins of error are reported as both "plus or minus" numbers). In this case, the Republican likely voters' 49 percent might actually be as high as 53.1 percent (49 *plus* 4.1) or as low as 44.9 percent (49 *minus* 4.1), and the Democrats' vote share could range as high as 49.1 percent or as low as 40.9 percent. In other words, there's a statistical possibility that neither party has an edge. More accurately, the outcome of this particular survey can only be described as a toss-up, not an "edge."

Horse race polling can tell us whether one candidate is beating the other *outside* the survey's margin of error, or it can tell us whether the race is a toss-up. If the results fall within the margin of error, as they usually do, a survey cannot even *suggest* to us which side might win, or which side gains an edge. Yet that is usually how they are reported out.

SHAPING PUBLIC OPINION

Prior to 2004, using their survey data, both Republicans and Democrats ran big campaigns aimed at the middle of the electorate. The theory, known in political science as the median voter theorem, works like this: If you survey voters' political ideologies and plot those ideologies on a graph with "liberal" on the left and "conservative" on the right, you'd see a bell curve. Most voters would land in the center, at or near the highest point of that curve—the median. The median voter theorem presumes the political party that best aligns with the people in the center of that bell curve—the one that best reflects the preferences of the median voter—would win over the most voters. This weeded out extremists in primaries on both the right and the left as both parties sought to maximize candidate electability, and we ended up with more moderate elected leaders.

Then, in 2004, the GOP shook things up. *Instead of gauging public opinion and adapting to it*, they thought, *why don't we just shape public opinion in our favor to push voters to the polls to vote for Republicans?* Whether that was clearly articulated or not, functionally that's exactly how Karl Rove, President George W. Bush's chief political adviser, ensured a second term for one of America's least popular presidents.

In 2004, Rove worked behind the scenes to put constitutional amendments banning gay marriage on the ballot in eleven states. Rove knew banning gay marriage was a passionate issue that elicited strong emotional opinions, especially from the Christian Right. But the issue clearly struck a nerve with moderates too—those swing voters in the conversion pool. Even in my bright blue home state of Oregon, 57 percent of voters supported changing the state constitution in 2004 to declare that "only a marriage between one man and one woman shall be valid or legally recognized as a marriage."

Pay close attention to Rove's strategy. Gay marriage didn't start off high on the list of issues that voters were focused on in 2004, but the presidential election cycle sure ended that way. Through his ballot initiative strategy, Rove *made* gay marriage the defining domestic issue that year, motivating social conservatives and right-leaning moderates to vote. He also defined Democrats as cultural and moral extremists, and that pushed swing voters away from supporting Democrat John Kerry.

The GOP's message to moderates in the conversion pool was essentially this: "Democrats are destroying the 'sanctity' of *your* marriage." For a voting conservative, that is *red meat* political messaging, and we'll cover this soon too. Rove used the issue of gay marriage to execute negative partisanship strategy, galvanizing the Republican coalition while pushing swing voters away from Democrats. His strategy also ushered in an electioneering revolution on the right: wedging grievance politics as a way to win general elections. And remember, this all happened well before the Tea Party movement, Trump's nightmare presidency, and the Supreme Court's overturning of *Roe v. Wade*. Back in 2004, Democrats did not have the organizational strength, or even the broad cultural support, to harness national furor among the Left and use it to turn out voters and win elections.

Today we see the Republicans' negative partisanship strategy and their grievance politics baked into almost every hot-button issue. Take immigration. Any scientific survey will tell us that voters on the right have incredibly strong opinions about immigration and the way our

government deals with immigrants and our borders. Well, no shit. It's
not because most Republicans have always cared about immigrants and
immigration policy; it's because the news media they consume—the
media controlled by the GOP—*make them care.* Immerse yourself in
right-wing media for a day and you too just might believe America's
border issues are the most pressing and important issues facing this
nation. Research from Chapman University in 2022 found that "the
fear of illegal immigration is much stronger among those who consume Fox News and talk radio," and "those who consume more left-
leaning media sources like CNN have no correlation to fearing illegal
immigration."

Remember when Donald Trump said this, after riding down a gold
escalator to announce his White House bid in June 2015?

> When Mexico sends its people, they're not sending their best. . . .
> They're sending people that have lots of problems, and they're
> bringing those problems with us. They're bringing drugs. They're
> bringing crime. They're rapists.

Whether Trump truly believed this or simply knew it would resonate
deeply and emotionally with voters conditioned by right-wing media is
debatable, but the fact that he said it on his first day as a presidential
candidate was no accident. The GOP spent years giving life and credibility to the issue of immigration, cramming it full of racism and negative emotions (like fear, perceived unfairness, and even violence), and
making it a controversy that struck a chord with an entire half of America. Trump said what GOP leaders and their media allies primed him to
believe, and for him and tens of millions of other Americans those beliefs were as good as facts. Republicans didn't just measure and respond
to the electorate; they pulled the electorate along for the ride!

And while Republicans were busy changing human behavior at its
foundations, most Democrats were still simply measuring it. While Republicans were shaping public opinion by manipulating messages to
their voters and motivating new voters—by making them care about the

issues that are politically advantageous to the GOP—Democrats were still banking on the old strategy of appealing to the median voters in the middle of a bell curve via policy appeals, and they were losing. Democrats were—and for the most part still are—asking swing voters what they care about, then shaping their campaigns and policies around those concerns.

For any Democrats who still believe they can win by appealing to and winning over votes from moderate Republicans, I'll say it again:

THAT'S NOT HOW ANY OF THIS WORKS.

You Are What You Eat

To be clear: I don't blame the news media for putting American democracy on its deathbed. The Republican Party is squarely to blame for that. So why devote a whole chapter to the news media in a book about saving democracy? Well, the simple answer is because a whole lot of news organizations willfully ignore, or have at least deprioritized, their most important responsibility: *to hold democracy accountable to the truth*.

Good journalism in any functioning democracy really is that simple.

But because most Americans no longer give a shit about politics or maintaining the health, integrity, and sustainability of their own government, and because political identity and partisanship are so baked into American culture, the news media—especially profit-driven, corporate-owned news organizations—have conditioned themselves to meet consumers where they are. There's much better money in giving consumers the content they want, not the boring political news they *need*. No attempt to save our democracy can ignore our news media system and how its farting under the sheets played a significant role in divorcing Americans from their interest in governing themselves.

And it gets even more concerning. The much bigger problem with a news media system more interested in ratings, likes, shares, clicks, and page views than in protecting democracy is that this system is *exploitable*, and the Republican Party knows exactly how to exploit it. They do it with devastating effect, landing punch after punch in their effort to replace democracy with authoritarianism, as too many news media organizations go along for the ride. And no, I'm not just talking about the Right's propaganda organizations like Fox News; I'm talking about the whole corporate news media system.

I spent the first few years of my teaching career focused on our news media, criticizing sensationalism, ideological bias, and corporate consolidation. *Be skeptical of all political news you consume,* I'd tell my students. *Not everything you read is true, and it's your duty to sort accurate and objective information from noise and spin. The truth is out there!*

Then, during Donald Trump's rise in politics, I had to shift the focus of my lessons. Many of my students came to class already doubting even legitimate news media, especially political coverage—*all* of it. They had lost trust in news organizations and shrugged off any interest in the consequential events those organizations covered. Maybe they grew weary of the round-the-clock conversation about Trump and his bombastic candidacy, then the unsettling idiocy of his administration. Maybe they believed what the Right tells us to believe: that it's okay—patriotic, even—to dismiss uncomfortable truths as "fake news." Whatever the reasons, my college students didn't believe much of anything they read or saw.

So instead of teaching media skepticism, I set out to convince them that Pulitzer Prize–winning news organizations don't just make shit up. I had to assure them that bona fide news organizations actually have rigorous publication standards and verification processes, and if real journalists do screw something up, or make something up, or deliberately lie to their audiences, then they face serious professional repercussions.

By "real journalists," of course, I don't mean the people over at Fox News. No real journalist would ever do the bidding of a political party. And while Stephen Colbert jokes Fox is "the GOP communications office," there's plenty to suggest that joke hits pretty damn close to home. In May 2022, Media Matters for America, an advocacy organization devoted to tracking right-wing news organizations and trends, claimed "Fox News is the Republican Party," citing more than four hundred examples.

"Fox has retained its influence since Trump left office, emerging as perhaps the single strongest force in GOP politics," Media Matters wrote. "Its daily cacophony determines the party's message and policy aims on issues large and small, while its biggest stars are kingmakers whose endorsements can make or break Republican candidates and elected leaders."

While Fox may not, arguably, be *officially* tied to the Republican Party, the cable channel and its bevy of popular right-wing personalities play an inarguable role in the GOP's intentional dissemination of disinformation and propaganda.

No, by "real" political journalists, I mean the rapidly dwindling cadre of reporters, editors, producers, researchers, interviewers, and opinion leaders whose only North Star is *the truth*. I'm lucky enough to know some of them. They're good journalists, even if they are caught in the cogs of a profit-driven media system. Real journalists don't do their difficult work so their parent companies can report impressive quarterly earnings. Nor do they do it because it pays well. They do it because they understand that independent news media are essential to maintaining the health of a democracy.

Honest, independent journalism reveals the truths needed to check and balance the power we give to the people who lead us, who tax us, who protect us and take us to war. Journalism guarantees accountability and transparency in our government. Real journalists hunt for the truth and present it as objectively as possible, even when they're threatened with violence, or dismissed as "fake news" by half the nation, and jeered at, at the encouragement of the ex-president of the United States.

The problem is, the deck is now stacked against real political journalists. They're losing to a system more loyal to algorithms and ad revenues, one that has already streamlined itself to deliver consumers exactly, and only, what they want. So let's shine some light on the way modern Americans consume their news and political information, how news organizations meet the demand, and where it all falls short.

THE AGE OF THE ALGORITHM

Corporate-owned media companies make billions selling your precious time and attention to advertisers. For the most part, online media companies are machines that maximize profits by understanding exactly what earns the time and attention of their consumers, then using custom-tailored, automatically generated, proprietary computer codes—algorithms—to serve up whatever their individual users are looking for. Information? Entertainment? Sort of. Algorithms make clear that the majority of Americans who now get their news from social media, news websites, or apps engage with content that elicits *emotion*.

We news consumers want to feel justified in our values and beliefs. We want to feel safe and reassured. We like to feel morally superior to crooks and cheats and couch potatoes. Sometimes we want to feel shocked and outraged, but generally we'd rather be amused and inspired. Mostly, we just want to feel good. And thanks to the rise of digital media and the age of the algorithm, our corporate media system knows exactly how to deliver—very precisely—these emotions to you.

Unlike the front page of an old-fashioned, print-edition newspaper, social media algorithms also tend to deliberately exclude content that challenges their users' beliefs or existing worldviews. This is known as the filter bubble. Algorithms are, after all, designed to generate corporate revenue at the individual level, not to provide a public information service. But the social media filter bubble doesn't mean it's all puppies and unicorns for modern news consumers.

The Pew Research Center found that "social media users frequently encounter content that sparks feelings of amusement but also see material that angers them," leading to "widespread concerns that these sites are promoting content that is attention-grabbing but ultimately harmful to users—such as misinformation, sensationalism or 'hate clicks.'"

In 2018, Facebook changed its algorithm that determines which posts show up in a user's news feed and in what order. The new algorithm ranked the stories in the user's personal feed based on what that user will most likely *engage with,* or, as Facebook put it, "to create more opportunities to interact with the people you care about."

"A like, comment, or share is one sign that a post matters to you, so posts you're likely to interact with generally get higher ranking scores," Facebook acknowledged. Higher-ranking scores mean a greater likelihood you'll see those stories in your news feed—presented like the top stories on the front page of an old-fashioned newspaper. Facebook's prioritization of posts I'm more *likely to interact with* explains why, after I get into an argument with my old Don't-Tread-on-Me classmate who posts about crazy conspiracy theories, I keep seeing that guy's other right-wing shit at the top of my news feed, whether or not that content is true.

Facebook's news feed "doesn't differentiate between factual information and things that merely look like facts," the business news website *Quartz* points out, but it "can predict what you'll click on better than anyone you know."

> [Facebook] follows the videos you watch, the photos you hover over, and every link you click on. It is mapping your brain, seeking patterns of engagement. It uses this map to create a private personal pipeline of media just for you. In doing this it has essentially become the editor-in-chief of a personalized newspaper that 2 billion people read every month.

So why does information via algorithm matter to the health of American democracy? If you're a political news hound plugged into a social media news delivery system, your "personalized newspaper" probably prioritizes all sorts of political news from a variety of sources. But we've already established that tens upon tens of millions of Americans aren't political news hounds. Their algorithms elevate articles about golf tournaments or new kitchen gadgets over stories about the horrifying bills your Republican legislators are passing.

And you'd better believe the Republican Party is well aware of this concerning soft spot in American news consumption. For them, it's a twofold opportunity: They know most Americans aren't paying attention to the day-to-day news coverage of their success in destroying democracy, and thanks to algorithms, the GOP and conservatives can find, target, talk to, and ultimately influence the people who already subscribe to their beliefs and messages, or who might become new believers, then get them to engage (and vote) accordingly!

Unlike Democrats, who rely almost exclusively on decentralized, uncompensated, grassroots influencers to elevate their messaging, Republicans have developed a veritable influencer empire filled with folks like Charlie Kirk, Ben Shapiro, and Candace Owens. They're paid big bucks by conservative media outlets like *The Daily Wire* and *The Daily Caller*, which are funded by Republican billionaire megadonors, like the Wilks brothers and the Koch brothers, to shape public opinion.

IF IT BLEEDS, IT LEADS

What about the more traditional news media? The Pew Research Center says as of 2022, 5 percent of American adults still prefer to get their news from print publications—ink on newsprint—and 7 percent prefer to listen to the radio to stay informed. A third of adults in this country, including 56 percent of seniors sixty-five and older, prefer to get their news from good old television.

Of course national TV newscasts cover the day's top political stories. To a lesser degree, so do local TV newscasts. But before I pick on the political coverage we get from network television, remember that the primary goal for any news program interrupted by ads is the same as it is for online media: to attract as many eyeballs as possible. For that to happen, given most of America's aversion to politics, a political story has to be pretty damn juicy to become a top story—think career-ending scandals, or fiery Supreme Court nomination hearings, or election night results. Though TV news viewers want to be informed, most don't tune in for thorough and thoughtful public affairs reporting. No. A colleague of mine who produced network TV news for years in a "Top 25" market tells me this is content viewers tune in for, and come back for:

1. *to know whether they're safe* (hence the glut of TV stories about crime, court proceedings, and natural disasters);
2. day-to-day *practical information* (weather forecasts, traffic reports, health studies, financial news, product recalls); and
3. *sensationalism* (royal weddings, scandals, celebrities, and cute clips of water-skiing squirrels).

Stories about government, politics, and politicians usually take a back seat to these more sensational components of a newscast. And when political stories do make the cut, they're often simplified for mass audiences and truncated to match their interest level.

On October 6, 2022, for example, the 7:30 A.M. segment of NBC's *Today Show* devoted only twenty-four *seconds* to a story about an accident involving a Secret Service vehicle transporting Vice President Kamala Harris three days earlier. Sure, nobody was hurt, and in fairness the host Hoda Kotb did mention the newsworthiest part: "The incident was initially reported to Secret Service leaders as a mechanical failure, then later corrected." But twenty-four seconds wasn't nearly enough time for the whole story. As *The Washington Post* reported the day before, the Secret Service *falsely* characterized the incident as a mechanical failure, raising alarming questions about the way the entire agency operates.

The *Post*'s nearly thousand-word story said the driver of Harris's Secret Service SUV struck a curb in a tunnel, which destroyed the vehicle's tire, snarled traffic, and prompted a scramble for a new vehicle. The incident "concerned both the Secret Service director and the vice president and revived worries about the agency's history of concealing its mistakes," the *Post* wrote. "The Secret Service has had a long, troubled history of covering up its own mistakes and misconduct, with the most senior leaders and managers often relying on the shroud of secrecy covering presidential security to cover up agency foibles and failures."

That is a much bigger political story than a twenty-four-second blurb about a minor "mechanical failure" involving one of the most protected public leaders on the planet. Political stories simply don't get prime real estate in TV broadcasts. They often avoid the bigger picture, with no real analysis, nuance, or deep dive into the larger truths behind the extraordinary story of the world's most powerful government.

What about the millions of people who watch cable news all day? Who doesn't have a feisty relative glued to CNN or MSNBC, or Fox News, all of which seem to feature politics—and people *talking about* politics—around the clock? This should be no surprise by now, but your relative isn't a *normal* American either. According to Pew, roughly six and a half million TVs tuned to cable news every night during prime time in 2020 (just under half of them watched Fox; CNN and MSNBC split the rest). Even if you consider multiple viewers in front of some of those TVs, that's only a small fraction (about 2.5 percent) of the roughly 258 million adults who live in America. These outlets serve niche audiences and focus heavily on the *conflict* inherent in American politics— the disagreements, the hurt feelings, the indignation.

America's deliberately tedious political system was not designed for today's instant, viewer-driven, for-profit news media. The boring grind of policymaking on Capitol Hill or governing at your statehouse rarely breaks through as a top story—at least to ordinary news consumers. Yes, news consumers have a duty to govern and sustain their own democracy despite their growing disinterest in politics, but the news media have an equally important responsibility to give American politics the gravity and top billing our fragile democracy deserves. Faced with profits pressures, America's consumer-facing news media organizations have abdicated their responsibility to deliver political news with depth, complexity, and nuance, and the proof is in the hot mess of our sick democracy.

After all, a healthy democracy is what guarantees America's corporate news media organizations the very freedom to make news profitable in the first place, allowing the gathering and selling of information without interference, influence, or censorship from an authoritarian government. A sick democracy allows politicians to manipulate the free flow of objective facts and information, or to prevent it from reaching people altogether. That's exactly what today's Republican Party is doing.

THE RIGHT'S OWN MEDIA MACHINE

Vilifying the "mainstream media" is hardly a new trend in politics, but it has intensified since the failed vice-presidential candidate Sarah Palin referred to nonconservative news outlets as the "lamestream media" back in 2009. *The Independent* reported that by the end of Trump's time as president, he had used the term "fake news" to describe legitimate journalists and news organizations more than two thousand times— averaging more than once a day. For the leaders of today's Republican Party, delegitimizing reporters and news organizations has become a constant, albeit uncreative, way to diminish damning accusations, to dismiss tough questions, and to rationalize unproven accusations of bias—at least to the people willing to believe them.

What are the mainstream media, anyway? I define them as all news organizations with editorial processes and codes of ethical conduct that strive for objectivity, balance, and fairness in their work to hold democracy accountable to the truth. Some mainstream media outlets are much better at this than others. Many are driven by corporate profits, but some, like NPR and ProPublica, are not. All of them make mistakes from time to time. I have my share of complaints about the shortcomings of modern journalism, but no "mainstream" media organization deliberately shills for a partisan political agenda like Fox News.

But the Republican Party wants voters to believe the deck is stacked against conservatives, that the mainstream media are controlled by liberal elitists persistently pushing a partisan, left-wing agenda onto them, somehow threatening conservative values and sullying whatever was the American way of life of yesteryear. Ironically, as Republicans leaned into this strategy, they've been building up their own news media ecosystem—a juggernaut of a right-wing propaganda machine—to win political power and subvert American democracy with their own disinformation.

Sure, some news organizations, like the *New York Post* and *The Wall Street Journal,* have conservative slants. Others, like MSNBC and Vice, have liberal slants. And both political parties host a slew of online political outlets that are rigidly biased, functional equivalents to Fox News. But the Left certainly has nothing equivalent to a whole *media ecosystem* built around the goal of deliberately delivering disinformation like Fox News and its minor-league cousins (like *Breitbart,* Newsmax, and One America News Network).

Loyal Fox News viewers may represent a small fraction of the overall population, but they, along with consumers of other right-wing media, are a significant factor in America's unhealthy political environment. These consumers are conditioned to believe whatever their favorite conservative media organizations tell them, and that all other news organizations are wrong at best or lying to them at worst. Fox and the other organizations in the Right's media ecosystem radicalize their audiences and silo them off from more mainstream news sources that do not push partisan political ideologies. The Right didn't design their own media ecosystem to hold democracy accountable to the truth; they designed an echo chamber to sow and grow divisive political controversies and to advance their antidemocracy agenda.

Here's an example: Fox and other right-wing outlets rigorously covered the Black Lives Matter protests in Portland, Oregon, following the murder of George Floyd in 2020. When those protests turned into riots, pitting demonstrators against police officers and right-wing hooligans, Fox covered the situation as if it were a domestic war, creating a national illusion for its viewers that the Rose City had turned into a lawless hellscape overrun by left-wing nuts. In fact, data analysts who tracked the story found that Fox covered the unrest in Portland 6.7 times more than CNN and MSNBC combined. But fast-forward to 2022: Fox refused to air *any* live coverage of the January 6 Committee hearings, which investigated an armed, riotous attack on law enforcement officers protecting the U.S. government. Pay no attention to *that* lawless hellscape, Fox decided for its viewers. Man, *that* is how you shape public opinion in the crucible of your own media ecosystem.

But the most dangerous example is when Fox convinced its viewers that Trump's decisive 7,059,526-vote loss to Joe Biden in 2020 was stolen, despite no shred of credible evidence and even after months of Trump's signaling he would falsely claim fraud if he lost. Unwilling to accept that outcome, Fox hosts entertained conspiracy theories about illegal votes, missing ballots, polling-place shenanigans, and even that Dominion Voting Systems somehow rigged its ballot machines to switch Trump votes to Biden—an accusation that prompted a $1.6 billion defamation lawsuit against Fox. In the court filings that followed, Fox hosts admitted they didn't even believe the BS from Trump and his lawyers. In private messages, the former Fox host Tucker Carlson called election fraud lies from Trump's adviser Sidney Powell "insane." (Let the record show Tuck also called Powell "a fucking bitch.")

"It's unbelievably offensive to me," Carlson complained to his fellow host Laura Ingraham on November 18, 2020, adding, "Our viewers are good people and they believe it."

Bingo. *Fox viewers believe the election fraud lies they hear on Fox.* Remember when I said there's better money in giving consumers the content they want than the objective political news they should want?

Former congressman Adam Kinzinger, one of only two Republicans who formally investigated the January 6 insurrection, told CNN in 2023 that Fox News viewers have "been programmed by Tucker Carlson for many years" to suspend any disbelief. No matter what Fox tells its viewers, Kinzinger added, the network knows its audience "is vested in that tribal narrative."

The Right knows how to gaslight and infuriate millions of their own "news" consumers, but also countless other Americans who aren't particularly discerning when it comes to the information—true or not—blipping across their algorithms. This is how millions of hapless people see baseless conspiracy theories that can seem legitimate and believable, courtesy of the Republican Party and the media it controls. Oh, there's not a shred of credible evidence suggesting that a fair presidential election was stolen?

That's just what the liberal media want you to believe! Some Republicans (hat tip to you, Kinzo) have the gall to push back? *Kick 'em out!*

When you control your own narrative in your own media ecosystem, you can manipulate the beliefs and behaviors of your audience by the millions. You can also manipulate the news for a much wider slice of the electorate.

DUPED INTO DOING DIRTY WORK

Again, no legitimate *mainstream* media organization deliberately shills for a partisan political agenda. But news outlets are fallible and predictable, and that makes them vulnerable to another dangerous GOP strategy: duping legitimate news organizations into doing the dirty work of spreading false narratives. For an example of how threatening this is to our democracy, come with me back to March 24, 2019.

On that day, Trump-appointed U.S. attorney general Bill Barr released his own sneak peek of Special Counsel Robert Mueller's report on Russian interference in the 2016 presidential election. Barr knew that as the nation's "Top Cop," he—not Mueller—would be first out of the gate with a response to the long-awaited report, and that meant Barr could characterize the unpublished report's conclusions for the *whole world,* for right-wing media *and* for the mainstream news media. In other words, Barr knew his telling of the story *was the story.* A savvy political operator, Barr knew his assessment of the Mueller Report would be breaking news around the globe, thanks to the norms of the modern twenty-four-hour news cycle and its quest to deliver developments and content as soon as possible. Barr was well aware his response as AG would be treated as a legitimate first look at an investigation Americans had waited years to see.

So, in a brief letter to Congress intended to be immediately made public, Barr asserted that Mueller's investigation "did not find that the Trump campaign or anyone associated with it conspired or coordinated with Russia in its efforts to influence the 2016 U.S. presidential election." Problem is, the Mueller Report argues the exact opposite.

Nobody could fact-check Barr, of course, because the full 448-page report wasn't public yet. The mainstream media, conditioned to feed immediate headlines to their consumers and churn out their profits, ran with Barr's summary anyway, wrapping it up in a tidy "No Collusion" narrative that persists today.

A few days after Barr published his summary, a diplomatic Robert Mueller complained that Barr "did not fully capture the context, nature, and substance" of his yearslong work and caused "public confusion"—to say the least. Hardly anyone noticed or cared by then. Old news. And neither Mueller nor the media could unring the bell. Barr's version of history was set in concrete, and this was exactly his plan all along. He kicked the soft underbelly of the news media by duping them into doing the dirty work of the Trump administration and, boy, did it hurt— millions of Americans now call the entire affair the "Russia Hoax."

The attorney general relied on the mainstream news media's need to produce immediate headlines, and in doing so, he successfully obscured an objective fact. Ask even a politically informed friend what Mueller's investigation found and the likely answer is "no collusion." Bill Barr's mastery of manipulating the mainstream media effectively muted a controversial saga that had plagued Donald Trump and his administration for years.

THE PITFALLS OF POLITICAL JOURNALISM

Given what we've just discussed, it's no wonder so many ordinary Americans are skeptical of political headlines and wary of every blurb of political news they hear. No wonder even politically interested citizens, like my college students, distrust the information they get from the media. No wonder the Right is taking advantage of the whole system.

The mainstream media have a responsibility to address this malaise if we're going to nurse America's democracy back to health, and we news consumers have a duty to keep ourselves informed with more journalistic discernment and civic literacy. So as I share some of the bones I have to pick with the media, know that it's meant as tough love.

Our democracy isn't going to recover on its own. In fact, we can't do it without help from the mainstream media.

These criticisms are specifically intended for journalists who cover politics, but they're important for all news consumers to at least be aware of, no matter what kind of news consumer you are.

1. Keep Covering Both Sides, but Quit Bothsidesism

Covering both sides of a story is one of the tenets of ethical journalism. I would never suggest journalists abandon this fundamental principle of fairness, *ever*. But let's take a look at the difference between covering both sides of a story and the unfortunate tendency of mainstream media organizations to commit *false balance*, also known as bothsidesism.

First, a definition: bothsidesism is when, in the pursuit of fairness, political journalists give equal weight to competing perspectives in a story, policy issue, or debate—even if objective facts and evidence don't warrant equal weight. By learning to recognize bothsidesism in the political news we read and watch, we can see exactly when the Republican Party and conservatives abuse the journalistic expectation of fairness.

The spectacularly disastrous derailment of dozens of Norfolk Southern railcars in 2023 made lots of room for bothsidesism. A mechanical problem in one of the cars caused the accident, which resulted in toxic chemicals spewing all over the rust-belt town of East Palestine, Ohio—deep-red Trump country. Though the derailment drew an immediate emergency response from federal authorities, Secretary of Transportation Pete Buttigieg was slow to physically tour the site, prompting conservative media pundits to make up a narrative that Buttigieg and Biden specifically, and Democrats in general, don't care about the rural pockets of America that supported Trump. Seeing a political opening as a presidential candidate, Trump himself visited East Palestine almost three weeks after the derailment to hand out bottled water to affected residents. Buttigieg showed up the day after Trump.

Here are the facts of the matter on "the Left's" side of this story: Democrats certainly didn't cause the train derailment, and they have a much stronger history than Republicans of championing regulations designed to prevent such environmental disasters, as well as ample federal funding for emergency response, prevention, humanitarian aid, and disaster cleanup—nationwide. Buttigieg acknowledged he should have shown up earlier, but the timing of his physical presence wouldn't have changed the pace of the cleanup, the recovery, the federal aid, or the investigation. Democrats also pointed out that President Obama had, in fact, enacted a rule in 2015 requiring certain "high hazard" chemical transport trains to improve their braking systems.

Now here are the facts on "the Right's" side of the story: Trump repealed Obama's train safety rule in 2018 under pressure from the rail industry. The train that derailed in Ohio wouldn't have been affected by said rule, but it highlights the fact that Trump, like many other Republicans, generally *oppose* stricter safety and environmental mandates that they believe hurt business and commerce.

The only reason the train derailment in Ohio became so politically divisive is that Republicans, not Democrats, turned the accident into a political opportunity. It was a political hot potato because conservatives dipped the potato in boiling oil! And it's fair to expect that any news story would provide this critical context. But when *The New York Times* weighed in on the political fallout following the East Palestine disaster, the story gave so much equal weight to both sides that it characterized the ordeal this way, under the headline "In Fog of East Palestine's Crisis, Politicians Write Their Own Stories":

> In some sense, both sides are right, both sides are wrong and, in the bifurcated politics of this American moment, none of the arguments much matter.

Oof. Now that is, quite literally, bothsidesism—a failure in delivering to news consumers the full, fair context of a story about Republicans making political hay off an accident that Democrats had no part in causing.

Here's a less obvious example of bothsidesism: In the summer of

2022, NPR's *All Things Considered* interviewed former Australian prime minister Malcolm Turnbull, who had recently lambasted Rupert Murdoch, the Australian former CEO of Fox News.

"Fox News has played, by far, the largest single part in the polarization of American politics, in the amplification of political hatred," Turnbull told NPR's Ari Shapiro in late August 2022. "I would challenge anyone—any of your listeners—to nominate which individual alive today has done more to undermine American democracy than Rupert Murdoch."

Any trained journalist will tell you that if you broadcast an accusation like that, you need to give the accused a chance to respond. Of course NPR did. Presumably, the network had asked for an interview with some Fox executive. But instead Fox provided NPR with a written, twenty-three-word statement, which Shapiro attributed to an unnamed corporate spokesperson and read aloud:

> Fox News routinely has a larger audience than CNN and MSNBC combined, and the most politically diverse audience of any cable news network.

Wut? That throwaway sentence isn't a response to a fair accusation from a former prime minister that Fox News is responsible for undermining American democracy! It was just more propaganda: a snarky thumb in the eye; a red herring that neither addressed the criticism nor allowed for follow-up questions or scrutiny. It was a cheap, free shot for Fox News, an organization that specializes in propaganda. But NPR read the statement aloud anyway, likely because it reflected at least its attempt to get both sides of the story.

To maintain fairness and accuracy without committing bothsidesism, NPR should have instead said something to the effect of "We reached out to Fox News for a response, but the network chose not to specifically address Turnbull's accusations."

Journalists, refuse to be an outlet for political propaganda, or a mouthpiece for any person who holds a position of public trust, or for any organization that holds political power or influence, even if it means forgoing the coverage of "both sides." And if a politician doesn't directly answer or address your question, then you are not obligated to publish that politician's nonresponse.

2. Call a Lying Spade a Liar

Here's another soft spot within the mainstream news media: the persistent tendency to let known liars—especially Republicans—off the hook by being cute with words. Look, I understand why journalists have traditionally frowned upon using the word "lie." It's "a loaded word," the Associated Press wrote in a 2018 story with the ridiculously ironic headline: "News Media Hesitate to Use 'Lie' for Trump's Misstatements."

"Many news organizations resist using the word [lie] because of the question of intent," AP's David Bauder wrote back then. "Editors feel it's important to establish whether someone is spreading false information knowingly, intending to deceive, and it's hard to get inside a person's head."

With the benefit of hindsight, I'm calling bullshit on that dangerous line of thinking—at least when it comes to covering politics and politicians, especially Republicans. In fairness, following the 2020 presidential election, some of the most credible news organizations in the world no longer have a problem calling Trump's insistence that he won "the Big Lie." But we can't stop there, because the Republicans' aversion to the truth is much bigger than the Big Lie.

In March 2023, three Democratic state lawmakers, two of them Black men, participated in a gun violence protest at Tennessee's overwhelmingly Republican House of Representatives. The protest—in the wake of a mass school shooting in Nashville—might have been loud and disorderly, but nobody was hurt. It wasn't a riot. Nobody was armed, looking to start a revolution by overthrowing the government. Yet Republican House Speaker Cameron Sexton told a conservative radio show that the Black lawmakers' participation "was equivalent—at least equivalent—maybe worse, depending on how you look at it," to the January 6 insurrection at the U.S. Capitol. I don't care how you slice it, *that* is a lie—a deliberate intent to deceive.

The mainstream media should never get cute by characterizing lies like this as "false statements," or "inaccurate," or "misrepresentations." Sexton, an elected leader entrusted with extraordinary political power, said an intentional, hyperpartisan, racially charged *lie* in order to create a false narrative for a specific audience. As long as the entire Republican Party loses no sleep over intentionally deceiving the American people to advance their ideological agenda, journalists should lose no sleep over calling lies and liars who tell them exactly what they are.

My trench buddy Rick Wilson, an outspoken, disenchanted "Never Trump" ex-Republican who co-founded the Lincoln Project, points out there's a "cultural subset" of the reporting class who "still think that this country and its politics during this democracy crisis and the Age of Trump are a story about process." Another way to put it: Too many journalists cover the Republican Party's war on democracy and truth the same way they cover congressional hearings—like another "news of the day" story out of Washington, D.C. The Republican Party's endgame ought to be covered as the existential crisis it is, and the news media cannot, Wilson adds, "treat the truth and the lie like the same thing":

> You can't treat madness and real policy as the same thing. The madness is rising on the right. [Republicans] don't care about the truth. They are determined to use whatever tools they have to end democracy. Reporters who mistake the Republicans for anything but an authoritarian movement are playing a very stupid game.

Journalists, call out lies and any other form of intellectual dishonesty rigorously and unapologetically. Do not tolerate any politician or candidate or organization that knowingly and verifiably tells lies, do not hesitate to report lies as lies, and do not allow liars to abuse or hide behind the expectation of journalistic fairness.

3. Don't Overcompensate to Avoid Accusations of "Liberal Bias"

Legitimate news organizations and journalists strive for fairness and objectivity in every word they write. They report on the (real) scandals of Democrats just as much as they report on the scandals of Republicans (again, this is *journalistic fairness*, not to be confused with bothsidesism). Political journalists are in the business of refereeing politics and politicians, so any accusation of bias can immediately and forever destroy their credibility and ability to court trusted sources and to keep loyal followers.

Too many political journalists—sometimes unaware they're even doing it—give more airtime, ink, and benefit of the doubt to the *Right's* perspective in an attempt to convince audiences that they *don't* have the liberal bias the Right accuses them of. This insecurity results in overcompensation, an unintentional overcorrection journalists make in order to preempt the accusation of any bias. This overcorrection is why we end up with a disproportionate number of conservative pundits on the Sunday morning talk shows.

And what does the mainstream media get for overcompensating? Pssh. These journalists certainly aren't impressing conservatives, a majority of whom no longer trust any mainstream news. In 2021, only 35 percent of Republicans interviewed by Pew researchers said they had "some trust" in national news organizations, down half, from 70 percent, just five years earlier.

But 78 percent of Democrats, and independents who lean Democratic, "have 'a lot' or 'some' trust in the information that comes from national news organizations." This isn't because the news media are pushing some liberal agenda. It's because many politically informed Democrats tend to get their news from a buffet of trusted sources, whereas Republicans tend to stick with a single source they personally trust—one that consistently reaffirms their worldview and provides a safe space from reality.

So, journalists and editors, check your coverage for overcompensation with as much care and diligence as you check for facts and fairness.

Overcompensation doesn't provide a full accounting of the story; it distorts the truth.

4. Cover Political Discourse Relentlessly

As the Republican Party dismantles the political institutions and norms that have built our democracy since its founding, America's inattention and indifference to political news coverage allows them the time and cover they need.

My plea to all mainstream news organizations: Cover America's political discourse and civic processes relentlessly, with the same intensity, frequency, and accuracy that your news organization covers crime, weather, and traffic. Covered properly, politics is never, ever "boring." Educate your audience on civics whenever you can. If your audience doesn't understand basic government functions and political processes, or the rights afforded by our Constitution and the responsibilities necessary to preserve those rights, your very right to gather and disseminate information unfettered—and our democracy itself—is at risk.

Today's entire Republican Party has declared war on objective truth. We may not live in a country where everyone is interested in politics, but we certainly get to demand stronger and smarter accountability from our news media when it comes to liars, deniers, and cheaters entrusted with political power.

And of course we cannot forget that while the news media may be the front line of our culture, *we* are that culture. That means the rest of us are ultimately responsible. It belongs to us, average Americans and news hounds alike. If the news media are failing us, then we are failing ourselves. If we get manipulated news or water-skiing squirrels instead of hard facts about our complicated system of government and those among us who want to control it, it's because water-skiing squirrels are more important to us than preserving our democracy.

Trust me, no water-skiing squirrel is *that* cute.

4

A Critical Culture War

Cancel culture . . . Colin Kaepernick . . . Bud Light . . . Tan suits . . . Dr. Seuss . . . Drag queens reading books . . . Books themselves! . . . Pronouns . . . Gas stoves . . . Paper drinking straws . . . Green M&M's new sneakers . . . The emasculation of a plastic potato toy . . . Americans have been inundated with dumb Republican controversies over the last few years (never let Republicans tell you that modern conservatism is about free enterprise and limited government). Their only strategy today is to invent wave after wave of culture war battles in their deliberate effort to split America apart.

Of all the controversies the Right and Republicans have made up in recent years, few compare to the effectiveness of the one that shaped the 2021 gubernatorial election in Virginia. It's a case study in what happens when, with the help of their own media ecosystem, the Republican Party injects artificial controversies into an unengaged, uninformed electorate.

Virginia is unique because one year after every presidential election, voters there go back to the polls to elect a new governor (Virginia's constitution also prohibits governors from running for consecutive terms). Political analysts pay close attention to this stand-alone bellwether race in the Old Dominion because the results give us important indicators about the broader political landscape across the rest of the country.

Virginia's metamorphosis from a swing state that slightly favored

Democrats before 2016 to a "safe blue" state in 2020, when Joe Biden trounced Donald Trump there by ten points, depended on the combined effects of pure independent voters breaking against the in party (the Republicans) and surging coalitional turnout among Democrats and Democratic leaners.

This trend applies to Virginia's gubernatorial elections too. Fifty years of data don't lie: The rule is that pure independent voters swing away from whichever party controls the presidency, which usually means the out party's candidate becomes governor. We saw an exception to this rule in 2013, a year after Barack Obama won his second term. That year, former Democratic National Committee chairman Terry McAuliffe capitalized on a weak Republican opponent and a libertarian spoiler (who got 146,000 votes) to buck a decades-long trend. McAuliffe became Virginia's in-party governor after winning by more than 56,000 votes in 2013.

Understandably, in 2021, Virginia Democrats attributed their recent successes to demographic change, which made Virginia more diverse. Some believed Virginia would stay blue.

"No, no," I told them. "Your recent wins aren't due to the brilliance of our party's electoral strategy. They were conditioned on favorable out-party fundamentals and backlash to Trump's election. That drove Democratic coalition voters out to vote, pushing swing voters away from Republicans."

As you can imagine, my explanation went over like a vegetarian in a steak house. The Democrats who believed Virginia would stay blue forever never fully appreciated how much they actually benefited from the long pattern of pure independents breaking against the in party, or from the uncommonly strong *negative partisanship* response to Donald Trump's disastrous presidency that drove higher turnout for their own coalition.

Republican strategists, however, understood *exactly* how their new out-party status would benefit their fortunes in Virginia's 2021 race for governor. They hatched a plan designed to enhance their built-in advantage with swing voters *and* the strong enthusiasm advantage among their coalitional voters. Then they wrapped their strategy into a single, purposely ambiguous issue nobody had ever heard of, taking full advantage of America's screwy civic culture.

POLITICAL OPPORTUNITY, POLITICAL MISCHIEF

Let's rewind back to September 1, 2020, a full year before Virginia elected a new governor, and only ninety-nine days after George Floyd's brutal murder under the knee of a white cop.

That Tuesday night, Tucker Carlson hosted an unknown conservative think-tank geek named Christopher Rufo on his popular primetime Fox News show. Rufo, introduced as a research fellow for a right-wing think tank called the Discovery Institute, also had ties to another, better known conservative think tank called the Manhattan Institute.

With millions of people watching, Rufo complained to Carlson that something called critical race theory had "pervaded every institution in the federal government" and was "being weaponized against the American people." Before that TV appearance, the term "critical race theory" wasn't even part of America's political vernacular.

Earlier in 2020, according to reporting by *The New Yorker,* a City of Seattle employee sent Christopher Rufo documents from a recent online "antibias training session." The documents, which Rufo shared on his website in July 2020, urged employee participants to examine their "white silence" and "white fragility" and offered advice for "processing white feelings" and "retraining." Rufo then requested materials from other government diversity workshops and seminars, and people from around the country started sending him screenshots and slide decks from their own online antiracism trainings. The common denominator, Rufo said, was references to an obscure, strange-sounding principle unfamiliar to most people who weren't legal scholars.

"I've obtained new documents from the city's segregated 'whites-only' trainings," Rufo wrote in July 2020, "which induct white employees into the cult of critical race theory. . . . Under the banner of 'antiracism,' Seattle's Office of Civil Rights is now explicitly endorsing principles of segregationism, group-based guilt, and race essentialism—ugly concepts that should have been left behind a century ago."

Rufo had a pile of what was admittedly nutty training materials documenting what he claimed was a government-led effort to make well-meaning white people feel guilty about being white. And he saw what I admit I would've seen in them: a political opportunity. On Fox News, Rufo detailed a specific anecdote about a diversity trainer hired by the U.S. Treasury Department to conduct seminars on critical race theory:

> And [the trainer] told Treasury employees essentially that America was, fundamentally, a white supremacist country and I quote, "virtually all white people uphold the system of racism and white superiority." And [he] was essentially denouncing the country and asking white employees at the Treasury Department and affiliated organizations to accept their white privilege, accept their racial superiority and accept, essentially, all of the baggage that comes with this reducible essence of whiteness.

Rufo then used his platform to appeal directly to Fox News's most famous viewer, asking President Trump on live TV to "immediately issue an executive order abolishing critical race theory trainings from the federal government."

Trump heard the plea and clearly understood the opportunity for his own political gain. Three days after Rufo's appearance on Fox, the head of the Office of Management and Budget sent a memo to the leaders of all federal departments and agencies stating "the President has directed me to ensure that Federal agencies cease and desist from using taxpayer dollars to fund these divisive, un-American propaganda training sessions."

"These types of 'trainings' not only run counter to the fundamental beliefs for which our Nation has stood since its inception," wrote the OMB director, Russell Vought, "but they also engender division and resentment within the Federal workforce." The move turned the issue of CRT from a feisty complaint on *Tucker Carlson Tonight* into an actual news story and hurled it smack into the lap of mainstream news organizations that covered the daily shitstorms of the Trump administration. And let's not forget, the "antibias training" material at the center of it all was hardly representative of most government literature; it was an outlier. But a single example is good enough to feed the outrage for Fox viewers and the Republican Party. *If one document goes overboard,* their thinking goes, *then all the other government training documents must be pushing some weird, woke agenda!*

The next morning, Trump took to Twitter to call CRT "a sickness." A couple weeks later, on September 22, he issued his own executive order stating that "it shall be the policy of the United States not to promote race or sex stereotyping or scapegoating in the Federal workforce or in the Uniformed Services." Trump's order quoted the well-known words from Dr. Martin Luther King Jr., hoping that his children would "not be judged by the color of their skin but by the content of their character."

Like Trump, the Republican Party establishment immediately saw CRT as a political opening wider than the Potomac River. They had their own media ecosystem and useful idiots in the media. They had an emotional controversy they could dishonestly yet effectively frame as reverse racism. And they had plenty of uninformed Americans—some of them independent voters in Virginia—to believe it. Mischief, managed.

WTF IS CRT?

Now, if you knew anything about critical race theory before the fall of 2020, you are certainly not an average American political junkie or news consumer, and you know a whole lot more about arcane legal scholarship than a vast majority of America. As I told the neo-fascist Charlie Kirk on his YouTube show *Debate Night,* I was happy to argue CRT with him, but just like the rest of America, I had no fucking idea what it was (of course that didn't stop Charlie from calling me a "CRT Advocate," and it didn't stop me from showing up in my "Fascism Sucks" shirt).

The New Yorker wrote that the idea of CRT emerged from legal scholars in the 1990s who "argued that the white supremacy of the past lived on in the laws and societal rules of the present." The mainstream media characterizes CRT as an "intellectual movement" or a "framework." Informed white liberals might conceptualize CRT as a social responsibility to acknowledge and unwind the lingering legacy of institutionalized racism and to acknowledge that being white in America means we've benefited, intentionally or unintentionally, from that painful legacy.

For the rest of America, the ambiguous phrase "critical race theory" becomes whatever message it *needs* to be, which is exactly why the GOP used it in Virginia's 2021 gubernatorial election. The right-wing Heritage Foundation quickly demonized it as "an unremitting attack on Western institutions and norms." The Republican National Committee called it "corrosive and antithetical to the history and founding of our nation."

Though voters struggled to define or understand the literal "theory," the emotional subtext Republicans intended all along came through loud and clear: *Democrats want to make your kids' school curriculum all about shaming your sweet, innocent children for being white. In fact, Democrats hate white people like you. They think you are racist, and now they're trying to undermine you by teaching your children about your racism while they're away at school.*

Even worse, CRT was the brainchild of academic elitists. The very term annoyingly invokes wonkiness and activates a latent sense of anti-intellectualism among plenty of Americans, especially the ones who watch Fox News in prime time.

"ANOTHER RIGHT-WING CONSPIRACY"

According to an analysis by *The Washington Post*, the phrase "critical race theory" was mentioned only 132 times on Fox News throughout 2020. By late June 2021, CRT had been mentioned nearly 2,000 times on Fox. By then, Republican legislatures in nine states had already passed laws banning the teaching of CRT or "the discussion, training,

and/or orientation that the U.S. is inherently racist as well as any discussions about conscious and unconscious bias, privilege, discrimination, and oppression," as characterized by the nonpartisan Brookings
Institution.

Back in Virginia, many Democrats still felt pretty good about their
election prospects—at least for the first half of 2021, but stuck on the
sidelines, I had my doubts.

Terry McAuliffe, the Democratic candidate, was a familiar face with
lots of name recognition following his first successful term as a relatively popular governor. Now McAuliffe was running again, this time
against a political newb: a Trump-endorsed, mild-mannered multimil-
lionaire in a sweater-vest named Glenn Youngkin. Most Virginians had
never heard of him. According to publicly available survey data, McAuliffe held a comfortable lead well into the fall of 2021. In August, a survey
conducted by Roanoke College even suggested McAuliffe led Youngkin
by eight percentage points—*well above* the survey's 4.2 percent margin
of error.

But the GOP's strategy to win by turning out their coalitional voters
and pushing swing voters away from Democrats didn't hinge on Youngkin or any other candidate for that matter. As planned by Republican
strategists, making CRT a central issue was all they needed to bring
enough negative partisanship into the equation.

As angry parents crammed into school board meetings to demand
an end to critical race theory, Youngkin fully embraced this GOP strategy and made the threat of CRT at public schools his main campaign
theme. Days before Virginia's May 8 primary election, he released four
ads attacking CRT over the course of twenty-four hours. He bemoaned
CRT in a May 4 interview with Tucker Carlson, claiming it was the reason McAuliffe and Democrats wanted "to take accelerated math out of
the curriculum." Lo and behold, *The Washington Post* debunked that lie
a week before Youngkin repeated it on Fox.

Through the summer of 2021, Youngkin claimed that CRT had
"moved into all our schools in Virginia," which the Pulitzer Prize–winning
fact-checking organization PolitiFact found to be false. But as long as Fox

News told viewers CRT was a threat to children and to the ability of parents to have a say in their kids' education, viewers believed it.

In June, Fox News published a recording of McAuliffe calling the debate over CRT "another right-wing conspiracy." He said the issue was "totally made up by Donald Trump and Glenn Youngkin." Why did Fox even air the "leaked" recording? Presumably it was to show that the Democratic candidate was an out-of-touch liberal elitist, and dismissive of a deeply emotional issue that Fox had convinced its viewers was real.

And while what McAuliffe said was true, it wasn't an effective response, at least politically. He then tried to reframe the debate over public education on his terms:

> Why are we not paying our teachers? Why are we down a thousand teachers today? Why? And why are 50 percent of our schools 50 years old? This is what people want to know about. So let's pay our teachers, let's get our children access to broadband. Let's make sure we get at-risk children taken care of with pre-K. Those are what the Virginians care about.

His public education message, though, didn't stick. A shortage of teachers, crumbling schools, and at-risk children didn't strike the gong of visceral emotion the way critical race theory did. By luring McAuliffe into contesting an election on the GOP's terms, and on the GOP's proven issues like reverse racism, Republicans ensured that they kept the ball while we Democrats got stuck playing defense, and you don't score many touchdowns playing defense.

And just as you might expect, the debate over CRT, brimming with conflict, chaos, and controversy, didn't just stay in the echo chamber of right-wing news organizations. Soon after the primary, *The Washington Post*'s Robert McCartney mentioned Youngkin's opposition to critical race theory in a column suggesting the Republican had "a surprisingly good chance of winning."

By early summer, as Republican talking heads and politicians across the country banged their pots and pans about critical race theory, most of the mainstream media began covering its growing role in Virginia's race for governor. Spoiler alert: *No* public schools in Virginia or anywhere else in America were even teaching critical race theory. The mainstream media reported this too, but none of it mattered, at least politically.

The mere threat of Democrats indoctrinating *your* children was all Republicans needed for voters in Virginia and everywhere else to file a grievance with the status quo. This forced McAuliffe to do what so many other Democrats are used to doing: he had to persistently explain and defend an ambiguous issue that most people don't even want to understand.

Critical race theory provided Republicans with the perfect opportunity to wedge race, children, and racial identity overtly into the election. But it pulled even more important strategic weight for Republicans than that. The main benefit of the GOP's CRT strategy—and others like it—is the response it predictably elicits from us Democrats.

WHY LET LITTLE DETAILS MATTER?

Throughout 2021, countless Americans started *believing* what Tucker Carlson, Chris Rufo, the RNC, and other conservatives with microphones said critical race theory was: reverse racism imposed by woke elitists on non-racist white children and "seeping into classrooms" funded by *your* tax dollars.

As with other issues in our hot mess of contemporary politics, Democrats know we can beat Republicans on substance. We know that the facts, the ethics, and the morals of the issues are on our side, even with made-up, hyperbolized controversies like CRT, and we simply can't resist any opportunity to tell you so because we are smart and because we are right. And every time Republicans lay out a baited trap like CRT, we Democrats can't help but oblige. After all, fighting racism is our issue! So is public education! And damn it, facts matter!

I can't stress this enough: *the Democrats' response, or lack thereof, is half the point of the Republicans' strategy!* So what was our response to critical race theory? Great question, which the *Washington Post* columnists Paul Waldman and Greg Sargent accurately answered:

> When Republicans turned an obscure academic topic known as critical race theory into a national boogeyman supposedly poisoning the minds of our youth, Democrats were caught flat-footed. They weren't sure how to react: Debate what it actually means? Explain that it isn't something that gets taught to kids? In the face of relentless conservative demagoguery, they were flummoxed.

"Flummoxed" here is just a polite word for fucked. While the GOP and its allies used critical race theory to effectively convince countless Americans that *wokeness is racist*, progressives and the Democratic establishment had no singular counter-message, no cohesive strategy, no media ecosystem, no simple way out.

Through most of 2021, McAuliffe and other Democrats responded by explaining that CRT is not what many voters think it is. We scrambled to try to define the literal and academic intentions of critical race theory, to give it context, and to swat down falsehoods. We said CRT was "made up," as McAuliffe did. We presumed voters would proactively seek the truth from the mainstream news media, which invited scholars and professors and progressive do-gooders to walk their audiences through the academic history of untangling the legacy of institutionalized racism. We used a whole lot of clunky, confusing words you'd never hear on Fox News or at a MAGA rally, like "intersectionality," "heteronormativity," and "differential racialization."

We responded by acknowledging "racial insensitivity" and with generalizations like "people don't want to hurt other people's feelings," as Joe Biden did when asked about CRT during the September 29, 2020, presidential debate.

When the Trump administration banned antiracism trainings in the federal government, Democratic senator Cory Booker of New Jersey quickly requested a Judiciary Committee hearing to address "serious constitutional questions . . . while the nation is confronting a historic moment with racial justice."

But none of these responses were strong enough, clear enough, or convincing enough to push back against the Republican Party's critical race theory strategy. The GOP and its allies didn't (and still don't) give a rat's ass what CRT actually is. Their unspoken motto: *Why let little details matter when you've got all the powerful, simple, emotional messages on your side?*

It's like the Republican Party's freestyle use of the words "socialism" and "cultural Marxism." GOP strategists know that most average Americans don't really understand what socialism or Marxism is. But over the course of decades, they vilified those words and conditioned their coalition to believe that socialism and Marxism are bad and un-American. If you call Democrats socialists, technicalities aside, Americans will believe Democrats are bad through association. If you say CRT is wrong and has Marxist roots, as the Heritage Foundation and the RNC did, conservatives will believe CRT is un-American because it's Marxist—whatever that means.

In politics this is called branding, by the way, and we'll cover it extensively soon.

"INVOLVED PARENTS"

By September 2021, the fight over critical race theory in Virginia evolved into another controversy that bolstered the GOP's coalitional turnout against Terry McAuliffe. Like CRT, this controversy had a powerful grip on mostly white voters, and like CRT it had a racial subtext that forced the former governor to play defense on what most of us would consider a pretty damn stellar record on public education.

In 2016, then-governor McAuliffe vetoed a Republican bill requiring schools to tell parents when their children were assigned books with sexually explicit content. State lawmakers passed the legislation after a parent objected to her son's assigned reading of Toni Morrison's Pulitzer Prize–winning post–Civil War novel *Beloved*. Though considered one of the great works of modern literature, the concerned mom objected to scenes in *Beloved* that depict sex, rape, and bestiality.

"This legislation lacks flexibility and would require the label of 'sexually explicit' to apply to an artistic work based on a single scene, without further context," McAuliffe said of his veto, also noting that Virginia's "school systems have an obligation to provide age-appropriate material for students."

Now fast-forward five years to the final debate between McAuliffe and Youngkin, in late September 2021.

"You believe school systems should tell children what to do," Youngkin told McAuliffe, making a clear connection between sexually explicit books and the bogeyman of critical race theory. "I believe parents should be in charge of their kids' education."

"I'm not going to let parents come into schools and actually take books out and make their own decisions," McAuliffe retorted. Then he added a line that dogged him for the rest of the campaign—something that neatly rested the GOP's case against him: "I don't think parents should be telling schools what they should teach."

Republicans immediately seized on that line, using it to punctuate the CRT argument Youngkin and the right-wing media carefully laid out to Republican voters, Republican leaners, and swing voters across Virginia: *Moms and Dads, Terry McAuliffe thinks the government knows better than us when it comes to parenting, and critical race theory is just the beginning.*

Youngkin also launched a minute-long ad featuring the parent whose complaint about *Beloved* prompted the legislation in the first place. In the viral ad the mother, a white woman named Laura Murphy, sits in front of a fireplace literally wringing her hands with anxious sadness.

"When my son showed me his reading assignment, my heart sank," Murphy says, without ever mentioning the title of *Beloved* or the name of its Black author, or that her son was a senior taking an Advanced Placement class when *Beloved* was assigned. "It was some of the most explicit material you can imagine." Oh, honey.

To anyone unfamiliar with the finer nuances of critical race theory or the heated race for political power in Virginia, CRT was now about more than woke liberals pushing a radical agenda to make white kids feel guilty. According to Youngkin and the Republicans, now it was also about *pushing pornography on your children, and if you're a parent, those crazy Democrats don't think it's any of your damn business!*

Another Youngkin ad featured a woman at a school board meeting resigning from her job as a teacher and sobbing as she says, "I quit. I quit your policies. I quit your trainings that tell me to push highly politicized agendas." A narrator then pipes in and says, "McAuliffe caused chaos in our schools" as Virginia's governor, and then a clip from Fox News claims, inaccurately, "McAuliffe's administration actively pushed CRT." McAuliffe watched his lead over Youngkin dwindle as Election Day approached—as Youngkin claimed his opponent *caused chaos* in public schools.

Perhaps with no choice left, Terry McAuliffe had to go on defense on the issue of public education, one of his strengths. In mid-October he launched his own ad featuring pics of his smiling children:

> As parents, Dorothy and I have always been involved in our kids' education. We know good schools depend on involved parents. That's why I want you to hear this from me: Glenn Youngkin is taking my words out of context. I've always valued the concerns of parents. It's why, as governor, we scaled back standardized testing, expanded pre-K, and invested a billion dollars in public schools.

The fact that McAuliffe had to produce and run that ad, in order to defend himself as a champion of public education, was a clear sign of political danger. The red check-engine light flashed on the dashboard. We political insiders could almost see the smoke billowing from under the hood of his campaign.

NIBBLING THE SQUIRMY WORM

As for *Beloved*, the McAuliffe campaign released another TV ad addressing what Youngkin and the Republicans never publicly admitted: that the fight over whether an important, celebrated novel by a Black author should be taught in public schools was, as McAuliffe repeatedly said, "a racist dog whistle," like the entire debate over critical race theory.

The first half of McAuliffe's sixty-second ad, called "Our Voice Matters," features Barack Obama and Oprah Winfrey praising Toni Morrison. Then a narrator comes in for a pitch to Virginia's Black voters:

> Now, in the final days of this campaign, Glenn Youngkin supports banning books by Toni Morrison and other Black authors in Virginia classrooms. We know what this is. Just like Donald Trump, Glenn is trying to silence our voices, to silence the truth. But our voice matters and together our collective power will keep this great Commonwealth moving forward. Make your plan to vote.

As a stand-alone ad, "Our Voice Matters" is an example of powerful political communication. The message—that Glenn Youngkin, like Donald Trump, is a rich white *racist* who wants to silence Black voices—is a bold and powerful gut punch. And bonus: It's true! But rather than responding to Youngkin's attacks on CRT, McAuliffe needed to launch a counteroffensive, forcing Youngkin into a defensive posture. The Republican Party wanted to make *public education* the centerpiece of their strategy, and the McAuliffe campaign should have made them regret it by hammering the Republican Party's record on education and by painting Glenn Youngkin as a dangerous extremist bent on destroying Virginia's public schools.

Instead, McAuliffe closed his campaign exactly where the Republican Party wanted him: on defense.

"[Youngkin] wants to ban Toni Morrison's book *Beloved*," McAuliffe complained to Chuck Todd on NBC's *Meet the Press* just two days before

Election Day. "So he's going after one of the most preeminent African American female writers in American history—won the Nobel Prize, has the Presidential Medal of Freedom—and he wants her books banned. Of all the hundreds of books you could look at, why did you take the one Black female author? Why did you do it?"

I'd make the same argument if I were sitting in a room full of ultra-informed, well-read, die-hard political activists having a chat. I'm sure we'd have a substantive policy conversation about good government, and of course that includes important discussions about racial identity, white supremacy, and American literature. But *this* book is an in-your-face reminder that *Republicans don't play that game*. All they care about is holding on as white hegemonic power collapses around them. And they're pretty good at it.

Charles Siler, a self-described former pitchman for the "libertarian-conservative movement" who now advocates for well-funded public schools, confesses that the GOP's strategy to manufacture panic around CRT builds on "a centuries-old tactic that has been trotted out whenever conservatives have felt left behind by social progress."

"From the critiques of evolution being taught in science classes culminating in the Scopes Monkey Trial of 1925, to rabid opposition to sexual-health classes from the 1960s to today, their industrial media machine feeds on outrage," Siler wrote in *The Economist* in 2022.

Still, it was a winning strategy for the GOP. I'm quite certain Glenn Youngkin, his well-paid team of D.C. consultants, all the suits at the Republican Governors Association, and all the operatives at all the right-wing think tanks and media organizations grinned like Cheshire cats as they watched Terry McAuliffe gripe to Chuck Todd on *Meet the Press*. Mischief managed, again.

We cannot forget what he *wasn't* talking about. He and the Democrats weren't making a case to key voters about the GOP's long-held plans to destroy public education to fund private Christian schools. We weren't talking to voters about the Republican Party's plans to end abortion nationwide, gut their healthcare, steal their Social Security money, and let their kids be slaughtered at their schools. We weren't talking about the Republicans' effort to end democracy. We weren't even talking about the Virginians who'd been sickened or killed by COVID because Republicans brainwashed them into exposing themselves to a deadly virus; 10,300 Virginians died of COVID in the single year leading up to Election Day.

When we should've been talking about Republicans, Virginia's 2021 race closed with *them* talking about *us* and *us* talking about *us*. Rinse and repeat.

Glenn Youngkin beat Terry McAuliffe by more than 63,000 votes—almost two full percentage points—on November 2, 2021. The next day Fox News reported that according to their own survey a quarter of Virginia voters said critical race theory was "the single most important factor they considered when deciding who to support for governor," and nearly three-quarters said CRT was an "important" factor.

Turns out, talking about race in America, especially in the frame of a threat to white identity, was *good* for Republicans in Virginia. They knew we Democrats would take the bait—that we would keep nibbling the squirmy worm as long as it dangled from their hook.

We couldn't help ourselves. And Virginians got left with the check.

"EDUCATIONAL GAG ORDERS"

Critical race theory evolved into a much bigger animal since its debut in American politics in the fall of 2020. The Right built a parallel universe around CRT, relying on misinformation, a largely apathetic electorate, negative partisanship, and emotional conflict to redefine it as something much broader than some legal theory about racism and racial identity.

In late 2021, the pro-free-speech organization PEN America published a report about the political response to the furor over critical race theory. The Republicans didn't just push CRT to win an election; they made the whole issue up, then legislated on it with horrifying consequences. PEN America examined twenty-four state legislatures that had, over the course of the year, "introduced 54 separate bills intended to restrict teaching and training in K–12 schools, higher education, and state agencies and institutions."

> The majority of these bills target discussions of race, racism, gender, and American history, banning a series of "prohibited" or "divisive" concepts for teachers and trainers operating in K–12 schools, public universities, and workplace settings. These bills appear designed to chill academic and educational discussions and impose government dictates on teaching and learning. In short: They are educational gag orders. . . . Their adoption demonstrates a disregard for academic freedom, liberal education, and the values of free speech and open inquiry that are enshrined in the First Amendment and that anchor a democratic society.

Through 2021, critical race theory had indeed become a convenient and familiar strawman—an umbrella issue that allowed the GOP and the political Right to lay battle plans for their bigger culture war. Chris Rufo admitted on Twitter that his goal all along was "to have the public read something crazy in the newspaper and immediately think 'critical race theory.'"

And it didn't take long for the Right to take the manufactured moral outrage over CRT and the well-being of children to an even uglier right-wing conspiracy theory that gained traction in right-wing media. Fox personalities and Republican politicians falsely accused the Left of indoctrinating and sexualizing *children*.

"The Left is *obsessed* with teaching children about sexual and gender identity," Fox's Laura Ingraham complained on April 7, 2022. Then she attacked Disney, which had just infuriated conservatives by publicly opposing Florida's controversial "Don't Say Gay" bill. Chris Rufo had also just claimed (on Fox) that Disney was "injecting queerness" into its children's programming. "Marketing sneakers or those goofy mouse ears to kids—that's one thing," Ingraham told her viewers, "but marketing complicated topics of sexuality and gender—that's *grooming*."

A few months earlier, Tucker Carlson had accused California teachers of "grooming seven-year-olds and talking to seven-year-olds about their sex lives."

So why, you might be asking, is the Right so hell-bent on fighting this fight and twisting their narrative to the point of lunacy? For a simple answer, let's turn to Republican congressman Jim Banks of Indiana, who served as chairman of the Republican Study Committee in 2021. *Politico* obtained a memo Banks sent to his GOP colleagues that year titled "Lean into the Culture War."

"The Democrat Party has wholly embraced Critical Race Theory and all its conclusions," Banks falsely claimed of an issue most Democrats can't even define. Then he added,

> We are in a culture war. On one side, Republicans are working to renew American patriotism and rebuild our country. On the other, Democrats have embraced and given platform to a radical element who want to tear America down.
>
> Here's the good news: **We are winning.**

Jim Banks underlined and bolded those words, by the way. And when an extreme MAGA Republican like him calls a made-up issue in a culture war "good news," we can count on it being terrible news for American democracy.

The Republican Party understood from the get-go that the political bonfire of critical race theory would create a blanket of smoke everyone else had to choke on. The issue touched on deep fears and emotions that Republicans knew they could stoke within their base and across the broader electorate, proactively, without ever having to worry about the *actual* consequences of whatever they claimed critical race theory would bring. Candidates, voters, and the news media played right into their hands, coughing along the way.

While Republicans waste no time shaping the electorate over made-up fears, Democrats point to very real ones that are already making us sicker, poorer, and less secure. Overturning *Roe v. Wade* was never just a pie-in-the-sky *threat* from the Republican Party, for example; it was a decades-long promise. And they delivered.

So just how do they do it? How do Republicans control so much of the narrative with shit that isn't true? How does their world work? How do they shape so much of America's political landscape? How do they end up with more convincing messages? And how do they get so many Americans to come along with them?

For answers, let's go where no Democrat has gone before: deep inside their playbook.

PART II

CHESS VERSUS CHECKERS

Our party needs to reconcile bottom-up, not just top-down . . . to begin to reconcile. We do not have the surround sound; we don't have the anger machine that those folks have on the other side. And we're going to have to do better in terms of getting on the offense and stop being on the damn defense.

—GOVERNOR GAVIN NEWSOM,

D-California, *The Takeout,* November 2, 2022

5

This or That?

Let's get a few things straight about the playbook of today's Republican Party. First, there's nothing all that sophisticated about it. In fact, *simplicity* is one of its most admirable attributes.

Like a social media algorithm designed to agitate followers enough to keep scrolling and engaging, Republicans have figured out how to manipulate information and the delivery of that information (and misinformation) in order to fire up their followers and convert new ones into their fold. The Republican Party can drive entire news cycles and distill complex political issues into uncomplicated, emotive talking points—facts, logic, decorum, and compassion be damned. Any strategy as basic as appealing to tribalism, fear, and instinctive emotion—which is exactly what Republicans do so well—may be devastatingly effective, but it's hardly innovative. The same strategy was used to launch the Third Reich.

Second, there's nothing secret about the GOP playbook. Republicans don't whisper their strategies behind clipboards like coaches on the sideline. Their playbook is wide open for the world to see. I've spent my career researching it.

Third, the GOP's playbook is not sustainable because it is hostile to democracy. Today's Republican Party openly supports fascism, aspires to authoritarianism, and embraces racism and violent insurrection. That only lasts so long before your democracy either triumphs or crumbles. It also means Republican strategies have increasingly relied on falsehoods, ignorance, conspiracy theories, and overrepresentation in political power. MAGA Republicans have shitcanned any allegiance to the truth, they couldn't care less about moral inconveniences (like violence and hypocrisy), and they've made plenty of room for weirdos, extremists, and dimwits who deserve no place in any part of our elected government.

And fourth, though the GOP playbook has furnished winning plays for the Republican Party in recent years, resulting in key electoral victories, appointments, and policy outcomes, it's neither visionary nor intellectually honest. Politicizing the federal debt ceiling and risking the stability of the entire U.S. economy in order to force drastic spending cuts that directly hurt seniors, children, and veterans is ultimately a zero-sum game. Convincing millions of voters that a free and fair election was stolen is only possible in a party that is no longer moored in intellectual honesty.

But the GOP playbook is, for the most part, disciplined and dogged. It took *decades*, after all, to install enough conservative justices on the Supreme Court to overturn *Roe v. Wade*. Achieving that also required the creation (and ample funding) of two right-wing organizations devoted wholly to the cause: the Federalist Society, tasked with recruiting new followers of "constitutional originalism" (whatever that is, because it seems to be in the eye of the beholder), and Judicial Watch, which was instrumental in making up the right-wing narrative that America's federal courts were full of liberal "activist judges" hell-bent on "legislating from the bench." After half a century of careful political positioning, the GOP got a handsome return on their investment in a whole slate of conservative judges who actually do legislate from the bench (like the Texas judge Matthew Kacsmaryk, a Trump appointee, who put a hold on the abortion drug mifepristone in April 2023, overruling a twenty-three-year-old, science-based decision by the Food and Drug Administration).

Today's Republican Party benefits from a well-financed, vertically aligned system that finds and elevates conservative causes and candidates, helps their campaigns, and—using their own news media ecosystem and shrewd, well-funded think tanks—saturates their coalition with cutthroat messages carefully crafted to earn Republican votes and to persuade swing voters to *not* vote for Democrats. Of course, this is all easier to do when Republican leaders lose no sleep over lying, or making false accusations, or adopting the preschool logic that *everyone else* is to blame for their own political losses. And of course it's easier to do when most Americans don't care about politics and when 100 million of them refuse to even vote.

As for the Democratic Party's playbook? Sure, Democrats are generally united by the progressive principles agreed upon and codified in their platform. They stand for big-ticket values like equal rights and representation, fair pay and fair taxes, public education, access to healthcare, and protecting the environment. But do Democrats have some sort of centralized electioneering strategy designed solely to win political power? Nope, they do not. While Democrats are stuck with checkers, Republicans are playing chess.

To understand why, remember what I pointed out earlier: America's democracy has opened up to a lot more eligible voters since the middle of the last century. What was once the exclusive, heteronormative domain of wealthy, educated, mostly Christian, white men before the civil rights movement is now *everyone's* political domain—at least in principle. For the most part, today's Republican Party represents what *used to* control and shape our political system. The slow collapse of white male dominance in American politics means Republicans represent an ever-diminishing slice of the electorate. As the Republican Party began representing a shrinking chunk of America, the Democratic Party represented almost everyone else by default—becoming a much bigger tent with a lot more varying opinions and perspectives.

That progress has most certainly been for the better in a modern, globalized democracy that values multiculturalism, identity, and diversity, but it's also been, well, clunky. As necessary as it is, it isn't easy representing and giving voice to "everyone else," especially when the Republican Party has waged war on multiculturalism, identity, and diversity.

TWO IS THE LONELIEST NUMBER

You might be wondering by now: *Why are we stuck with only two parties, anyway?*

In 2022, the Pew Research Center conducted a major nationwide survey exploring "partisan hostility" and found that nearly half (47 percent) of the voters surveyed between the ages of eighteen and forty-nine "wish there were more parties to choose from"—Democrats more so than Republicans. Pew's survey, of more than six thousand American voters (margin of error: +/− 1.8 percent), also found that only 41 percent of them "have a very or somewhat favorable view of the Democratic Party." Only 37 percent "have a favorable impression of the Republican Party."

America is far too huge and diverse for our entire political system to be split into a binary choice between Republicans and Democrats, isn't it? Why are there no other viable options? We political scientists get asked these questions all the time. Our two-party system controlled by Republicans and Democrats isn't going anywhere anytime soon. And it's important to understand why before we get into the real nitty-gritty of comparing the two parties.

Some political systems, like many across Europe, choose their national leaders through *proportional representation*. Voters in the U.K., for example, don't elect a prime minister. They elect members to Parliament; then those members choose a prime minister based on which party holds the majority of seats or can "team up" with other parties to form a governing coalition. Their job is to figure out how to form a government among all the parties that represent various interests across the political spectrum proportionally. If the Green Party earns 5 percent of the vote, they get 5 percent of the seats in parliament.

That's not how it works in America. We choose our political leaders in majoritarian elections—where whoever gets a plurality of popular votes wins and losers, even those who nearly won, get nothing. And we elect our presidents independently from our federal lawmakers. In majoritarian, presidential political systems like ours, voters *consistently* express *preference for* a two-party system, even when they say they don't. This phenomenon is called Duverger's law, named for the French political scientist Maurice Duverger, who first documented the tendency in the mid-twentieth century. Under Duverger's law, it doesn't matter *which two* political parties dominate our political system; the point is that voters tend to favor a system that elevates only two viable options. And in the modern era of American politics, those two parties are the Republicans and the Democrats.

Does this mean we're stuck with only Democrats and Republicans? Not necessarily! Any other political party could replace one of the dominant two parties, but it would have to represent a significant share— roughly half—of the electorate. In other words, unless a third party can muster enough votes to actually win an election, and not just a smattering of votes from principled ideologues and protest voters, that party stands no chance. This also means third-party and independent candidates tend to be spoilers, not realistic options.

In 1992, the independent presidential candidate Ross Perot garnered nearly 19 percent of the popular vote (just over 19.7 million votes). That's an impressive share, but it wasn't enough for Perot to win a single Electoral College vote, which is all that matters in presidential elections. The Green Party candidate Ralph Nader didn't even come close in the shitshow of the 2000 election. Nader earned only 2.8 million votes nationwide. More than 97,000 of those votes, however, came from Florida, where George W. Bush officially eked out a win with only 537 more votes than Al Gore, ultimately clinching Florida's Electoral College votes to become president (let's never forget that Bush lost the national popular vote in 2000 by more than half a million votes). Ralph Nader's candidacy, as my Democratic friends from Florida like to remind me, gave America Dubya's disastrous presidency.

But the Nader Spoil of 2000 doesn't hold a candle to what happened in the "Blue Wall" states of Pennsylvania, Wisconsin, and Michigan in 2016. Among those three blue-leaning swing states that year, more than 700,000 voters supported third-party candidates over Hillary Clinton or Donald Trump (namely the Libertarian Gary Johnson, the Green Party's Jill Stein, and the independent Evan McMullin—none of whom came close to even winning participation ribbons). Why did those candidates get so many votes? Mostly because their voters didn't trust Clinton (more on that soon). And instead of focusing efforts on mobilizing Clinton's base supporters, her campaign tried, in vain, to recruit Republicans wary about Trump. And so, thanks in large part to the third-party spoilers of 2016, Donald Trump won Pennsylvania, Wisconsin, and Michigan by only 80,000 votes and by earning only a plurality of the vote. That gave him 304 Electoral Votes and the presidency (let's also never forget that Trump lost the national popular vote in 2016 by more than *2.8 million* votes).

Now you know why political dweebs like me are so skeptical of efforts by groups like No Labels to fund and field a Third Party "consensus" candidate. No Labels is a secretly funded, well-endowed political organization trying to become a viable political party (it actually *is* a registered political party in some states). No Labels claims to be a "national movement of consensus Americans" who don't consider themselves extremists on the left or the right. No Labels says it wants to be a moderate party representing the political middle, and for the 2024 presidential election it was "preparing for the possibility of nominating" a unity ticket that includes a moderate Democrat and a moderate Republican as "an insurance policy that the American public wants and needs." That might seem like a creative, noble concept peppered with swell-sounding platitudes, but we're still stuck with a fundamental problem: Unless No Labels supersedes either the Democrats or the Republicans in our majoritarian, two-party system, which it won't do anytime soon, it will just be another spoiler that will likely screw Democrats again. And I'm not alone in splashing cold water on No Labels.

"No Labels is committed to fielding a candidate that will, intentionally or not, provide a crucial boost to Republicans—and a major obstacle to Biden," the center-left, nonpartisan think tank Third Way pointed out in 2023. "As a result, [No Labels would] make it far more likely—if not certain—that Donald Trump returns to the White House."

While No Labels points to research suggesting that a plurality of American voters identify as independents and want a "different choice" than Trump or Biden, Third Way highlights the same fine print in voter behavior that I pointed out in chapter 2: If you ask voters who claim to be politically independent which party they *lean toward*, most will answer "the Republican Party" or "the Democratic Party," and they'll vote accordingly. Subtract out all those party leaners, and you're left with a much smaller percentage of *pure independents*—definitely not a plurality, and certainly not enough to replace one of our two established political parties. Like it or not, and for the foreseeable future, America is stuck with a two-party political system controlled by Democrats and Republicans.

PARTY OF THE PEOPLE

While I can understand the frustration with American politics and the parties that make up our two-party system, it's much more difficult for me to accept sweeping mischaracterizations like "all politicians are corrupt," or "the Democrats are just as bad as the Republicans," or "both parties are to blame."

The Democratic Party is far from perfect, and, sure, we have our share of bad eggs and scandals like any other endeavor that involves human beings. But the Democratic Party isn't actively trying to destroy American democracy and hijack our freedom as today's Republican Party is. For decades, for crying out loud, Democrats played the aces when it came to winning elections and controlling power at all levels of government—using their legislative power to build America's economy and to expand its middle class.

What can we thank the Democratic Party for? If you ever find your-

self debating anyone who questions the record of Team Blue over the
past century, keep this list handy:

- the rise of organized labor, allowing unionized workers to
  collectively bargain for fair pay, benefits, and safe working
  conditions;
- the New Deal, which made unprecedented investments in physical
  infrastructure across the nation, brought electricity to rural
  America, allowed middle-class families to finance home ownership
  through the Federal National Mortgage Association (Fannie Mae),
  and implemented agricultural reforms that ended the Dust Bowl;
- Social Security (1935);
- the Fair Labor Standards Act, which established the federal
  minimum wage, the forty-hour workweek, and overtime pay and
  put limits on child labor (1938);
- the Servicemen's Readjustment Act, better known as the GI Bill,
  which provided higher education and job opportunities, and home
  loans, to millions of American veterans (1944);
- the Federal-Aid Highway Act of 1956, which built the U.S.
  Interstate Highway System;
- the Clean Air Act of 1963;
- the Civil Rights Act of 1964, which outlawed discrimination based
  on "race, color, religion, sex or national origin";
- the Voting Rights Act of 1965, which outlawed racial discrimination
  in voting;
- the Higher Education Act of 1965, which established Pell Grants;
- Medicare (1965);
- the Title X amendment to the Public Health Service Act, now
  known as Title X, which provides family planning services and
  reproductive healthcare—including preventive cancer
  screenings—to lower-income women (1970);
- the Title IX amendment to the Higher Education Act, now just
  called Title IX, which prohibits gender discrimination in schools
  that receive federal funding (1972);

- health insurance for all Americans, regardless of preexisting conditions, through the Patient Protection and Affordable Care Act, better known as Obamacare (2010).

While some of these accomplishments earned bipartisan support (like Title X, which passed the Senate with unanimous support), or began as bipartisan ideas (like the GI Bill), Democratic lawmakers championed *all* of them. And this is just a partial list!

So what exactly is the problem for Democrats today? Democrats are still the "party of the people," right? Of *smart* people. Of people who think for themselves and care about others. Why is it that Democrats have sound principles, better-qualified candidates, and smarter policies that benefit more Americans, yet we keep losing so often in the court of public opinion and at the ballot box? Why don't more people vote for the party of the people, especially when the alternative is likely to be a candidate who has no problem trampling on your rights and dismantling American democracy as we know it, making you and your family sicker, poorer, and less secure?

Better messaging is certainly part of the answer, and we'll tackle that in the next chapter. But the other big reason that Republicans continue to earn so many votes from the American electorate is that today's Republican Party is a product of stronger, older, more centralized, better organized political *infrastructure*.

Sure, Democrats have political infrastructure. Democrats, along with their alphabet soup of affiliated electoral organizations and their progressive allies (namely not-for-profit social welfare organizations), are good at mobilizing grassroots volunteers, identifying voters, and getting them to vote on or before Election Day. Many Democrats get elected and reelected thanks to some of the savviest campaign strategists and political minds in the world, even when the odds are stacked against them. The Democratic Party has accomplished lots of difficult, impressive things in its complicated history. But its political infrastructure trails way behind the system that props up today's GOP for two main reasons: billionaires and corporations.

HERITAGE: FOUNDATIONAL POLITICAL INFRASTRUCTURE

Half a century ago, as the Democratic Party experienced the growing pains of an expanded, Vietnam War–weary electorate, the newly re-aligned Republican Party wrestled with its own problem: President Richard Nixon, dogged by one of the most consequential scandals in American history. But Watergate wasn't what really bothered the right-wing ideologues of the early 1970s; they were frustrated with Nixon's politics, which they thought were *too liberal*. A conservative historian named Kevin Roberts claims Nixon's political fallout "left the conserva-tive movement in shambles—even though he had governed as anything but a conservative."

So in 1973—the same year the Supreme Court ruled that women have a constitutional right to our own reproductive freedom in *Roe v. Wade*—a group of conservative operatives founded a powerful organiza-tion *outside* the official infrastructure of the Republican Party: the Heri-tage Foundation. Kevin Roberts, by the way, has been its president since late 2021.

Though there are countless other right-wing think tanks, public pol-icy centers, special interest organizations, nonprofits, and watchdog groups, the Heritage Foundation stands above the rest in terms of its influence over modern conservatism and the Republican agenda in Congress, at the White House, and in statehouses across the country.

The Heritage Foundation, whose eight-story headquarters faces the U.S. Capitol complex, officially claims it doesn't "work on behalf of any special interest or political party." That's as honest as me telling you I'm a former supermodel. The mission of Heritage is "to formulate and promote public policies based on the principles of free enterprise, lim-ited government, individual freedom, traditional American values, and a strong national defense." You could say it professes the quaint, conser-vative values of the Republican Party of decades ago. But in the critical infrastructure of today's Republican Party, the Heritage Foundation is a double-decker suspension bridge between Washington and the rest of America. It rewrote the how-to manual on shaping public opinion and driving conservative agendas through public policy at the highest levels of American government.

When *The New York Times* wrote about the influence of the Heritage Foundation back in 1985, it noted the think tank's conservative staffers weren't pressured to "develop highly original ideas" that "shape scholarly thinking on an issue" in academic books or boring articles. Instead, Heritage analysts were "expected to cultivate sources in Congress and the Administration, sense what issues are becoming ripe and produce terse position papers that can be used to sway political argument."

In 1980, just ten days after voters ousted Jimmy Carter and elected Ronald Reagan, Heritage gave the president-elect a three-thousand-page document detailing some two thousand conservative ideas, which it called the *Mandate for Leadership.* The twenty-volume *Mandate* thoroughly detailed what the Heritage Foundation saw as problems within the sprawling federal government and suggested conservative solutions to them. President Reagan gave copies to members of his cabinet during his first meeting with them.

Heritage estimates it got most of those ideas implemented during Reagan's first year as president, then had the gall to tell Reagan even he wasn't conservative enough! After Reagan's first year in office, the think tank blasted the president's administration for moving too slowly on political appointments, calling the Justice Department a "major disappointment" and the State Department a "nagging embarrassment" while throwing some perfunctory praise to Reagan's "personal leadership." The entire process cemented the Heritage Foundation's influential new place in the unofficial infrastructure of the Republican Party.

You don't move the needle by just sitting around talking about ideas, the Heritage Foundation's political strategy suggests. *You have to make those ideas stick with leaders who are empowered and motivated to turn them into political outcomes, and you have to give them effective language needed to make it stick!* If that sounds like common sense today, it's because the Heritage Foundation *made it* common sense decades ago. This strategy was revolutionary in its time. While some political think tanks emulate this strategy today, others stick to the much more traditional, passive model of simply making policy-based research and ideas publicly available with the hope that the right people will see them and incorporate them in their work.

Today the Heritage Foundation is a megalith institution that operates as a tax-exempt nonprofit. Public records indicate Heritage in 2021 employed 465 people and reported more than $100 million in revenue, mostly tax-deductible contributions from conservative corporate and family foundations. It has published multiple editions of *Mandate for Leadership* since 1981 and boasts that the Trump administration embraced 64 percent of the "policy solutions" from its 2016 edition.

In 2022, Roberts announced the 2025 Presidential Transition Project, which he described as the "most ambitious" in the Heritage Foundation's history. The project, Roberts added, will "arm the next [Republican presidential] administration with policy prescriptions, recruit and train 10,000 administration staff, and create a 180-day playbook." Now *that* is political infrastructure.

And now you can see how Heritage designed, built, and deployed a powerful system for delivering an agenda that it uses with great effect— one that serves as a model for similar right-wing organizations. That system has four (unstated) objectives:

1. to ensure that elected leaders and—just as important—their staffers and advisers, appointees, and media personalities understand the expectations to achieve real political outcomes;
2. to supply those allies with ideas and simple, emotive arguments that pivot from a defensive position to an offensive attack;
3. to popularize those ideas and other political opinions by ensuring they're talked about in a way that resonates deeply with both the political class and ordinary voters by distributing talking points and messages via right-wing media; and
4. to hold political leaders accountable to expected political outcomes.

The same year the Heritage Foundation was born, conservative activists founded another organization designed to push the conservative agenda—but not from Washington, D.C. The American Legislative Exchange Council, or ALEC, has also dramatically shaped the Republican Party since 1973, ensuring that Republican state legislators across the country—not just presidents and members of Congress—sing from the same sheet of music. It too is a critical component in the unofficial infrastructure of the GOP. And it too is unmatched on the left.

NATIONALIZING POLITICS, IN EVERY STATE

Like the Heritage Foundation, the American Legislative Exchange Council operates as a 501(c)(3) nonprofit, meaning that federal law technically keeps it a separate entity from the Republican Party (though it claims to be nonpartisan, it champions only Republican-aligned policies, which means it benefits only Republicans). ALEC describes itself as the nation's largest "voluntary membership organization of state legislators dedicated to the principles of limited government, free markets and federalism." You could call it a think tank *and* a chessboard membership club whose back rank is made up of major corporations, trade associations, lobbyists, and wealthy conservative donors. Hundreds of Republican state legislators from across the country, most of them politically inexperienced and low-paid citizen lawmakers, are the pawns in the front.

The progressive Center for Media and Democracy runs ALEC Exposed, a wiki devoted to tracking and illuminating the secretive work of the American Legislative Exchange Council. ALEC, the watchdog says, is a "pay-to-play operation where corporations buy a seat and a vote on 'task forces' to advance their legislative wish lists and can get a tax break for donations" (thanks to ALEC's tax-exempt status). Then, with the help of ALEC's lawyers and legislative experts, these wish lists get turned into draft legislative proposals—model bills—that lawmakers can and do claim as their own.

Among the hundreds of ALEC's model bills: legislation making it more difficult to vote, cutting corporate taxes, easing regulations that protect the environment, and codifying controversial "stand your ground" laws. (ALEC, which counts the NRA among its most powerful members, modeled its castle doctrine template after Florida's controversial Stand Your Ground law, allowing citizens to shoot and kill anyone unlawfully inside their homes.)

When the Wisconsin Legislature passed its anti-union so-called Right to Work law in 2015, ALEC Exposed compared the law's language, side by side, with ALEC's template. The language matched almost word for word. For ALEC, plagiarism is the whole point! And for understaffed, inexperienced Republican state legislators, ALEC is a one-stop shop that delivers premade conservative policies, slick talking points, and even expert witnesses to testify in committee hearings—on behalf of America's most influential corporate interests.

Almost all of ALEC's revenue, which totaled nearly $10 million in 2021, doesn't come from dues-paying legislators, who pay only $100 per year to be a member. No, 98 percent of its funding comes from corporate members and trade associations, which pay up to $25,000 per year—or more through sponsorships—for a seat at the table.

Several progressive organizations have tried to mirror ALEC's success, including the Progressive States Network and the State Innovation Exchange (which calls itself SiX). But these organizations haven't been able to make their work stick as effectively or broadly or uniformly as ALEC has, and none of them has been around as long; none has made decades-long investments as ALEC has. The Left has no ALEC.

I'm certainly not suggesting Democrats don't care about state-level or local politics and don't win lower-level elections. Of course they do! But as a party, Democrats haven't invested nearly enough time, money, or discipline into the hard work of driving a national political agenda, bringing it to the states, and making politics *convenient* for citizen legislators and the civically disenchanted constituents they serve.

Nor am I suggesting Democrats emulate the Republican strategy of courting corporate America to subvert the responsibilities of state lawmakers, then using those citizen legislators as pawns to enact beneficial policies across the country. But I am suggesting that Democrats nation-alize their agenda, as Republicans do, and bring that agenda to all levels of government, as ALEC and similar conservative organizations do.

For decades, the Republican Party has understood that if cultural wedge issues are important and incendiary enough for federal lawmak-ers to spend their time griping about in Washington (like gay rights, gun control, immigration, abortion), then they're certainly important enough for state and local leaders to address at other levels of govern-ment. In 2017, for example, as the national furor over Trump's han-dling of U.S. immigration policy boiled over, and as progressive activists advocated for sanctuary cities and demanded the abolishment of U.S. Immigration and Customs Enforcement, ALEC offered ready-made leg-islation for Republican state and local lawmakers to stake a claim in the national narrative, even if only symbolic. ALEC's Mad Libs–style so-called Rule of Law Community resolution looked like this:

THE [Insert Governing Body] OF THE [Insert Jurisdiction] HEREBY RESOLVES AS FOLLOWS:

Section 1. The [Insert Governing Body] of the [Insert Jurisdiction] does hereby pledge support of Federal Immigration enforcement through the adoption of local measures within the scope of local authority in accordance to the state and US Constitutions.

Section 2. The [Insert Governing Body] of the [Insert Jurisdiction] does hereby declare that [Insert Jurisdiction] is not a sanctuary community and is in fact a Rule of Law Community in regards to upholding our nation's immigration laws.

Nationalizing politics can look like this too: In 2023, as multiple Republican-controlled state legislatures introduced and passed similar bills limiting the rights and freedoms of transgender people, Senator Marco Rubio of Florida and Congressman Jim Banks of Indiana introduced Republican legislation in Congress to "regulate" transgender people serving in the U.S. military.

When Democratic House Speaker Tip O'Neill famously popularized the adage "all politics is local" in 1982, he might have been right for the moment, but that adage no longer holds up in today's landscape. Democrats have gotten too comfortable taking that advice with too much rigidity as the Republican Party has injected national politics into everything. Today, *all politics is national.*

HELLOOOO, GERRYMANDERING

If I still need to convince you that the Republican Party has been playing strategic chess while the Democrats have played checkers, let's look at the electoral map.

In the 2012 general election, Democratic candidates for the U.S. House of Representatives earned 1.36 million more votes than Republican candidates. That's more votes than the total populations of Wyoming and Alaska *combined.* But Republicans kept control of the House with a thirty-three-seat majority that year. How the hell did that happen?

The Republicans' 2012 House victories were the fruit of a massive, $30 million project the Republican Party had launched, with financial support from corporations and special interests, two years earlier. The GOP called its coordinated strategy the Redistricting Majority Project— REDMAP, for short. The idea behind REDMAP was to invest significant resources to help elect Republicans in 107 congressional districts, as well as to state legislatures, in sixteen critical swing states—including the Blue Wall of Pennsylvania, Wisconsin, and Michigan.

With Republicans controlling state legislatures following the 2010 census, the GOP knew it could gerrymander congressional districts in their favor, and that's exactly what they did. After 2010, Republicans had full control over the fate of nearly two hundred House districts, whose maps they redrew—precisely, using street-level data—to favor Republican and Republican-leaning voters, especially in the Blue Wall states. The Democrats, by the way, had the ability to redraw only forty-four districts after 2010.

We're still living with the effects of REDMAP today. In fact, as *The New Republic* pointed out in 2020, more than fifty million Americans live in states "where one or both chambers" of the legislature are controlled by Republicans—even though Republicans won fewer votes than Democrats. REDMAP was brilliant, if you consider bending the rules brilliant. It was a relatively cheap investment that paid dividends by guaranteeing minority rule in a majority-rule political system by winning enough power in the right places at the right time to stack the deck against American democracy for *decades,* while most Americans, including many Democrats, weren't paying attention.

THE DATA RACE

There's another piece of political infrastructure that matters a great deal to both the Left and the Right: *information.* Collecting, maintaining, and using data to win elections are some of the most valuable components of political warfare.

Both parties and numerous political advocacy groups collect as much info as they can about voters—especially the ones inclined to vote for and give money to their candidates. Sure, cellphone numbers and email addresses are important for fundraising and marshaling volunteers. But what campaigns really want to understand, well in advance of Election Day, is exactly which voters support their candidate and with how much enthusiasm, who might donate money, which voters are persuadable, where those voters live, and when they cast their ballots.

Political campaigns are often on the hook for gathering their own data within their districts. Staffers and volunteers still cold-call publicly available phone numbers or go door-to-door, canvassing thousands of households for information. They start with voter files from state governments, which include names, addresses, voting histories, and, sometimes, party affiliations. Well-funded campaigns can also purchase more sophisticated data from commercial data brokers through expensive consulting firms. If you can afford it, you can buy consumer data as specific as internet browsing histories, cellphone locations, net worths, and even pet ownership! At least one data firm claims it offers data about *individual* voter interests—from golf to natural foods to board games.

How do Democrats use data? Democratic campaigns across the country can purchase access to a privately owned, Democrats-only database called NGP VAN, which insiders simply call VAN. VAN stood for Voter Activation Network when it was founded by a staffer for Iowa senator Tom Harkin in 2001. Several years later, as chairman of the Democratic National Committee, former Vermont governor Howard Dean required all state Democratic Parties to subscribe to and have access to the VAN, and Senator Barack Obama used its data with great effect in his 2008 bid for the presidency. In 2010, VAN merged with NGP Software, which specialized in fundraising and compliance.

If they can afford to pay for the access, candidates, labor unions, and progressive nonprofits can use voter data in NGP VAN for grassroots field organizing and fundraising. When these campaigns gather updated data from "the field," they log it into the VAN, where other subscribers, usually future Democratic campaigns in the same district, can access it. That's how the voter files stay somewhat fresh for the next election. The VAN was once a groundbreaking system that catapulted Obama and other Democrats to the front of the data race. Plenty of Democrats across the country have won with its help. But it is still an expensive, pay-to-play resource for Democrats.

And here's where you might expect me to tell you Republicans now have a better voter data system. Why, yes. . . . Yes they do.

Following the national successes of Democrats in 2008 and again in 2012, Republicans and the right-wing billionaire brothers Charles and David Koch began investing heavily in a new data operation to help improve the electioneering performance of GOP candidates. The end product: a $50 million private data firm called i360, which keeps tabs on some *quarter of a billion* Americans with *trillions* of data points. i360 boasts that it offers "a unique combination of hard data points and predictive modeling" in order to "build the most complete profile for every individual possible." As its name suggests, i360 runs circles around NGP VAN.

As *Politico* reported in 2014, i360 connects the dots between individual voter information and consumer data, providing "superior profiles" of voters to Republican campaigns:

> Information from social networks is blended in, along with any interaction the voter may have had with affiliated campaigns and advocacy groups. Then come estimated income, recent addresses, how often a person has voted, and even the brand of car they drive. Another i360 service slices and dices information about TV viewing to help campaigns target ads more precisely and cost efficiently.

Today i360 assigns scores (0.0 to 1.0) to voters within various "models." Want to know what Joe Q. Voter feels about restricting gun ownership? If his score is 0.9 in i360's "Gun Control Model," there's a very good chance that Joe Q. Voter is a pretty staunch supporter of gun rights, and he's worth contacting, either face-to-face or through targeted advertising, to make sure he votes against an antigun Democrat. i360 offers individual scores in models for a bunch of other cultural issues, like criminal justice, taxes, marriage, and even "Trump Approval." It also scores voters on the likelihood that they'll go out of their way to vote, streamlining the task of getting out the vote on or before Election Day.

The power of i360 complements the Republican National Committee's own data firm called Data Trust, which serves as an information hub for GOP candidates, consultants, and vendors. According to *The Washington Post*, at the urging of conservative donors who feared "a duplication of resources," i360 and Data Trust agreed to share data *with each other* in recent elections, creating what is perhaps the world's most sophisticated political data collection effort. This has allowed Republicans to reinvent the science of electioneering.

In 2016 the Republicans' superior data system benefited the dysfunctional (and broke) Trump campaign to boost their state-level voter turnout operations, allowing the GOP to drive up their coalitional turnout and push swing voters *away* from Democrats. Sound familiar? They're using their infrastructure to win with *negative partisanship.*

POST–*CITIZENS UNITED* POLITICAL FUNDING

If the Democrats had political infrastructure like the Heritage Foundation (and the constellation of other similar right-wing organizations), ALEC, REDMAP, and i360, they would be able to play on an even field, and they would regularly beat the less popular party that no longer represents a majority of Americans. But the Democratic Party is still stuck playing checkers.

Why? Why can't the Democrats build a system like i360 to replace or modernize NGP VAN? Why can't they benefit from a handful of effective think tanks whose singular mission is to drive the political narrative of progressives and elected Democrats, and to push purely independent swing voters away from Republican candidates? Of course they can! But like everything else in the modern era of politics, it comes down to money. And that too is where Team Blue falls far behind.

Though tax-exempt, nonprofit political organizations are required to be nonpartisan and unaffiliated with any political party, most of them have missions that align with one political party or the other. We should consider progressive organizations that support the official work of elected Democrats as part of the party's *unofficial* political infrastructure (Republicans certainly count conservative nonprofits as part of theirs!). Many of these progressive advocacy groups, think tanks, and public policy centers are made up of smart people who work hard and care deeply about our country and its future. I have yet to meet one of them who does it for the pay.

These progressive organizations tend to rely on financial contributions from philanthropic foundations that award competitive grants. If a progressive nonprofit needs funding for a specific project, it'll probably have to "win" its slice of the pie by beating out other organizations that want to fund their own projects. Under this model, left-leaning organizations often cannot count on their funding year to year, which affects their ability to invest in the most talented minds and plan long-term strategies. Their funding is spread thin, which means their work is spread thin and often duplicated. The Left has myriad well-intentioned nonprofits that step on each other's toes, court the same wealthy funders, and get stuck in the mud of bureaucracy, mission creep, and groupthink.

Conservative funders, however, provide the Right's advocacy organizations with reliable, multimillion-dollar, no-strings-attached block grants, allowing them the luxury of long-term planning and the ability to onboard the brightest conservative minds in the country. Conservative funders also invest heavily—*billions* of dollars—in the GOP's unofficial infrastructure. Most conservative organizations are run like Michelin-starred kitchens, with a strict *brigade de cuisine* hierarchy. Their funding goes toward hiring expensive, experienced staffers (the Heritage Foundation's president disclosed a nearly $1 million salary in 2021).

Since the Supreme Court's *Citizens United v. Federal Election Commission* ruling in 2010, special interests, ridiculously wealthy Americans, and big businesses have had unlimited rein influencing American elections with money. That controversial decision changed the game again for American democracy, creating a system where eight-, nine-, and ten-digit checks outweigh individual votes—dealing democracy another kick to the head.

Since *Citizens United*, the Republican Party actively courted wealthy donors and corporate interests, then put their dollars to work building its infrastructure and laying plans to win elections and impose their agenda on the rest of us. Even if you don't follow the ins and outs of politics, you probably know the names of the billionaires who write enormous checks to Republican candidates and conservative causes.

The Democrats rightfully rebuked *Citizens United* and have bemoaned the decision ever since. Democrats chose to be less competitive, believing elbow grease and grassroots organizing alone would deliver their political victories. The problem is, Democrats are still on the same checkered board as Republicans, and they're still playing a lesser game.

To this day, many Democratic candidates reject money from corporate political action committees or any political effort they deem as dark money. Progressives have a few wealthy donors who give to Democrats and progressive causes (you've no doubt heard the name George Soros, most likely if you've ever listened to right-wing media), and they have a few powerful political action committees (like Priorities USA and Future Forward).

But Democrats today are far behind the curve when it comes to the money needed to play the same game. They have yet to unlock the full capabilities of the progressive Left. They have no centralized Mission Control—no entity whose sole charge is to craft a national brand, or to develop clear and convincing messages that our allies can use to drive voters to the polls, or to play offense against the other side.

Our ideas are better. Our democracy is more important. And for crying out loud, *there are more of us than there are of them.* So let's start playing some chess.

6

All Politics Are National

Let's go back to another unsurprising but bizarre moment in recent history: August 8, 2022—the day the FBI executed a search warrant at Donald Trump's Mar-a-Lago estate. That Monday in Florida, federal agents seized a trove of unsecured sensitive and classified documents—some purported to contain nuclear secrets and intelligence. Before Republican lawmakers had any facts about the situation, they started framing the narrative within and for the news media, not unlike what Bill Barr had done with the Mueller Report. Shortly before 6:00 P.M., the Twitter account of the GOP members of the U.S. House Judiciary Committee shared these sixteen words with its 350,000-plus followers:

If they can do it to a former President, imagine what they can do to you.

That evening on the GOP's own media channel, Fox's Laura Ingraham told her viewers this:

The real target of this investigation isn't Trump. The real target of this investigation is you.

And Republican senator Tim Scott of South Carolina said this to the right-wing radio host Mark Levin:

If they can target a former president, you know they can target me and you.

The MAGA congresswoman Lauren Boebert of Colorado tweeted a video statement that included this:

It was Trump today. But you're next if we don't take a stand.

The following day, the Heritage Foundation's president, Kevin Roberts, released his own response to the FBI's search of Mar-a-Lago:

If they think they can treat a former president this way, imagine what they think they can do to the average American.

Then Ronna McDaniel, the chairwoman of the Republican National Committee, weighed in:

If the Democrat establishment can do this to a former president, what can they do to you?

And MAGA senator Marsha Blackburn of Tennessee told Fox Business this:

I know Tennesseeans are looking at this and they're saying, "If they can do this to Donald Trump, they can do this to me."

Was it a coincidence that all these Republicans (and more!), their media, and their conservative allies used nearly identical language to deflect the reasoning behind the FBI's search and make the story not about Trump but rather about some ridiculous, fear-fueled, police-state threat to all Americans? Hardly.

The Republican messaging around Trump's mishandling of classified documents is just one example of the GOP's mastery of the Message—another strength that gives them yet another advantage over the Democratic Party, which, well, could learn a thing or two from Team Red. Superior messaging is part of the Republicans' political infrastructure, but their messaging strategies are so highly refined—and so simple, synced, and disciplined—that they deserve their own chapter.

THE ART AND SCIENCE OF THE MESSAGE

So what exactly is the Message in politics, anyway? Simply put, the Message is a reason—real, imagined, or fabricated—to support or oppose a candidate, a politician, a political party, a policy, an idea, or a course of action. The Message is usually conveyed in language, but it can also be communicated in imagery, or even music. It can be lofty and abstract, or it can be specific and small.

Campaign managers and press secretaries constantly remind their bosses to "stay on message!" We praise a particularly effective piece of political communication, like a debate zinger or a powerful TV ad, as "on message." A hot-mic comment, or an unprepared response to a gotcha question, is usually "off message."

A good message can convey an entire political brand in a single, aspirational word that characterizes what a candidate or politician stands for, like "authentic" or "experienced." For Barack Obama in 2008, it was two words at first—"hope" and "change"—then three: "Yes we can." Or the Message can be variations on a theme in order to persuade the electorate and drive a narrative or flip a script, like "If the FBI can search the home of the former president, imagine what they can do to you."

I don't know who first came up with the GOP's messaging of the FBI's search of Mar-a-Lago. But I'd bet folding money that some conservative pollster somewhere pored over survey data, which scientifically suggested the best way to protect Donald Trump was to pivot the whole issue away from the ex-president by focusing instead on the fear factor of manufactured government overreach. And the best way to do that? For the GOP in August 2022, it was to frame the lawful search for unsecured nuclear secrets as, somehow, a threat to the security and privacy of everyday American citizens who have zero access to nuclear secrets.

Does the Message have to be intellectually honest? For the GOP, it most certainly does not.

This particular "they're coming for you next" victimization messaging strategy, by the way, lives on in MAGA America, where the concept of the law applying equally to all citizens is apparently confounding. In March 2023, as the ex-president faced federal indictment for hush-money payments made to the porn star Stormy Daniels, his campaign responded, "If [they] can do this to President Trump, they can do it to you." Other prominent Republicans quickly repeated the line. Even one of his long-shot rivals borrowed the messaging a few days later, after Trump was indicted. "It's not even about Donald Trump," the GOP presidential candidate Vivek Ramaswamy told Tucker Carlson (a few weeks before Fox fired Tuck). "It's about every American because if they can do it to Trump, they can do it to you."

Most of the GOP's messages are as simple as this. They're made of easy-to-understand words that communicate and reinforce shared values, ideals, and emotions—*especially* fear and threat. Pollsters repeatedly test which words resonate best as political messages by asking samples of the electorate—just like basic market research. And as with good marketing, you don't just hear Republican messaging; you *feel* it. In the gut.

But where the Republicans really excel in the art and science of messaging is in their discipline and in their system of amplification. Most Republicans who hold positions of power, their think tanks, and their partisan news media use and repeat effective messages uniformly and regularly. If a message works, there's no need to reinvent it or to be creative about it; the goal is to make a message become so familiar and thematic that it becomes part of the vernacular—to lift up the Republican Party's brand while simultaneously shitting on the Democrats' brand.

The GOP has cracked another nut in their political messaging: meeting the civically unsophisticated electorate where it actually is. The Republican Party knows damn well that average Americans are unconcerned about politics. Even among those attuned to politics enough to vote, interest basically begins and ends at 1600 Pennsylvania Avenue. Sure, voters pay *some* attention to the most consequential developments in Congress or at the Supreme Court, but if it's not meaty enough for a roast on *Saturday Night Live,* it probably didn't register as a significant story among a good chunk of the electorate.

As for state and local politics—*pssh!* In 2018, researchers from Johns Hopkins University found that a third of the fifteen hundred Americans they surveyed couldn't even name their governor. And Portland State University learned that in nineteen of America's largest cities, less than one in four eligible voters participated in mayoral elections in 2016. In Las Vegas, turnout was only 9 percent; in Dallas, only 6 percent.

This helps explain why the Republican Party frames messages for candidates at all levels of government using well-known national political figures and state-level issues that overlap with hot-button national culture-war issues such as gun reform, abortion, and more recently, trans rights. Under the Republican system, household names that are deeply unpopular among Republicans and Republican leaners, like Chuck Schumer, Barack Obama, Joe Biden, Nancy Pelosi, and Alexandria Ocasio-Cortez, are staples of Republican messaging, even though those folks have little to do with state and local policies.

This strategy of nationalizing local political messaging has its roots in the 2010 midterm elections. In the fall of 2010, Michael Steele, then the chairman of the Republican National Committee, launched a forty-eight-state, fourteen-thousand-mile "Fire Pelosi" bus tour to gin up voter enthusiasm and turnout, riding the momentum of the Tea Party movement. The "Fire Pelosi" pitch was essentially: *Vote for Republican John Doe in the upcoming election for the Tennessee state house because he will stop Nancy Pelosi and Barack Hussein Obama.* That's it. That is nationalization at its core. You increase the stakes and interest in obscure elections voters don't care much about like state legislative elections and state judicial elections by using guilt by association. Voters may not know who John Doe is, or even care, but they sure know who Nancy Pelosi and Donald Trump are and have strong feelings about both.

Linking lesser-known state-level Republicans to well-known political heroes and villains has proven to be a winning strategy for Republicans.

The all-politics-is-national strategy certainly worked beautifully for the GOP in 2010. In those midterms, Republicans not only gained sixty-three seats in the U.S. House, they also flipped twenty-two state legislative chambers from Democratic to majority Republican control. Republicans also replaced or unseated twelve Democratic governors (plus Florida's Charlie Crist, who was an independent in 2010), in addition to holding eleven more seats. Overall, Republicans gained six governorships for a twenty-nine-seat majority (Democrats had twenty governorships, and Lincoln Chafee governed Rhode Island as an independent).

Until recently, Democrats have not emulated this critical, simplified pivot in electioneering strategy. Many Democrats who run for state or local office still stick to "all politics is local" messages about state or local issues, bipartisanship, and candidate biography. This finally started to change in 2022 in Michigan's state legislative elections and in the special election for the Wisconsin Supreme Court race in 2023 where Wisconsin Democrats defined the election as the last chance to protect women's reproductive freedom in the state.

Despite the strategic ship beginning to turn, Democrats have plenty of catching up to do when it comes to nationalizing their down-ballot messaging. Meanwhile, after more than a decade, Republicans have mastered the Message with devastating effect. They have turned words and rhetoric into weapons. They cast themselves as permanent victims, even when they hold political power, convincing the members of their tribe that everything they believe in is under attack. The GOP is also playing with fire by leaning into wild, disproven conspiracy theories in order to turn out their voters as they seek to replace American democracy with authoritarianism. This is low-hanging fruit to increase the negative partisanship they need to reel in their voters and to push swing voters away from Democrats, but it's brought American democracy to its knees.

The good news is, we can fight their fire with our own. The Democratic Party's famously poor messaging is one of the easiest problems to fix, once we understand how.

THE WEIGHT OF WORDS

You've heard plenty of razzle-dazzle political messages, even if you don't wake up and read political headlines. The most effective of them get absorbed into our everyday language. Think "stand your ground," "illegal alien," "religious freedom," "politicizing our courts," and, of course, "Make America great again." Now think of the moral framing behind these messages. What underlying values do they represent? Fair or false, right or wrong, what are these messages *really supposed to mean* to their intended audience of Republicans, Republican leaners, and, most important, pure independent swing voters?

- **Stand your ground:** *You're not a wimp! If someone's not welcome in your home, or if that person could harm you or your family, it's okay to shoot to kill—no questions asked.*
- **Illegal alien:** *The poor, brown-skinned, uneducated, non-English-speaking foreigners sneaking across our border aren't even worthy of descriptors we use for human beings, like "undocumented," "refugees," or "immigrants."*
- **Religious freedom:** *If you're a God-fearing Christian, your freedom to believe whatever you want supersedes lesser rights, like a gay couple's freedom from discrimination.*
- **Politicizing our courts:** *It's okay to distrust and even disregard court rulings you disagree with because the judges who made them are just liberal activists anyway.*
- **Make America great again:** *This country was doing just fine for people like you when politics was the exclusive, heteronormative domain of wealthy, educated, mostly Christian white men.*

The most famous example of Republican message framing may be the two-word term "tax relief." In his famous book *Don't Think of an*

Elephant!, the language expert George Lakoff points out that "tax relief" became so common that even liberals use it, but the antitax moral framing behind this phrase is clear:

> For there to be relief, there must be an affliction, an afflicted party, and a reliever who removes the affliction and is therefore a hero. And if people try to stop the hero, those people are villains for trying to prevent relief. When the word *tax* is added to *relief*, the result is a metaphor: Taxation is an affliction. And the person who takes it away is a hero, and anyone who tries to stop him is a bad guy.

Here's another example of political messaging that benefits Republicans more than Democrats: the moral imbalance between the framing of "pro-choice" and "pro-life" to describe supporters and opponents of abortion rights. Life is just about the most powerful moral value there is, no matter which party you belong to. The message "pro-life" immediately evokes images of cute babies—just as intended. Also by design, "pro-life" sets you up to argue that your opposition is pro-death, which immediately gives you the moral high ground. The frame of "choice" is a much weaker moral value—even when it comes to women making their own decisions about their own bodies. Compared with life, choice sounds like deciding between chocolate and vanilla when ordering a shake from a drive-through window.

Words carry the weight of values, morals, and ideas, so they matter more than anything else in politics. Republicans figured out long ago that using precise words at the right time, even if for the wrong reasons, is like playing pocket aces in hold 'em poker; the odds of winning the hand are in your favor even before you see the flop. The phrase "tax relief" is a particularly good example because it seems and sounds so innocent that even Democrats use it; it has, well, a poker face. "Pro-life" is designed to establish the moral high ground even before the argument begins. It's hard to argue against *life*, which is something Republicans are learning the hard way now that real women, not hypothetical babies, are doing the suffering.

Republican pollster and word wizard Frank Luntz might understand this better than anyone else in contemporary American politics. Luntz is a household name among political insiders, famous for coming up with, testing, and deploying the Right's most notorious messages, including "tax relief." Luntz helped Newt Gingrich, the Republican House minority whip and future House Speaker, write the GOP's *Contract with America* in 1994. Luntz has, by his own admission, "advised almost every Republican senator and congressman since then," conducting countless surveys and focus groups to find which political messages work and which messages don't.

Frank Luntz regularly offers messaging advice memos for Republican members of Congress (and their spouses, who, he once told lawmakers, "are your eyes and ears, a one-person reality check and truth squad combined"). His messaging guidance, detailed in his book *Words That Work,* suggests using simple, visual language and short sentences, focusing on the future, and speaking aspirationally. And in a leaked copy of an internal 170-page messaging memo he prepared in 2005, titled "The New American Lexicon," Luntz reminded his clients that the American public "absolutely positively NEVER wants to be told what it thinks":

> They want empathy rather than statistical declarations. They want to know that they are more than just a number, so give them something worthy of optimism rather than the latest economic results. . . . It is tempting to counter-attack using facts and figures. Resist the temptation.

Of course hard data have their place in civic discourse. This book, after all, is full of facts and figures, and I will never, *ever* suggest elected leaders shy away from the facts or abandon them altogether as the Republican Party gleefully has. But trying to win votes and political loyalty with facts and figures, as Democrats often do, is ineffective messaging. Psychologically, it doesn't work on most people, because our brains, just like our opinions, are too stubborn! If we are presented with evidence that doesn't jibe with our existing beliefs and worldviews, we often don't put much stock into that evidence, or we dismiss it altogether—especially if we don't have the intellectual wherewithal for critical thinking outside our comfort zones or the emotional maturity to admit when we are wrong. The scientific term for this is "confirmation bias." And, man, does it make things complicated for progressives because it takes reason and common sense out of our quiver of arrows when it comes to political messaging.

Confirmation bias explains why, in a 2023 CNN survey of more than a thousand Republicans and Republican leaners, a staggering 63 percent of them said Joe Biden "did not legitimately win enough votes to win the presidency." That's overwhelming even when factoring in the survey's +/− 3.8 percent margin of error. And among those Republican election deniers, more than half—52 percent—cited "solid evidence" for their beliefs, even though there literally isn't any (the other 48 percent admitted they based their beliefs on "suspicion only"). Years of hearing Trump lie incessantly about his election loss, and the Republican leaders who repeated the Big Lie for him, and the right-wing media ecosystem that amplified it, made that lie seem like the truth to Republican voters who are incapable of believing otherwise.

Here's another example of how conservatives take advantage of confirmation bias in their messaging: Let's say that I am a churchgoing Christian. Like most Americans, I don't follow politics with zeal, but I know that all Americans enjoy the constitutional right to practice whichever religion they choose. While I observe Christmas, I appreciate the First Amendment's prohibition on any law "respecting an establishment of religion, or prohibiting the free exercise thereof."

Then, one night, I turn on my favorite news channel (the only one with real news, I'm told). The host tells us that saying "happy holidays" is the product of political correctness gone overboard; that Christmas, after all, is a Christian holiday. *It's your right and duty as a Christian to keep saying "Merry Christmas,"* he says. The next night, the TV host turns up the heat. *The phrase "happy holidays" isn't just wokism,* he says, *it's anti-Christian! The liberal, godless mob,* he adds, *is waging a war on Christmas.*

Well, that's a fair point! I might tell myself. That's when my confirmation bias overpowers my previous reasoning. Now I'm starting to think "happy holidays" is no longer a polite way of accommodating everyone else's First Amendment right; it is actually *an invasion* of my values. The word "war" signals to me that shit is getting real, that this is an all-out attack on Christianity. A "war on Christmas" is a message frame that fits neatly inside my preexisting beliefs, which means it short-circuits my ability to separate passion from reason. I'm unable to excuse it as the ridiculous metaphor it is. The fact that our government intentionally separated itself from religious beliefs more than two centuries ago no longer matters; this is now *a war on my religious freedom*. Now the issue is stuffed with emotions that support my values and identity as a Christian, which means I'm not changing my mind anytime soon.

Do Democrats use emotional messages like this to frame their arguments? Sure they do! But as we'll see in a moment, Democrats are not nearly as good at it. They fail to harness the power of the most effective words and messages to change hearts and minds, they rarely use the same words and messages in unison (as so many Republicans did after the FBI's search of Mar-a-Lago), and they rarely repeat messages ad nauseam—until they become part of our language and culture—the way Republicans do.

The Democratic Party has not prioritized the weight of words. Too many of them still use words they're comfortable with rather than words that win elections. Too many Democrats still believe they can win arguments by presenting facts and figures with the false assumption that truth and reason will ultimately prevail. Too many of them don't think about the moral framing of the Message—about how they can persuade voters by appealing to their values and emotions, and to their basic instincts. For an important case study, let's go back to the fall of 2016, to the first presidential debate between Donald Trump and Hillary Clinton.

KEEPIN' IT ELEMENTARY

"I will bring back jobs," candidate Trump declared that September night at Hofstra University, during a feisty back-and-forth over the economy. "You can't bring back jobs," he told Clinton.

Clinton's response, though perfectly reasonable in substance and frequently interrupted by her opponent, violated several rules in the Republican Party's playbook for effective political messaging:

> I think my husband did a pretty good job in the 1990s. I think a lot about what worked and how we can make it work again, with a million new jobs, a balanced budget, and incomes went up for everybody. Manufacturing jobs went up also in the 1990s, if we're actually going to look at the facts. . . . When I was secretary of state, we actually increased American exports globally 30 percent. We increased them to China 50 percent. So I know how to really work to get new jobs and to get exports that helped to create more new jobs.

In this response, Hillary Clinton essentially told millions of Americans *what to think* (that her husband did a good job as president and that the 1990s were prosperous, which dangerously presumes that the audience agrees—if they even remember!). She focused on the past rather than the future, then used hard data points ("a million new jobs," 30 and 50 percent increases in American exports) to underscore her argument.

Now, don't get me wrong. I think Hillary Clinton did an admirable job taking on Trump and suffering through his infantile debate performances. But this is a book about learning lessons from the GOP, so let's look at Trump's much more powerful message, from the same debate question:

> I'm going to cut regulations. I'm going to cut taxes big league, and you're going to raise taxes big league. End of story.

In these twenty-three words, the future popular-vote loser made not one but two optimistic promises to *relieve* voters from government burdens, he warned that voting for the alternative would result in higher taxes, he framed his statement as the final word, and he even evoked America's favorite pastime, cutting taxes, twice!

In 2015, back when much of America laughed off the prospect of Donald Trump becoming the world's most powerful person, *The Boston Globe* published an analysis of the speaking comprehension levels of all nineteen Republicans and Democrats running to become president of the United States. The *Globe*'s analysis used the Flesch-Kincaid readability test, which "crunches word choice and sentence structure and spits out grade-level rankings," using factors like sentence length and syllable count. Trump's speech, the paper found, registered the lowest comprehension level; he could have been understood by a fourth grader. As for Clinton? She spoke in 2015 at an eighth-grade level. The *Globe* also found that Senator Bernie Sanders spoke at a tenth-grade level and former Republican governor Mike Huckabee was even higher.

Why does "Trumpspeak" resonate with tens of millions of Americans? That's a question that has annoyed the hell out of tens of millions of other Americans. Trump's speech is rudimentary—liberated from the confines of political complexity and nuance. It unfolds in real time like the unpolished, impolite, internal monologue of a nine-year-old in search of some nerd's lunch money. It requires no intellectual circuitry, no innuendo, no abstractions between the lines. But here's the thing: no matter what we think of the former president and his intellect, all of us *understand* his language.

In fact, according to data from Gallup and the U.S. Department of Education, 54 percent of Americans between the ages of sixteen and seventy-four read *below* a sixth-grade level. In other words, Trumpspeak is even simpler than the language of most of America, and it is basic, direct, and devastatingly persuasive. I don't give Donald Trump much credit for anything, but intentionally or not he uses language masterfully to uncomplicate politics for a nation of voters who are utterly disinterested in complicated politics. Democrats may never follow that lead, but they should at least understand that voters aren't enamored with intellectual elitism, nor are they persuaded by facts or reason. There is a reason they once had a game show called *Are You Smarter Than a 5th Grader?*

WINNING WITH MESSAGES ABOUT LOSING

If you've ever donated money to any candidate online, odds are your email address has been sold, traded, or donated to other candidates looking to raise campaign contributions. It's also likely you still receive regular fundraising emails from these candidates with urgent subject-line messages like "One last chance," "Now or never," or "Everything's on the line."

This is a strategy borrowed from basic marketing, based on the principle of *loss aversion:* Ordinary people *hate* losing, or losing out on, things we like or think we might like—with more intensity than we like gaining those things. A simpler way to put it: Losing makes us feel twice as bad as winning makes us feel good.

The science of loss aversion behavior says if I have only "one last chance" to make a campaign contribution that will be matched by someone else, I'm more inclined to do so because I don't want to miss the opportunity. Or if I don't donate today, I won't be able to later. If I'm told "everything's on the line," I might risk losing everything if I don't pitch in to help the candidate asking for money. These might sound like extreme examples, but they are subject lines from actual political fundraising emails.

Of course, loss aversion applies to more than just obnoxious fundraising appeals. For the same reasons loss aversion works in marketing, the Republican Party frequently uses this tactic in much of its messaging. Think "gun-grabbing Democrats," "death tax," "tax and spend liberals," or even "war on Christmas" and "if they can do it to a former president, imagine what they can do to you." All of these messages speak to an underlying threat of loss more than a promise of political or personal gain. When Republicans oppose policies like gun safety, vaccine mandates, or taxes, watch how they use loss aversion to vilify Democrats:

- Democrats are going to come and take away whatever you hold dear.
- Democrats are going to force you to do what you don't want to do.
- Democrats are going to make your life worse than it is now, and they'll lie, cheat, and steal to do it.

I still see one of the most effective loss-aversion responses to President Obama's "hope and change" message on bumper stickers across Oregon: "I'll keep my guns, my freedom and my money. You can keep the CHANGE!" See how this message creates tension between the desire to keep guns, freedom, and money and the perceived threat of losing all three under Barack Obama? Effective messages like this, even when they exist only on the bumpers of pickup trucks, play into the Right's strategy of framing Democrats as know-it-alls who want to take away your freedom of belief, your rights, and your money—things conservative America says it holds dear.

Democrats use loss-aversion messaging too, to a lesser degree. "Hands off my health care" comes to mind. So does "they're coming after your Social Security," or "my body, my choice." But remember, Democrats do not have the centralized infrastructure that Republicans do to make their most effective loss-aversion messages part of the vernacular.

Here's another, similar psychological strategy that the Republican Party uses in its messaging: *grievance politics.* The GOP and their allies constantly frame themselves as permanent victims of progressives and Democrats. Even when Republican majorities comfortably pull the levers of political power, their messaging is designed to convince their coalition that *they* are always underdogs, that everything they stand for—that everything America itself stands for—is under attack, and that their opponents always have the upper hand . . . *even after they win political power.*

Texas, for example, was a comfortably red state in 2020. Trump won Texas by more than 631,000 popular votes that year, meaning he captured all thirty-eight of the Lone Star State's Electoral College votes. But political victory wasn't good enough for the GOP. The Texas secretary of state, John Scott, a Republican, decided to audit election results anyway from four urban counties, three of which Biden had won. In the end, the Republican audit found no significant issues with the state's election despite, as *The Texas Tribune* reported, "repeated, unsubstantiated claims by GOP leaders casting doubts on the integrity of the electoral system." Then, as sore winners, the Texas Republican Party in 2022 formally adopted a resolution rejecting "the certified results of the 2020 Presidential election," falsely claiming Biden "was not legitimately elected" due to unproven, unsubstantiated fraud. The underlying message from the Texas GOP: *Because of Democrats, you should doubt elections even when Democrats lose.*

Framing messages through the lens of grievance and loss aversion is how the GOP casts itself as a permanent out party, and it's working well for Republicans everywhere by tapping into negative partisanship and freaking the hell out of swing voters, just as intended.

WINNING WITH A SINGULAR MESSAGE

In electoral politics, especially in big, statewide federal races, Democrats essentially run two messaging campaigns aimed at two different sets of voters. The first is aimed at the base: reliable Democratic voters and Democratic leaners. These voters don't need to be persuaded whom to vote for; they just need to be motivated and reminded to vote. To do that, a Democratic campaign will target base voters with specific messages, usually using online ads, about lefty bread-and-butter issues they care about—issues like ~~lowering student debt~~ debt relief, fighting climate change, and promoting equality. Democrats also use "victory lap" messages to remind their base voters of Democratic successes.

The second messaging campaign Democrats usually run is aimed at persuading pure independent swing voters. This is where Democrats broaden their appeals to the voters in the middle of the median voter theorem bell curve, in hopes of earning votes using both ideological and temperamental "moderation." The messages swing voters receive are ones that resonate with the political middle. They're focused on centrist kitchen-table issues like fighting inflation, investing in infrastructure, and "working across the aisle." There's nothing wrong with this dual strategy if you don't mind losing. So let's see how Republicans approach their persuasion game.

Republicans tend to use a *singular message* that accomplishes two goals, and those goals should sound familiar: to turn out as many reliable Republicans and Republican leaners as they can while simultaneously pushing independent swing voters to *not* support Democrats. This means modern Republican messaging tends to boil down to a general partisan theme—say, crime, guns, the economy, or taxes. But these themes funnel into a singular message, which is basically this: *Democrats are dangerous on all these critical issues, so don't vote for any of them.* This GOP strategy isn't about earning votes from undecided voters; it's about disqualifying the other option so Republicans can win by default.

Let's go to Wisconsin for a recent example. In 2022, Lieutenant Governor Mandela Barnes challenged the incumbent Republican, Ron Johnson, for a seat in the U.S. Senate. Barnes ran a traditional Democratic campaign with two traditional sets of messages. While announcing his candidacy in August 2021, he echoed themes familiar to Democratic base voters:

> We do this for opportunity for everyone. For jobs that we can support a family on, and education that we can build a future on . . . health care that actually protects our health, not the wealth of corporations, the courage to tackle climate change, and the principles to protect our democracy and the right to vote.

But for a presumably different audience, during a late-season debate with Johnson, Barnes used his closing argument to speak directly to issues that resonate with independent swing voters:

Women's lives and women's health are on the line. For our veterans who may have been victims of burn pits: you don't want a senator who's going to play politics with your life. For our retirees: we don't want a person who's going to take your retirement away from you—what you've worked hard for your entire life. Working people live with the constant threat of their jobs being shipped out of state or overseas.

The message for Democratic base voters: Mandela Barnes is the Democrat who shares your progressive values, so vote for him. The message for swing voters: Mandela Barnes aligns with the critical issues you and your family care about, so vote for him. Two different messages for two different sets of voters.

Now let's take a look at the Republican effort to ensure another Senate term for Ron Johnson, who entered his 2022 reelection as one of the most vulnerable incumbents in the country. Public polling suggested more than half of Wisconsin voters disapproved of his job performance in late 2021, and that Johnson had fallen out of favor with independent voters. So Republicans stuck to their playbook by delivering a singular, silver-bullet message for base Republican voters *and* swing voters that zoomed right past their flawed, nothing-to-see-here candidate. Their message? It was essentially this: *Mandela Barnes will get you killed.*

"Mandela Barnes coddles criminals and mocks victims," proclaimed one of Johnson's many TV ads framing Barnes, a Black man, as a weak-on-crime candidate. Another ad from Senator Mitch McConnell's Senate Leadership Fund super PAC called Barnes "too dangerous for Wisconsin." The short ad featured all sorts of dire visuals, including the phrases "Reject Extreme Mandela Barnes" and "Advocated to Defund the Police," and even an image of the lieutenant governor holding an "Abolish ICE" shirt. A longer ad from the super PAC linked Barnes to terrifying footage of armed robberies, carjackings, and "violent attacks on our police."

And in his closing argument of the same debate with Barnes, notice how Johnson went directly after Democrats in his effort to disqualify Barnes by association:

Wisconsin voters ought to be asking, "Are you better off or worse off since Democrats took control?" Considering forty-year-high inflation, record gas prices, skyrocketing crime, an open border flooded [with] deadly drugs, I think it's pretty obvious most people are worse off. What's important to notice is that these problems didn't just happen. They were the direct result of Democrat policies and Democrat governance. And Lieutenant Governor Barnes supports all these policies, causing you and your family so much pain. If elected, he would be a rubber stamp for President Biden and Senator Schumer, and together they would make matters even worse.

I'm not saying Mandela Barnes didn't take issue with Ron Johnson or his dumpster of a record. Of course he did. The problem was, Barnes didn't effectively frame his messaging to persuade independent swing voters to *vote against Johnson,* a Republican who wants to wipe out American democracy, who wants to take away your freedoms, and who is harming you and your family. The Barnes campaign instead tried to paint Johnson as a flawed leader—as someone whose business paid no income taxes, who believes "climate change is bullshit," and who even suggested mouthwash can kill the virus that causes COVID. In other words, they relied on Johnson's problems as problems for problems' sake and not problems that will hurt voters. The reason loss aversion works is because it's *personal* loss.

See how wickedly simple and functional the Republican messaging playbook is? Thanks to the power of negative partisanship, it doesn't need to be sophisticated. For the GOP in Wisconsin, this strategy worked well enough to reelect one of America's least popular U.S. senators. Ron Johnson won his 2022 race by only 26,718 votes—a single percentage point.

A THREE-WORD MESSAGING DISASTER

The GOP strategy of going after Mandela Barnes on the issue of crime was no accident, and it points to another soft spot in the Democratic

Party's ability to drive simple, effective messages as a party that represents a whole lot more viewpoints and interests than the Republican Party does. Ron Johnson and the GOP simply swung at a T-ball of a progressive political message that hurt Democrats everywhere.

In fairness, the phrase "defund the police" didn't begin as a partisan political message. It emerged as a radical idea from frontline grassroots activists—many of whom were terrified, pissed-off, and utterly frustrated people of color who had run out of hope or faith that anything good can come from the police. The notion of yanking public funding from local law enforcement agencies, or abolishing them altogether, began well before May 2020, but it intensified following Officer Derek Chauvin's brutal murder of George Floyd in Minneapolis and the worldwide outcry that ensued.

Sure, some activists advocated, literally, for the abolishment of police forces since the rise of Black Lives Matter. The BLM movement took off in 2013 following the acquittal of George Zimmerman, who shot and killed Trayvon Martin, an unarmed Black seventeen-year-old. After decades of racially motivated police brutality and injustice, it's an understandable position, even if politically and functionally impractical. But for most others, the conversation about defunding police wasn't a call to allow chaos and crime to prevail; it was really about redirecting public money to build trust between law enforcement officers and communities of color.

As the president of the Minneapolis City Council put it, activists in marginalized communities—communities that have historically had to *protect themselves* from officers and traditional police tactics that violently targeted them—simply wanted "to end policing as we know it and to recreate systems of public safety that actually keep us safe." So rather than fund trigger-happy beat cops to, say, forcibly restrain—and kill— a Black man who bought cigarettes with a suspected counterfeit $20 bill, city leaders could use that tax money to fund programs and people to peacefully resolve such minor situations, to build trust within the community, and to ultimately stop the normalized killing of Black people at the hands of police officers.

Politically, this difficult, racially charged conversation wasn't the problem. The problem was the oversimplified, three-word political message that resulted from it. Misunderstood by millions, the phrase "Defund the Police" was used by the Republican Party as a blunt-force instrument against Democrats. That's because "Defund the Police" is easy to interpret literally whether you mean it literally or not. There's no room for nuance. There doesn't need to be!

"But 'Defund the Police' doesn't mean getting rid of *all* cops," many of my progressive activist friends would explain. "It doesn't *really* mean stripping law enforcement of the resources they need to protect our communities from rapists and murderers!" I'd reply, *If you have to explain your slogan, your slogan sucks.*

There was no unringing that bell. Republicans used the phrase to frame *all* Democrats as soft on crime, pro-crime, anti-police, or all three—even after the Republican Party formally sanctioned the violent, anti-police insurrection at the U.S. Capitol on January 6 as "legitimate political discourse." And it cost Democrats dearly.

In 2020, the two-term Democratic governor of Montana, Steve Bullock, ran for the U.S. Senate against the incumbent Republican, Steve Daines. Bullock, a popular former attorney general, had built a long record supporting law enforcement officers and their work. He oversaw the Montana Department of Justice and the Montana Highway Patrol. Bullock pioneered a successful initiative to crack down on drunk driving and doubled the number of officers monitoring the internet to prosecute child sex abusers. He repeatedly stated his opposition to "any efforts to defund the police." But when Bullock ran for the U.S. Senate in his overwhelmingly white, Republican-leaning state, Daines smartly forced him to carry the baggage of the Democrats' nationalized "Defund the Police" message.

"Steve Bullock refuses to stand up for law and order," a uniformed Montana sheriff with a horseshoe mustache says in a Daines TV ad depicting rioters stomping on police cars. "Bullock's campaign is being bankrolled by the liberal mob. That's why Bullock's been silent while left-wing radicals try to defund our police, erase our history, and turn America into a socialist country." Daines beat Bullock in 2020 by nearly ten percentage points.

In 2022, well after House Speaker Nancy Pelosi rebuked Democratic activists for calling to defund police, and after President Biden called for increased police funding during his State of the Union address, Republicans kept turning the screws on Democrats. Republican senator John Kennedy launched a TV ad about how "violent crime is surging" in his state of Louisiana.

"Woke leaders blame the police; I blame the criminals," Kennedy says in his ad. "I opposed defunding the police." Then Kennedy looks into the camera and delivers his punch line with a Southern drawl, almost sneering with delight in exploiting a bad political slogan: "Look, if you hate cops just because they're cops, the next time you get in trouble, *call a crackhead.*"

There's another important reason "Defund the Police" is so politically crippling, especially when contrasted with countermessages as effective as the Right's "Back the Blue" and "Blue Lives Matter." Both of these countermessages mean exactly what they say. "Back the Blue" supports and defends the status quo. "Blue Lives Matter" creates a false equivalency by tapping into racism and ignorance, but it no doubt feels like an innocent message of solidarity and justice to the people who use it. No nuance needed! But "Defund the Police" threatens a loss that could disrupt the status quo and result in danger, violence, and maybe even death. That makes it an endlessly exploitable message.

PUSHING BACK

In the opening pages of this book, I stated that American democracy has gone terminal, that our political system is barely wheezing by on life support. Then I gave you a reason to support my claim: *Today's Republican Party is a threat to your freedom, health, wealth, and safety.* These words hopefully raised the stakes and got your attention. This message isn't bluster or empty rhetoric; sadly, it's not even hyperbole. It's *true.* The question is this: How effective is it? Will Democrats across the country use variations of this message with enough consistency and uniformity that it will become part of their brand? Will they find a more powerful message? Will they use it? Will swing voters hear it and vote against Republicans?

With several important exceptions, the Democratic Party, its leaders, and many of its members have long struggled with our ability to find, use, and win with effective political messages. Democrats have no centralized national structure that regularly suggests effective messages the way Republicans do, let alone a whole ecosystem designed to enhance their repetition. We forget the importance of communicating the simplest emotional reasons for supporting Democrats and their values, morals, and ideas. And when we try, we don't do it nearly as effectively or as consistently, with as much discipline, as Republicans do.

"We have a messaging problem," California's governor, Gavin Newsom, admitted to MSNBC in September 2022 during a highly publicized visit to Texas. "We allow these culture wars to take shape and we consistently are on the back end of them. Eight of the top ten states with the highest murder rates—all are Republican states. How did Democrats not know that? . . . And we're losing *that* message? Crime is higher—as well as taxes here for the average citizen in Texas—it's higher. . . . *Why don't we push back?*"

Democrats are not predestined to lose the messaging war; they simply haven't made the Message their priority. We haven't pushed back because we haven't yet figured out how to do it while moving the ball down the field. Nor have we really figured out how to use messaging, or the power of elected office, to *control the narrative* as Republicans do.

Now we have no choice, because America risks forfeiting its democracy to MAGA. Democrats need their messages to be as pithy and precise as the GOP's, not weedy or weak. We've got to play the same game the Republicans have been playing for decades.

Controlling the Narrative

After House Republicans eked out their five-seat micro-majority from the sad remains of their failed Red Tsunami in the 2022 midterms, GOP leaders immediately formed the Select Subcommittee on the Weaponization of the Federal Government. Instead of prioritizing old-fashioned Republican concerns like the economy or national security, MAGA lawmakers created a brand-new congressional subcommittee to air their grievances and conspiracy theories while framing themselves as victims of government "weaponization."

Oblivious to the irony of creating a committee to weaponize the government against Democrats, and without offering any new details or compelling evidence, the GOP's panel held official hearings on the impeachments of Donald Trump, the politics of Twitter, the politicization of the FBI, and of course President Biden's son Hunter, whose business dealings have fueled right-wing conspiracy theories for years. The topics of these investigations might baffle you if you live in the real world and not the Republican one.

The House Oversight Committee also prioritized the investigation of Hunter Biden immediately after Republicans took over in 2023. With a straight face, the committee's chairman, the Kentucky congressman James Comer, told *Meet the Press* in January that the "only people" who considered his committee's investigation partisan were "the media and hard-core Democrats"—as if neither mattered.

Then, in May, Comer accidentally whoopsie-daisied a truth bomb about the GOP's weird fascination with Hunter Biden. It happened a few days after the conservative columnist Jim Geraghty wrote about the Oversight Committee's news-less probe of the president's son in *The Washington Post*. Geraghty had halfheartedly opined that the people of America deserve more answers about payments President Biden's family had received from foreign companies in the past (Geraghty did acknowledge the committee had no proof of bribery or corruption). Apparently, Geraghty's nine-hundred-word *Washington Post* column suggested to both Comer and Fox News that the Hunter Biden conspiracy narrative was finally gaining traction in the mainstream news media. On May 22, 2023, Comer appeared on *Fox & Friends First,* where he was asked if his investigation into Hunter Biden is what finally "moved this needle with the media."

"Absolutely. There's no question," Comer answered. Then he said the quiet part out loud: "You look at the polling, and right now Donald Trump is seven points ahead of Joe Biden and trending upward. Joe Biden's trending downward."

Aha! There it was: an admission that the Oversight Committee didn't *really* exist to uncover dark secrets about corruption in President Biden's family. Whether the polling Comer cited was accurate or not, for House Republicans, the whole taxpayer-funded investigation was designed to tank Joe Biden's reputation—on manipulating Republican base voters, leaners, and swing voters into believing that Biden himself was somehow corrupt and guilty by association, even without any evidence. The White House quickly seized on Comer's moment of candor and sardonically *praised* MAGA Republicans for "doing something they rarely do: telling the truth."

"They are admitting through their own words and deeds that these so-called 'investigations' are actually intended not to reveal facts but to hurt the President's political standing," the White House spokesman Ian Sams wrote in a memo obtained by NBC News.

This moment of clarity might have been a minor blip in the news cycle, but it gives us another valuable look inside the GOP playbook. In addition to sturdier political infrastructure and superior messaging, Republican leaders use yet another simple but effective tactic to usurp American democracy: *controlling the narrative* by using their government authority, particularly when they hold the majority.

When Republicans are in charge of things, especially in Congress, they know how to manipulate our system of government and the news media to drive their agendas via the news cycle. They govern politically. Their agendas have very little to do with the difficult work of actual policymaking; they have everything to do with *partisan politics:* building their coalition and giving that coalition reasons to vote against Democrats. This, like infrastructure and messaging, is another asymmetry between the two parties; Democrats simply don't control the narrative with as much cutthroat determination, or with disregard for the truth, as Republicans do.

Today's Republican Party has taken its use of official government power to a whole new level; they've abandoned any serious commitment to real governing altogether. Their commitment instead is to use their government power to strip certain Americans of their rights and to declare war on individual freedom. For many in today's GOP, serving in Congress really just means getting a larger megaphone to grift while using conspiracy theories to push conservatives into supporting fascism.

Republicans understand their audience. They're well aware that using, say, congressional hearings to fight skirmishes in their culture war, to investigate wackadoo theories, and to skewer the reputations and credibility of their villains looks and feels legit to most politics-averse American news consumers who don't know any better. Republicans also know damn well that when covering politics, the mainstream news media are always looking for controversy to spice up stories and to make them more marketable for their algorithms and their audiences.

But all of us—citizens and journalists alike—also have to see exactly how elected Republicans use and abuse their "official" government power, because it helped give us Donald Trump and it damn near wiped out our democracy. When Democrats better understand how Republicans control the narrative in their march to end democracy, we can learn to use narrative control to stop them.

HOW "BENGHAZI" BECAME A HOUSEHOLD NAME

On September 11, 2022, as many political leaders reflected on the world-changing terrorist attacks of 2001, Senator Ted Cruz used the somber anniversary to play politics with another tragic, but far less consequential, attack on American citizens.

"10 years ago Islamic terrorists killed 4 Americans in Libya," the Republican from Texas tweeted in 2022. "[That] attack was a direct result of the failed policies of the Obama-Biden admin."

Yep, a full decade after the assault on U.S. citizens in Libya, Ted Cruz was still making political hay out of *Benghazi,* trying his best to cast blame directly on the current president of the United States. And why would Cruz still see the attack in Benghazi as an opportunity to attack Joe Biden all these years later? Because with Benghazi, Republicans *controlled the narrative* so effectively that it remains a political success story for them to this day.

First, a refresher: On the evening of September 11, 2012, armed militants stormed a U.S. diplomatic compound in Benghazi, a city in Libya many Americans had never even heard of. Hours later, mortars struck a nearby covert facility used by American CIA operatives. Attackers ultimately killed four American citizens, including Ambassador Christopher Stevens, and wounded several more. It was a shitty day for our nation, as is any day when America loses public servants in the line of duty.

Sadly, attacks on American embassies and military compounds around the world aren't particularly rare, and the 2012 attack in Benghazi was far from the worst in terms of American casualties. On October 23, 1983, a suicide bomber blew up a military barracks in Beirut, killing 241 U.S. troops. Six months before that, a suicide bombing at the American embassy in Beirut killed 63 people, including 17 Americans. Back then, no one really pinned blame on President Reagan or Secretary of State George Shultz. The United States was doing dangerous work in a dangerous part of the world.

In the weeks following the 2012 attack in Benghazi, several congressional committees, the FBI, and the U.S. State Department got to work untangling what happened. A month after the attack, Secretary of State Hillary Clinton acknowledged she was ultimately "in charge of the State Department's 60,000-plus people all over the world." But none of the initial hearings warranted further investigation of Clinton. The Senate Homeland Security Committee's bipartisan 2012 investigation didn't even suggest Clinton might have been to blame. Instead, it found that in the months leading up to the attack, "there was a large amount of evidence . . . that Benghazi was increasingly dangerous and unstable, and that a significant attack against American personnel there was becoming much more likely."

Of course the attack in Benghazi made plenty of headlines after it happened. But Fox News, the voice of the GOP, gave the story extra TLC and breathed new life into the whole ordeal *for years*. Media Matters for America, an organization that closely tracks the patterns and trends of conservative news outlets, called Fox's coverage of Benghazi an "obsession." In the twenty months following the attack, Media Matters tallied 1,098 prime-time segments on Fox about Benghazi (the network ran 174 stories about it in October 2012 alone). Fox didn't just air new developments; it kept reinventing the old story by mixing in new opinions from various right-wing pundits. Fox entertained wild lies and conspiracy theories (including an alleged cover-up by the Obama administration, later proven to be untrue). Media Matters also counted 105 "attempts" on Fox "to link Benghazi to Hillary Clinton's potential presidential ambitions."

So it's no wonder the Republicans in Congress did what they could to extend the shelf life of the 2012 attack in Benghazi as a political narrative. With control of the House and the authority to conduct oversight investigations, Republicans formed the Select Committee on Benghazi on May 8, 2014—more than six hundred days *after* the attack. The GOP knew it too could build an untrue but convincing narrative around the events in Libya that suggested Democrats and their presidential front-runner not only were to blame but also wiggled their way out of any accountability by lying about it. It was a convenient, made-up controversy they could use to chip away at Democratic leadership in general and Clinton's leadership specifically. You could call it, well, a weaponization of the government.

Republicans in Congress manufactured a new narrative from an old story because they could. They also knew mainstream news consumers—voters and would-be voters—would pay more attention to their narrative because journalists have a duty to cover the official work of Congress, right? Of course they do! And their story kept producing more subplots. After the initial investigation into what happened at Benghazi came the other fracases over Clinton's personal email server, administration talking points, and that alleged cover-up—none of which pointed to any real evidence of wrongdoing. But, hey, it was a wide opening to manipulate public opinion from the top down, and Republicans rarely let a good political opportunity go to waste.

THE SINKING OF A SECRETARY

Now let's look at the timeline of Hillary Clinton and Benghazi through the lens of public opinion. Just a few months after the attack, in early December 2012, Clinton still enjoyed a comfortable average favorability rating above 58 percent (and a 33.7 percent unfavorable rating) based on the results of hundreds of public opinion surveys compiled by *HuffPost*. In plain English: Even several months after Benghazi, significantly more Americans liked Clinton than disliked her, which is an important distinction in electoral politics. She was very much "above water." If the number of people who dislike a politician is greater than the number of people who like her, we say that politician is underwater. And if that politician remains underwater, there's a good chance her career won't survive.

Hillary Clinton's favorability rating had temporarily dipped underwater a handful of times before Benghazi. But according to Gallup, which had conducted dozens of public opinion surveys about Clinton since she became First Lady in 1993, she mostly remained well above water. In December 1998, when the Republican House impeached Bill Clinton for lying about his affair with Monica Lewinsky, Gallup reported Hillary's favorability rating at a career high of 67 percent. And she earned these relatively high favorability ratings despite the Republicans' decades-long effort to brand her as an untrustworthy, untruthful, un-Christian "feminazi."

After First Lady Clinton pitched the idea of universal healthcare for all Americans by requiring employers to pay for most of their employees' coverage in the early 1990s, conservatives, including the president of the Heritage Foundation, called the idea "HillaryCare," and she swiftly became a favorite villain among right-wing talk radio hosts, then cable-news commentators. The GOP's ire at Hillary Clinton and her political trajectory persisted through her tenure as a U.S. senator and as a first-time presidential candidate in 2008.

But it wasn't until 2013 that Hillary Clinton's average favorability rating started *steadily* and consistently falling as her unfavorability rating climbed. A few days after the House Select Committee on Benghazi held its first hearing on September 17, 2014, Clinton's average favorability rating had sunk to 48.7 percent and her unfavorability rating had risen to 42.7 percent. On April 13, 2015, the day after she announced her second presidential candidacy, *HuffPost* reported Clinton's average favorability rating had finally dipped beneath the surface—47.1 unfavorable and 46.8 percent favorable.

Shortly after she appeared before the House Select Committee on Benghazi for her infamous eleven-hour hearing in October 2015— more than *three years* after the actual attack—Clinton's average favorability rating had fallen to 42.5 percent. Her overall unfavorability rating had shot up to 50.6 percent. By Election Day 2016, Clinton's average favorability rating had plunged to only 41.2 percent, well below her 55.4 percent unfavorability rating.

So what the hell caused this significant turnaround in the court of public opinion? Of course the unprecedented 2016 presidential election took a heavy toll on Hillary Clinton's reputation and favorability. You usually become less popular when you run for major office. Trump built his entire MAGA movement with Hillary Clinton as its chief villain—as a symbol for everything wrong with Washington and progressivism—and his fans followed suit, screaming "Lock her up!" at every political rally across the country. But Clinton's fall from favorability among the wider American electorate started measurably sinking well before Donald Trump even entered the presidential race, and there's no doubt that the GOP's obsession with Benghazi in Congress played a significant role.

After all, the purpose of the Select Committee on Benghazi, which gobbled up more than two and a half years of the congressional agenda at a cost of nearly eight million taxpayer dollars, wasn't even about Benghazi. We know that because then-Republican House majority leader Kevin McCarthy admitted it, just as Jim Comer did with his bogus investigation of Hunter Biden, on Fox News. McCarthy said this to Fox's Sean Hannity on September 29, 2015:

> Everybody thought Hillary Clinton was unbeatable, right? But we put together a Benghazi special committee. A select committee. What are her numbers today? Her numbers are dropping. Why? Because she's untrustable. But no one would have known that any of that had happened had we not fought to make that happen.

The lesson is this: Republicans understand that when they have majority control of Congress, they can set the agenda to benefit themselves politically. They had a hand in souring the public opinion of Hillary Clinton by forcing the narrative they wanted America to hear, with a government megaphone, congressional authority, persistence, and lots of help from their allies in the conservative media.

In 2016, the Republican Party nominated a known, documented compulsive liar as their presidential nominee. Even before that happened, Donald Trump had an objective, verifiable history of incompetence, bankruptcy, and corruption. *The Washington Post* counted more than 30,500 "false or misleading claims" Trump made during the four long years of his disastrous presidency—averaging 21 "erroneous claims" a day.

But when Quinnipiac University asked more than fifteen hundred registered Republicans, *Democrats, and independents* across the country what was "the first word that comes to mind" when they thought of Hillary Clinton in 2015, the top adjectives painted a devastating picture of how the GOP turned the narrative against her:

"First word that comes to mind when you think of Hillary Clinton?"	Number of times each response was given:
Crooked	11
Corrupt	12
Benghazi	12
Politician	13
Email	14
Intelligent	15
Democrat	16
Deceitful	18
Criminal	18
Untruthful	19
Crook	21
Smart	31
Woman	47
Bill	56
Strong	59
Experience	82
Untrustworthy	93
Dishonest	123
Liar	**178**

BACKED INTO A CORNER

As for Democrats? Sure, Democrats try their best to capitalize on Republican scandals. But ask anyone who's followed basic American politics for more than a decade: Do you recall a single Democratic equivalent to the GOP's yearslong, taxpayer-funded investigation into Hillary Clinton for the sole purpose of tanking her reputation? Your conservative friends will no doubt resort to whataboutism: "But what about the House's January 6 Committee," they might ask, "which was formed and designed to torpedo Donald Trump's reputation?" Hardly.

The January 6 Committee—established months and not years after the actual attack—zeroed in on an armed terrorist plot to overturn the will of American voters for the first time in the history of our republic. The January 6 Committee was designed to hold accountable the former president of the United States who called for the violent overthrow of democracy, the lawless bums who followed his lead, and the elected cowards who looked the other way.

Do Democrats know how to make a non-news story bleed so that it leads? I can't think of a single instance of that happening either—at least intentionally. Democrats are too focused on separating the facts from the weeds, even if it means losing the Message. Democrats tend to be too preoccupied with policy outcomes and civic processes to worry about something as mischievous as shaping public opinion from the top down. We wrap ourselves in information knots hoping for a political environment where concerned citizens educate, then motivate themselves to create a more perfect union from the bottom up. We're too concerned with politeness and decorum to play hardball the way Republicans do.

To be clear, most hearings on Capitol Hill have some sort of self-serving, political endgame for the party convening them. When Elizabeth Warren sternly grills CEOs during a Senate Banking Committee hearing, she is doing her job while also reinforcing her political brand as a consumer rights champion—giving her constituents another reason to vote for her again, and maybe giving grassroots donors another reason to send a few bucks to her next campaign. That's not my beef. My beef is that Democrats don't control the larger narrative when they can.

Here's an example of a missed opportunity: In May 2023, Senate Democrats convened a Judiciary Committee hearing following several bombshell news stories about Supreme Court justice Clarence Thomas. ProPublica first reported that Thomas failed to disclose luxury vacations, valued at hundreds of thousands of dollars, paid for by the billionaire GOP donor Harlan Crow. Then came a story about Thomas's failure to report selling the home where his ninety-four-year-old mother lives to Crow. Then CNN reported Thomas's mother wasn't even paying rent on the home Crow owns.

The committee brought in five experts to testify for more than three sleepy hours about the need for binding ethics rules for Supreme Court justices. Republicans, however, dismissed the gravity of the whole ordeal from the beginning. They accused Democrats of politicizing Thomas's challenges with ethics and transparency, suggesting the whole hearing was payback for the conservative court's overturning of *Roe v. Wade* in 2022. Senator Lindsey Graham of South Carolina, the senior ranking Republican on the Judiciary Committee, even characterized the hearing as "an assault on Justice Thomas" and as a "concentrated effort by the Left to delegitimize the court and to cherry-pick examples to make a point."

For Democrats, the oversight hearing went, well, just as you might expect for Democrats. They did not eviscerate Justice Thomas, whose wife, Ginni, was heavily involved in the events surrounding the January 6 insurrection and in efforts to obstruct the presidential election certification process. They did nothing to make the headlines about a conservative Supreme Court justice hiding gifts from Crow, who collected Nazi artifacts and paintings by Adolf Hitler and whose "Garden of Evil" art collection included statues of dictators like Lenin and Stalin. And even though they were being branded as political opportunists, Democrats didn't even take the opportunity to remind anyone that Thomas had suggested outlawing contraceptives and same-sex marriages in his concurring opinion to *Roe v. Wade*. No, Democrats showed up intent on a substantive, boring conversation about ethics reform. Republicans showed up to control the narrative.

Is ethics reform for the Supreme Court an important issue that deserves a substantive examination by our elected leaders? Of course it is! But Republicans have no interest in substantive investigations into Supreme Court ethics. As such, they predictably used their valuable committee time to attack Democrats.

So what can Democrats do in the face of such merciless, predictable behavior from Republicans? They can learn the art of electoral war, and they can play the GOP's game.

PART III

THE ART OF ELECTORAL WAR

Now the general who wins a battle makes many calculations in his temple ere the battle is fought. The general who loses a battle makes but few calculations beforehand. Thus do many calculations lead to victory, and few calculations to defeat: how much more no calculation at all! It is by attention to this point that I can foresee who is likely to win or lose.

—SUN TZU,

The Art of War

8

Stronger Messaging in Seven Steps

With democracy on its deathbed I hope you're wondering, *Well, what can we do about it?* What can we start doing right now to make the Democratic Party—the party of the people—tougher, smarter, and more efficient heading into future elections? And to win those elections? The rest of this book is my response.

First, think of all elections, big and small, as battles in a much larger and far more consequential *electoral war* whose victors will determine the future of this nation. The Republican Party certainly thinks of them that way. And while this electoral war remains a cold war of ideologies, never forget some on the far right are openly advocating for—and *using*—violence. We saw it on full display even before January 6, 2021. Unless you are one of those mob insurrectionists, you cannot afford to sit out. Politics is no longer a "season" most Americans have to put up with every other autumn; it is a 24/7 tug-of-war over the future of democracy. Even if you don't want a war with the Republican Party, they're already at war with you.

Second, understand the strategies and tactics of today's GOP. They have a decades-long head start in fighting this war. And the GOP has given us plenty more to work with after Donald Trump took over as their undeniable leader. If you've come along with me this far, you already have a pretty good grasp of how Republicans fight and how they win. We need to use every tool at our disposal—our new understanding of human behavior, the news media, political infrastructure, and control of the narrative—to tear up our old playbook and fight fire with fire. As the great military strategist Sun Tzu advised twenty-five hundred years ago, *preparation* is the most important step before battle. The same goes for the art of electoral war. We've got to acknowledge our weak spots, know the opposition's strengths and shortcomings, and understand every element of their strategy.

Third, let's start by picking the lowest-hanging fruit, which is improving Democratic messaging. Now that we understand what we're up against and where we've fallen short, let's win back the Message. With our freedom, health, wealth, and safety on the line, we really have no choice. This advice doesn't apply just to card-carrying Democrats, by the way. Anyone who's concerned about the future of America can use stronger messaging to help save democracy.

Before we get into the fundamentals of stronger messaging, here's the good news: this advice is actually pretty damn straightforward, by design. If you've ever worked in marketing, engineering, communications, or Republican politics, you've no doubt been reminded at some point to "keep it short and sweet," or its military slang equivalent, "keep it simple, stupid." This stuff may have something to do with brain science, but it ain't rocket science.

Simplicity, by the way, doesn't mean we have to dumb down our arguments. We don't have to sound as vapid and harebrained as Donald Trump. Simple messaging simply means using clear, easy-to-understand language to convey ideas that matter and resonate with ordinary people, just as Trump did so well.

1. RIDE FOR THE BRAND

In the old days of the American West (and in some places still today), cowboys were said to "ride for the brand," meaning they focused their time and attention only on the cattle bearing the brands of the livestock owners who paid them. Those brands were easy-to-identify symbols burned into the hides of calves, permanently scarring the animals so ranchers could easily find, sort, and separate them on the open range.

In politics, *branding* is what we end up with when political messaging is effective, for better or for worse. It's the end result of a deliberate attempt to get voters to believe something about a particular politician or political idea. A good way to find and test a political brand is through word association, as Quinnipiac University researchers did when they asked participants what was "the first word" to come to mind when they thought of Hillary Clinton. By far the most common answer, as we discovered in the last chapter, was "liar." Now *that's* a political brand—an unfortunate, inaccurate one. What's the first word to come to mind when you think of the Republican Party? Ron DeSantis? Congress? Joe Biden?

One of the most familiar branding successes in American politics shaped a strange conversation I had with a Lyft driver a few years back. Whenever I book a trip with a chatty rideshare driver, I like to ask a question or two about politics to see where the conversation goes. There's nothing scientific about these informal, one-on-one focus groups, but they usually yield interesting perspectives from complete strangers around the country.

"I respect Donald Trump," the driver, who spoke broken English and who happened to be an immigrant, happily told me as he navigated the streets of downtown D.C.

"But what do you think of him as . . . president?" I asked with my typical poker face.

"He's a wonderful president," he replied. "A good businessman. Successful!" Then the driver looked at me in the rearview mirror and, with a chuckle, imitated the *Apprentice* tagline: "*You're fired!*"

I don't need to tell you that Donald Trump is not and never was a particularly good businessman, do I? The failures of his myriad ventures—from fraudulent companies to sham universities to mail-order steaks—have been documented for decades. The man bankrupted a casino, for heaven's sake! It is an objective, established fact that Trump has driven businesses into the ground, screwing countless clients, contractors, and American taxpayers in the process. But millions of Americans immediately think "business success" or "art of the deal" when they hear the name Donald Trump. That's because Trump's carefully cultivated *political brand* was more powerful than reality. Despite all of Trump's failures, and despite copious news coverage of those failures, his brand as a successful tycoon—as a cutthroat dealmaker, as a problem solver—is stronger.

This brand crystallized in 2004, when NBC gave Trump a starring role in its hit "reality" TV show. *The Apprentice* not only boosted Trump's household name recognition and celebrity status, it completed a made-up circuit that the man *was* his TV show character: an embodiment of power, wealth, confidence, and success. This tightly controlled illusion was so effective that it was seared into the imagination of my Lyft driver, where it remained a fantasy twenty years later. Trump's brand as a successful businessman was as permanent as an actual cattle brand.

Political branding, of course, isn't necessarily a bad thing. In fact, as long as it's honest, political branding is essential for advancing and popularizing important political ideas, allowing voters to identify, separate, and process them. But "honest" is the key word here.

Republicans have an endless supply of dishonest brands for Democrats. The old Republican Party branded Democrats as "tax and spend liberals" who reject the conservative values of smaller government and low taxes. But today's Republican Party is painting a much more sinister brand for Democrats, convincing a whole lot of other Americans that all Democrats are woke, pro-crime socialists who are racist against white people and who want to groom children into sexual deviants. Of course this isn't true, but remember that for today's GOP inconvenient details like *truth* no longer matter. This is also strategic for Republicans; it's negative partisanship! Their branding motivates GOP voters and leaners, and it pushes independent swing voters away from supporting Democrats.

But how effectively do Democrats brand Republicans? How do they brand themselves? This is yet another vulnerability for Team Blue, because effective political branding doesn't happen without effective messaging, and we know our problem there. It also won't happen unless Democrats embrace basic marketing principles. Democrats, good at governing and making important policy decisions, well, just kinda suck at marketing.

Sure, Democrats have some brands for themselves and for Republicans, but which of them actually resonate with the electorate? If you were to ask all Americans the first thing they think of when they hear the word "Democrat," what would be the most common answer? Would it be something Democrats are proud of? Would it help them win elections? Would it be accurate? If past is prologue, probably not.

So when I say step 1 is "Ride for the Brand," I mean Democrats should rebrand themselves with a single guiding value—one symbolic word—and they should stick to it, using it whenever possible as a guiding star for their political messaging. This word should accurately reflect the Democrats' enormously complex and diverse party under one emotive umbrella, frame the stakes of every election, and be shaped by negative partisanship strategy. And the results of the 2022 midterms already tell us what that word ought to be.

2. REBRAND BOTH PARTIES WITH F-WORDS

Here are two truths that many Americans simply will not believe, thanks to the GOP's success in branding Democrats and themselves:

- Today the Democratic Party is the only political party truly fighting for and preserving American *freedom.*
- Though it brands itself with patriotic images and language, today's Republican Party hates freedom; they want *fascism.*

Democrats must take back the most powerful f-words in American politics by *rebranding themselves as the party of freedom and the Republicans as the party of fascism.* Democrats must make a clear, accurate case that every election, as well as almost every plan and piece of legislation in the Republican Party's agenda, is ultimately about keeping or losing freedom. The Republican agenda is making that challenge easier by the day, as long as Democrats frame the stakes for voters. For example, outlawing drag shows and gender-affirming medical care isn't just an LGBTQ issue; it is an *attack on freedom*. Banning books doesn't protect children; it *takes away their freedom*! "Raising questions" about a free and fair election with no evidence of fraud isn't just entertaining a conspiracy theory; it's an *attack on our freedom* to choose our own government.

The reason the Supreme Court's 2022 *Roe v. Wade* reversal angered and motivated so many Americans wasn't just that the decision allowed states to outlaw specific medical procedures. No, it fired up Democratic voters because of something much deeper and much more horrifying, and it resonated in every corner of our country. The Supreme Court's decision meant the freest people in the world suddenly didn't have control over their own bodies or medical choices. That argument stuck with voters when some Democratic candidates framed the stakes, starkly and accurately, as a loss of their own freedom. It was powerful stuff. And as we'll see soon, it worked well politically for most Democrats who used it.

Gavin Newsom understood the power of messaging the Republican attack on freedom too. On Independence Day in 2022, he launched an ad in Florida trolling Republicans about their efforts to undermine American democracy. The California governor, then rumored to be considering a presidential candidacy, called his thirty-second TV spot "Florida Freedom":

Freedom? It's under attack in your state. Republican leaders? They're banning books, making it harder to vote, restricting speech in classrooms, even criminalizing women and doctors. I urge all of you living in Florida to join the fight, or join us in California, where we still believe in freedom: Freedom of speech. Freedom to choose. Freedom *from* hate. And the freedom to love. Don't let them take *your* freedom.

For no good reason other than volume, discipline, and repetition, the political Right has laid claim to the value of *freedom*—simply because Republicans branded themselves with it. Everyone can and should own freedom as a deep-rooted American value, especially after we've worked so damn hard and shed so much blood to guarantee it. But now that the Republican Party is overtly yanking away our freedoms, Democrats get to own freedom as *their* political brand.

"It has frustrated me that Republicans love to cloak themselves in this blanket of freedom and feel as though they own it somehow, when in fact what they are selling to the people of Pennsylvania, or the American people, really isn't freedom at all," the then-candidate Josh Shapiro said during his successful 2022 run to become governor of Pennsylvania. What Republicans actually want, Shapiro added, is "far bigger government and more control over people's everyday lives."

Let's consider that our cue, then, for Democrats to reframe and redefine *freedom* when Republicans try to use it—or worse, when they claim only they own it. If a MAGA Republican claims a face-mask mandate during a worldwide pandemic is a violation of her freedom, reframe her objection as a violation of *your* freedom to not get sick from the shit coming out of her germy face. If a MAGA Republican claims losing his assault rifle is a violation of his freedom, reframe his objection as a violation of a third grader's freedom to go to school without getting murdered by an assault weapon.

Whenever possible, Democrats should center their branding and messaging—especially about the work and intentions of the GOP—on the maypole of American freedom, the growing threat today's Republicans pose to it, and how it directly threatens voters' health, wealth, and safety. The Republican Party's definition of freedom is a very narrow one—one befitting a time when politics was the exclusive domain of wealthy, educated, straight, mostly Christian white men. There's another f-word for forcing that narrow definition on everyone else: "fascism." And that should be the Democratic Party's new brand for the GOP.

Every election from this point forward boils down to an uncomplicated, fundamental choice between Democratic Party freedom and Republican Party fascism, and it falls on Democrats and their messaging to frame it that way.

3. LESS DEFENSE, MORE COUNTEROFFENSE

Politico published a leaked draft of the Supreme Court's decision overturning *Roe v. Wade* on the evening of May 2, 2022. The *following day,* the White House released a wordy statement from President Biden outlining "three points about the cases before the Supreme Court," detailing how the president had asked his advisers to "prepare options for an Administration response," and a ho-hum warning that "it will fall on voters to elect pro-choice officials this November." The Democratic National Committee also responded with the political equivalent of "get off my lawn, kids!"—a 147-word statement that ended with "we will fight back with everything we have, and Republicans will have to answer for their party's relentless attacks on Americans' rights."

Of course the decision to end women's freedom—and *Politico's* early preview of it—caused a national uproar among Democrats and millions of other concerned Americans who don't even identify with a political party. Progressive politicians, candidates, and organizations shared all sorts of furious opinions and statements about the historic decision and the legitimacy of the court. But did the Democratic Party immediately provide a cohesive, unified *message* strategically designed to put Republicans on defense? No. Not even close.

If there was any deep, strategic, poll-tested wordsmithing by Democratic leaders before or after the overturning of *Roe v. Wade,* a decision the Left had anticipated for years if not *decades,* the rest of us didn't get the memo! There was no centralized messaging plan akin to Frank Luntz's "New American Lexicon" widely distributed to Democrats, detailing words that work with clear messaging guidance and advice. So on May 4, two months before launching his "Florida Freedom" ad, Gavin Newsom got feisty about the state of the Democratic Party during a news conference in Los Angeles.

"Where the hell is my party?" the governor fumed, flanked by Planned Parenthood activists. "Why aren't we standing up more firmly? More resolutely? Why aren't we calling this out? . . . Where is the counteroffensive in the Democratic Party?"

Ah, the *counteroffensive*. Democrats are used to playing defense. But again, you don't score many touchdowns playing defense. A counteroffensive is a message that puts your opponent on defense on an issue that hurts *them* politically. When the Republican Party got behind Glenn Youngkin in Virginia in 2021, they didn't wait for Democrats to criticize Youngkin on his weak-ass vision for public education. No, the Republicans executed a counteroffensive strategy: They put Democrats on defense— on *their* issue of education—with critical race theory. Democrats should get much more comfortable with this kind of rougher, tougher play.

So what would a Democratic counteroffensive to the Supreme Court's decision have looked like? Justice Clarence Thomas gave us the perfect opportunity to play counteroffense when he wrote his concurring opinion. Justices "should reconsider all of this Court's substantive due process precedents," Thomas wrote, referring to previous court decisions that allowed contraceptives and same-sex marriages. In stronger words, the Supreme Court's conservative majority isn't just coming after abortion rights; they are coming after *all* rights you and I take for granted!

To wit, here's the counteroffensive response I would have suggested:

Republicans have stripped American women of their freedom. Will they come for YOURS next?

Note how I didn't bother getting specific about the case itself, or Justice Thomas and the decision-making process of the Supreme Court, or the Republicans' decades-long effort to game the system and stack the court with antiabortion justices. As we've already established, most Americans don't pay enough attention to civics for those kinds of distracting details. Keep it simple and make your audience actually feel your message in the gut rather than merely hear it.

Similarly, if Republicans complain about how crappy our economy is and blame a Democratic president for it, the Democrats' response shouldn't be to explain exactly why the economy isn't crappy with academic reasoning and numbers that few people understand. That's exactly what Republicans *want us* to do. When we take their bait, we put ourselves on defense. We wander in the weeds wondering why nobody's hearing us. Anyone listening certainly isn't hoping for an academic explanation, no matter how accurate or eloquent it may be.

No, the Democratic counteroffensive response to a crappy economy should be to talk about how the Republican Party destroyed the American middle class using their "voodoo" economic plan known as Reaganomics while marketing Bidenomics as the cure. Showing and reminding voters that they cannot trust Republicans with their money is a counteroffensive strategy on the economy, one of the most important issues to voters in every election cycle.

4. TAKE CREDIT, GIVE BLAME

In Congress, the Republican Party has largely given up on policymaking altogether and has instead shifted its entire focus to winning elections, messaging their culture war, and grievance politics. In both the Senate and the House, Republicans proudly brand themselves as obstructionists tasked with preventing Democratic majorities from doing the work of the people.

"One hundred percent of [the Republican Party's] focus is on stopping this new administration," Mitch McConnell admitted in May 2021 when talking to reporters about Joe Biden's months-old presidency. The Senate minority leader's comment echoed another infamous remark he made in 2010 about the GOP's top political priority being "to deny President Obama a second term."

Senator Ron Johnson took the new Republican strategy of obstructing over legislating a step further when he appeared on Fox News in the fall of 2021. "I hope for Democrat gridlock," the Wisconsin Republican told Fox's Maria Bartiromo with a straight face. "Oftentimes in Washington, D.C., gridlock is the better alternative, but when it's Democrat gridlock, *pray* for it."

I point this out because the Republican Party's strategy of embracing political brokenness presents another opportunity for stronger Democratic messaging: taking credit for being the one party that actually delivers tangible results for America while assigning blame to the party whose stated goal is to stand in the way. Doing this effectively requires delivering partisan messages, which too many elected Democrats—especially ones in swing states or traditionally red states—shy away from. Purposefully or not, Democrats often bleach partisanship out of their messaging, doing themselves no favors.

"If you're on Medicare and need insulin," a Democratic U.S. senator tweeted in late 2022, "it's capped at $35 starting in 2023." Democrats in Congress included the insulin price cap in their Inflation Reduction Act of 2022, which not a single Republican member of Congress voted for. So while there was nothing inaccurate with our Democratic senator's public service tweet, the message missed a critical branding opportunity. Instead, the message should have been this: "Because Democrats capped insulin at $35, American seniors no longer have to go hungry to pay for the medicine they need to live." *Our brand up, the Republican brand down.*

After Congress passed the American Rescue Plan Act along party lines in 2021, one Democratic governor hailed the achievement as a "once in a generation opportunity" and a "truly collaborative effort." Though his press release featured celebratory quotes from Democratic lawmakers from his state who supported the legislation, there was no mention that every single Republican in the delegation voted against it; there was no message telling voters that the landmark legislation happened only because of Democrats.

So why do too many elected Democrats fail or refuse to take credit or assign blame? Most likely they've been advised by consultants that the way to win their next election is to always stay above the fray. Maybe these Democrats incorrectly assume that their audiences of regular Americans magically know that when reporters say "Congress passed," they really mean "*Democrats* passed." Spoiler alert: they don't! If you want average people to know Democrats are delivering for them, you have to tell them it was Democrats even if two Republicans helped.

Some Democratic strategists seem to believe swing voters will punish their clients for "being partisan," but this fails to explain why extremely partisan Republicans like Ron DeSantis and Ron Johnson keep winning in swing states. If extremism is such a turnoff for swing voters, how do extreme candidates like DeSantis still win? As we'll see soon, the 2022 cycle rewarded Democrats who embraced partisan branding and punished those who did not. The old habit of taking the high road has to change because when Democrats lose, people pay.

Democrats: Get comfortable with partisan *credit claiming* and partisan *blaming*; get comfortable branding achievements as *Democratic* achievements and not just generic congressional achievements, even if a handful of Republicans come along. We're not in an accuracy war; we're in a messaging war. There's no Pollie Award for accuracy, folks. We need to make sure voters—all of them—know exactly whom to thank, whom to be disappointed in, and, most important, whom to vote against in the next election.

Do you know why Congress doesn't pass more effective anti-gun-violence laws, even as surveys consistently show a comfortable majority of Americans support stricter gun laws? It's because with the powers granted to the minority party in Congress, like that damn filibuster and the ability to block votes, the GOP throws monkey wrenches into nearly every Democratic effort to pass gun legislation. *It's their admitted strategy!* Stopping the Democrats' agenda is now the most important component of the GOP's agenda. Then they regularly claim credit for doing it, branding themselves as good guys protecting America from Democratic ideas and values.

So if you ask ordinary Republican voters who the "bad guys" are when it comes to "controlling" guns, the answer will almost certainly be *Democrats*. But when voters who care about a higher minimum wage go to the polls, do they know exactly which party and which candidates actively block higher minimum wages? Do they know that GOP leaders actively and consistently oppose raising minimum wages? Well . . .

On Election Day 2022, nearly 59 percent of voters in Nebraska approved gradually increasing their state's minimum wage from $9 to $15 per hour. On the same day, and by almost the same decisive margin, Nebraskans elected Republican Jim Pillen as governor even though he—like so many other GOP politicians—believes the government should not have a role in determining the minimum wage.

So why do voters who support increasing the minimum wage also vote for candidates who actively oppose increasing the minimum wage *on the same ballot?* It's because Democrats have not done an effective enough job of claiming credit for their progress on popular issues like this; we've failed to brand ourselves as the party of higher wages! Or maybe it's because we haven't done an effective enough job of blaming Republicans for low wages. Either way, we're getting our asses whupped, and we have been successfully branded as having "left working-class Americans behind" by a party that never brought working-class Americans along in the first place.

5. OWN OUR ISSUES, THEN OWN THEIRS

The next time you find yourself chatting with a rideshare driver or a barista, try conducting your own one-on-one focus group. Ask which political party your coffee slinger believes is better on the issues of taxes, the economy, and national defense. If that person is like the majority of Americans who only skim political headlines when they must, the answer you'll hear is Republicans. Which party is better when it comes to ensuring access to healthcare, minority rights, and, until recently, education? That'd be the Democrats.

In politics, this is called issue ownership, when voters—not politicians, journalists, or pundits—assign competency on particular issues to political parties based on brand identity. Democrats own all sorts of popular issues, like advocating for clean air and water (which too many progressives call "climate action," whatever that means), championing cheaper prescription drugs (not "drug pricing controls" or "reimporta-tion," whatever they mean), and legislating gun safety (stop calling it "gun control"; nobody who values gun rights wants to be controlled by the government!).

Here's the problem: Republicans are eager to own more of the popu-lar issues currently owned by the Democratic Party. They're making measurable progress, and Democrats are not reciprocating. The GOP made its fight against critical race theory in Virginia a national referen-dum on public education, which has been a slam-dunk, hallmark issue of the Democratic Party for more than half a century.

It was Democrats who passed the National Defense Education Act in 1958, increasing school funding in a Cold War effort to keep America's schoolkids competitive with students in the Soviet Union (which had just beaten America to the punch in successfully launching the first sat-ellite into orbit). Democrats passed the Elementary and Secondary Edu-cation Act less than a decade later. In 1979, Democrats established the U.S. Department of Education. And teachers' unions have long aligned with the values and organized labor objectives of the Democratic Party.

So it was no surprise when, in June 2017, a Gallup survey among a thousand respondents in all fifty states found that 54 percent of them believed Democrats "do a better job of dealing with" education, com-pared with only 35 percent who believed Republicans do better. Even factoring the survey's +/– 5 percent margin of error, Democrats handily *owned* the issue of education, without question.

Now fast-forward to November 2021. Just a few days after Virginians elected Glenn Youngkin as their new anti–critical race theory governor, a *Washington Post*–ABC News poll gave us an alarming look at just how much ground Democrats had lost on the issue of public education. Among a little more than a thousand respondents nationwide, only 44 percent said they trusted Democrats "to do a better job handling education and schools" compared with 41 percent who said Republi-cans (a whopping 15 percent said "both," "neither," or didn't register an opinion). Factor in the +/– 3 percent margin of error and statistically you could argue Democrats lost the issue to Republicans altogether!

Democrats did lose the issue according to yet another survey conducted the following summer. This survey, from a pro-charter-schools organization called Democrats for Education Reform, suggested voters trusted Republicans *more than* Democrats "to handle issues related to schools and education," 47 percent to 43 percent. The survey's +/– 3.5 percent margin of error means Democrats could still lead the issue, but that didn't stop *U.S. News & World Report* from publishing an article about the changing narrative under the headline "Democrats Cede 'Party of Education' Label to GOP." And from *USA Today*: "The GOP Is Strengthening Its Grip on Education. Parents Say Democrats Are to Blame." Oof.

So why are Democrats losing ground on the issue of education? One of the organizations tracking public education in America said it conducted focus groups of swing voters who "emphasized a lack of awareness for Democrats' priorities on public education and a perception that educational funding is misallocated." In simpler words, Democrats failed to reassert their brand dominance on education, then failed to hit back with a counteroffense attacking Republicans for decimating public schools. Instead, they let the GOP swoop in and claim our issue with a made-up scandal!

Today's GOP has an entirely different plan for claiming public education, and no, it's not because they want all children everywhere, regardless of their socioeconomic status, to have access to quality public schools and teachers. No, the Republican Party's official platform argues public schools should be stripped of their funding to subsidize private schools for rich kids with taxpayer money. It's literally welfare for rich people.

And don't even get me started on the economy. More Americans believe Republicans, not Democrats, are better when it comes to the economy, and survey after survey shows us Republicans have owned this issue for decades. That's because the GOP has successfully branded itself as the party of business-friendly policies, small businesses, and lower taxes, while branding Democrats as the opposite. It's easy to associate a good economy with the party that says it supports your small business, promises to stay out of your way, and claims it wants less of your tax money, isn't it? But which party truly is better for America's economy?

The National Bureau of Economic Research (a nonpartisan economic think tank) found, objectively, that "the U.S. economy has grown faster—and scored higher on many other macroeconomic metrics—when the President of the United States is a Democrat rather than a Republican." Nonetheless, the Republicans' pro-business brand sticks with most voters, even after their radical fiscal experiment popularly known as Reaganomics.

This bonkers idea, championed by President Reagan, dropped top marginal tax rates from 70 to 50 percent, then eventually to 33 percent, making federal deficit spending and the national debt that accompanies it a feature, not a bug, of governing in America. Not only did the Republican Party's radical Reaganomics tax scheme decimate American coffers and leave our country vulnerable and struggling after nearly fifty years of "starving the beast," the GOP also ushered in a second Gilded Age in America by making the gap between the rich and the poor even wider than it was in the Roaring Twenties.

So when folks say Republicans are "better on the economy," I don't know what the fuck they're talking about! Republicans have caused nine of the last ten recessions and have managed to reduce us to a debtor nation. Republicans in Congress deliberately force us to flirt with economic disaster. They regularly bring our entire economy to the brink of chaos, even threatening America's credit rating to "own the libs." It is long past time to prosecute the Republican Party for destroying the American middle class and leaving our country idling while the rest of the world develops state-of-the-art infrastructure and public education systems.

And have Republicans learned from the error of their fiscal policy ways? Hell no! In March 2022, the Republican Party unveiled a new tax plan that would have resulted in a tax increase of $4,500 for a family earning $50,000 per year. This from the same party that claims to be against higher taxes—at least for those who make seven digits a year or more. Senator Rick Scott of Florida, who's worth more than a quarter of a *billion* dollars, defended the Republican tax hike on us not-wealthy Americans by saying we should pay more to "have skin in the game."

Most Americans apparently missed the headline, so it's worth repeating: In 2022 the Republican Party pushed a real plan to force middle-class families to give up more of their hard-earned money to the government, not long after the same Republicans relieved millionaires and billionaires of paying their fair share of taxes. Of course the GOP's tax hike scheme went over like a fart in church, and after a few months the Republicans stopped pushing it.

Then, in 2023, Republican representative Buddy Carter of Georgia proposed replacing most federal taxes with a flat 30 percent national sales tax—on *everything*, for everyone. Under the GOP's so-called Fair Tax Bill, a $20,000 car would cost you $26,000. A $5 cheeseburger would cost $6.50. Your $30 haircut would cost an extra $9, before the tip! House Speaker Kevin McCarthy even promised a vote on this disastrous, expensive tax on every American.

So let's not allow the Republican Party to claim they're the party of lower taxes—at least for us ordinary taxpayers. It simply isn't true, and with better, louder, more consistent messaging voters will catch on. Through more effective messaging and branding via partisan credit claiming and blaming, Democrats can start building a convincing case that the GOP truly is a threat to America's economy and to *your wealth*.

6. STICK TO A SINGLE VILLAIN

One of the reasons Republican messaging is so effective is that it usually takes issue with a single villain: Democrats. Who causes the "border crisis"? The Democrat Party! Who wants to take your guns? Democrats. Who wants to turn your boy into a girl? . . . You get the point.

In 2023, when a Biden-appointed member of the Consumer Product Safety Commission indicated that his panel was considering an eventual ban on new gas stoves, citing concerns over indoor air pollution, the Republican Party didn't frame it as overreach from some group of bureaucrats in Washington, nor did they blame health advocates trying to protect children from asthma. No, no, no. The GOP pinned the blame directly on Joe Biden and his party, little details be damned.

"If the maniacs in the White House come for my stove, they can pry it from my cold dead hands," the MAGA congressman Ronny Jackson of Texas tweeted of the news. "COME AND TAKE IT!!"

Democratic messaging, on the other hand, is nuanced—focused more on the unelected middlemen and the special interests funding the Republican machine.

"As a nation, we have to ask: When in God's name are we going to stand up to the gun lobby?" President Biden said in an address from the White House in 2022, following the devastating mass shooting at Robb Elementary in Uvalde, Texas. The president used his prime-time speech to sharply criticize Congress's lack of gun reform legislation, but he did not once remind the people of America of the hundreds of Republican members of Congress preventing such legislation. This misdirected blame is all too common in Democratic messaging. Can't negotiate drug prices for Medicare? *Big Pharma won't allow it.* Why won't Congress pass any legislation to address climate breakdown as Earth burns? *Blame the greedy Big Oil bastards.*

Democrats quickly point fingers at the generic, nefarious forces we've vilified for having far more influence than they should over our government: the NRA, Wall Street, billionaires, oil profiteers, the military-industrial complex. Sure, we can assign a whole lot of blame for a whole lot of problems on these factions of influence and their legions of handsomely paid lobbyists. That influence is a genuine problem, and we need to hold these middlemen accountable to the truth, to the law, and to a livable future. But as a strategic message, blaming these bogeymen misses an important negative partisanship opportunity for Democrats.

At the end of the day, voters don't get to vote for or against the gun lobby or Big Oil or Wall Street. We only get to vote for Republicans or Democrats to represent us.

Why don't we have stronger gun safety laws on the books? Of course the NRA plays a major part, but the real answer that voters need to understand—and that we must say aloud—is this: *because the Republican Party won't let us.* Republicans might be in the pockets of the NRA and its lobbyists, but only Republican lawmakers get to vote for or against gun laws. And our messaging needs to reflect that in order for the negative partisanship strategy to work.

Worry less about the middlemen and more about the biggest bogeyman there is: the Republican Party.

7. SAY IT AGAIN. AND AGAIN. AND AGAIN.

Good messages, as the GOP knows, aren't abstract; they're easily understood value statements. They don't require explanation or deep knowledge or historical context to comprehend them. And most important, effective messages are repeated messages *whether or not they are true.*

This is the phenomenon of the *illusory truth effect,* first identified in groundbreaking research in 1977. Researchers showed volunteers sixty true or false statements that all sounded plausible, such as "lithium is the lightest of all metals" (true) and "Zachary Taylor was the first President to die in office" (false—it was William Henry Harrison). Then researchers asked their subjects to rate the validity (or, as Stephen Colbert would call it, the truthiness) of each statement. Two weeks later, the same volunteers saw sixty more statements, a third of which were repeats from the first round. Two weeks after that, volunteers participated in a final round with sixty more statements—another third of them repeats. Researchers found that volunteers scored statements they had heard before as *more valid,* whether or not they were true, simply because those statements were familiar. Bottom line: If it's familiar, it's truthier!

Why does this happen? We are confronted with millions of stimuli every day—data points that our brains must remember and sort, or discard altogether. And we are much more likely to retain information that resonates with, or specifically addresses, something we want or need in a given moment.

So, for example, if I watch a football game and see a hundred commercials for a new pickup truck, I'm probably gonna gloss over every single one of them. They fade into the background. But one day, when I'm actually in the market for a new truck, my brain will process those repeated ads differently; I'll start paying attention to their messaging, and I'm much more likely to remember them. Suddenly all those ads become extraordinarily relevant (and worth every penny to the advertiser). Same goes for those prescription drug ads that tell me to ask my doctor about some funny name I'll never recall. But if I've been diagnosed with diabetes and need to know which drugs are available to me, I'm much more likely to ask my doctor about Ozempic.

Like new pickup trucks and diabetes medications, American politics, sadly, is a product with limited appeal. So in order to sell voters on a political idea or a candidate, we have to repeat our messages until they resonate with our target audience. This is why it's more effective in politics to focus on a single simple, overarching message and repeat it over and over, like *The Republican Party is taking away your freedom.* How, exactly, are Republicans taking away freedom? We're happy to show voters exactly how, and we've got nothing to hide. But we have to sell the overarching message first, with repetition.

Here's a favorite, frequently repeated GOP message: "witch hunt." Donald Trump tweeted those two words nearly four hundred times before Twitter suspended his account following the GOP's January 6 attack on democracy. Even long after Trump lost his Twitter privileges, he called the FBI's 2022 search a "NEVERENDING WITCH HUNT" while asking supporters for money. A few weeks later, Trump called the New York attorney general Letitia James's quarter-billion-dollar civil lawsuit against him "Another Witch Hunt." And that was *before* federal prosecutors charged him for stashing classified documents at Mar-a-Lago and lying about them! Republican politicians and candidates use the phrase "witch hunt" all the time to characterize unflattering investigations, rumors, or accusations of wrongdoing.

So do the right-wing media, whether parroting Republicans or while describing what they want viewers to believe are unjust investigations into Republicans. In 2018, *The Atlantic* cited survey data in which a whopping 85 percent of respondents "whose most trusted network was Fox News believed that the Mueller investigation was a witch hunt . . . more than seven times the respondents for any other network." When political messages are repeated, they resonate with their target audience as truths!

Of course Republicans certainly aren't the first to harness the power of political message repetition. History's most sinister leaders have known its persuasive power for a long, long time:

> The receptive powers of the masses are very restricted, and their understanding is feeble. On the other hand, they quickly forget. Such being the case, all effective propaganda must be confined to a few bare essentials and those must be expressed as far as possible in stereotyped formulas. These slogans should be persistently repeated until the very last individual has come to grasp the idea that has been put forward.

This passage isn't from the GOP playbook.It's from *Mein Kampf,* Adolf Hitler's manifesto, written in 1925. But I think you'll recognize it all the same.

Unlike Hitler and the MAGA movement, Democrats have no need to repeat messages again and again in order to make them *seem* true. Our messages should never, ever be untrue! But we have to do better at repeating our true messages until the folks who don't live and breathe politics *understand* them to be true. And to get there, the Democratic Party must harness the psychological power of message repetition as the Republican Party and its allies have done so well for so long. We must make our messages more familiar, and therefore more valid, by repeating them until we're beyond sick of 'em.

As for the messages themselves? Well, friends, it's time to learn how to land your punches.

How to Land Punches

Plenty of progressives believe Democrats can and should win difficult elections by staying on the high road and never looking down. Many of them subscribe to the advice of former First Lady Michelle Obama, who famously told the 2016 Democratic National Convention, "When someone is cruel or acts like a bully, you don't stoop to their level. No, our motto is: 'When they go low, we go high.'"

Those were some of the most memorable words delivered during that year's national gathering of Democrats in Philadelphia, and most of us understood it as a plea for civility and kindness in a political landscape scorched by Donald Trump's GOP. But make no mistake; Mrs. Obama wasn't asking Democrats to stand down or wimp out.

"Going high doesn't mean sitting on the side of the road and watching injustice go by," she clarified in a 2022 interview. "Going high is about having a real, concrete strategy for change. It's taking the rage and turning it into reason."

Democrats certainly can and should win even the most difficult elections without ever resorting to dishonesty as Republicans do. But with the future of America at stake, we have to get tougher in our messaging and wiser in our electioneering strategies. But to do that—to turn rage into reason by winning electoral power—we need to land more metaphorical punches and we need to aim low.

We need to show the entire country that the clowns who've climbed their way to the top of the Republican Party are notorious for how ridiculously *unserious* they are about the grave responsibility of governing our nation. And if we treat these unserious politicians seriously, we end up making them sound and appear serious.

THE MORE YOU MOCK

Look, I get it. Mocking people is rude. I learned that in the first grade, and so did you. But you're interested in saving American democracy, not in manners lessons. So let's get comfortable with using a little more mockery in our political messaging.

And no, I certainly am *not* suggesting the use of cruelty, as the leader of the Republican Party has done for years. Donald Trump normalized disparaging his own vice president, for crying out loud. He openly made fun of a *New York Times* journalist with a physical disability. He belittled the late John McCain for surviving torture as a prisoner of war. He even mocked E. Jean Carroll, the woman who successfully sued him for sexual abuse and defamation.

No, that's not the kind of mockery I'm suggesting. I'm suggesting the kind of mockery that Democratic congressman Ro Khanna of California used in a tweet in 2021, after Democrats lost to Republicans, 13–12, in the annual congressional baseball game in Washington, D.C.:

I don't care if the scoreboard said Republicans 13, Democrats 12. Democrats won! The Republicans stole the game! I demand a recount! I want an audit! Democrats must introduce new rules to make it more difficult for Republicans to hit, run, score, and catch the ball for outs.

This particular use of mockery in political messaging might be tongue-in-cheek, but its humor allows ordinary, politics-averse voters to understand—and to see and process—something far more serious. Khanna's message cleverly called attention to a much more important issue: that many Republicans in Congress are cheaters who tried to wipe out democracy following Trump's decisive loss several months earlier. Khanna's tweet, however, is the exception, not the rule, in Democratic messaging.

The rule, as we've touched on already, is for Democrats to rebut Republican lies by trying to prove them wrong with facts. As intuitive as that sounds, it doesn't land any punches. In fact, it ends up hurting Democrats in the process. I'll explain.

In 2022, numerous prominent Republicans began spreading a widely debunked lie that some public schools were offering *litter boxes* to students who identify as "furries" (furries cosplay as anthropomorphic animals and wear Chuck E. Cheese–style costumes at events that happen to be popular within, but not exclusive to, the LGBTQ community). The litter-boxes-in-schools lie was as ridiculous as it sounds. Nothing more than a bizarre hoax. But because facts no longer matter to the GOP, and because Republicans have a powerful messaging machine, this urban myth got a lot more traction than it should have, apparently as some sort of wildly irrelevant riff on the debate over the freedom of sexual and gender identity. Colorado congresswoman Lauren Boebert accused schools in her own district of actually providing litter boxes to students (which was quickly shot down as false). Unsuccessful Republican gubernatorial candidate Scott Jensen repeated a similar lie on the campaign trail in Minnesota.

The following May, a furry convention planned for the fall of 2023 in Orlando announced that it would prohibit minors from attending, citing Florida's new Protection of Children Act. That Republican bill, signed into law by Governor Ron DeSantis, prohibits event organizers from "knowingly admitting a child to an adult live performance." GOP lawmakers passed the Protection of Children Act to prevent minors from attending any performance that "depicts or simulates nudity, sexual conduct, sexual excitement, or specific sexual activities." That apparently means drag shows for Florida Republicans.

Though the Orlando furry convention was never intended to be sexual in nature or a drag show, organizers decided to ban minors anyway, citing "legal reasons" around the uncertainty of the new definition of "adult live performance" and the threat of steep fines and revoked licenses. The GOP's made-up hoax about litter boxes in schools no doubt heightened the tension and confusion. And that's when one of Florida's Democratic state senators weighed in to try to clarify the matter in a mainstream TV news interview:

> The furry thing has nothing to do with the bill whatsoever. . . .
> The point I'm trying to make is that way beyond the words—the text in the bill—is the chilling effect of any kind of "adult entertainment" or even non-adult entertainment, like a furry convention, which is not necessarily sexual in any way, is being affected.

In the boxing ring of partisan politics, this "jab" completely missed the target. It didn't land. The state senator who said this tried to prove a false allegation wrong with facts and reality. While well intended, this Democrat unintentionally legitimized the whole argument and provided the news organization exactly what it needed to attract more viewers: *both sides* of a ridiculous situation involving the only political party that relies on lies and urban myths to attack basic freedoms.

Mockery would have been a much more effective response. Mocking strips away the assumption of legitimacy, and it forces any news coverage to focus on the overall merit of the debate instead of the facts and details from side A, then from side B. It's not a Democrat's job to explain a Republican law specifically targeted to deny the freedom of expression to LGBTQ people. A Democrat's job is to convince anyone paying attention that the entire law, as well as all the confusion around it, is another attack on freedom from the same party that believes in stupid hoaxes. Let Republicans explain what their laws do or don't do! Democrats should focus on showing voters that Republican politicians have no business being in charge by mocking them—by belittling their intentions and holding them accountable to the bigger, deeper problems they've caused.

Here's the message I would have suggested instead to land a punch in Florida:

While Florida Republicans were obsessing over people dressing up as cats, Florida homeowners are stuck living in trailers because they can't afford Ron DeSantis's skyrocketing property insurance rates.

This message mocks Republicans for wasting time on a silly cultural issue. It doesn't legitimize the debate over the Protection of Children Act by offering explanations and facts. It reminds voters that the GOP wants to take away freedom. And it's true! As Florida Republicans nanny-stated legislation about adult performances, they let property insurance rates rise to four times the national average, and they get to own that problem. This response also pivots the message to an issue that resonates with far more voters.

Embracing this tactic isn't just advice for elected Democratic policymakers. You too can mock the Republican agenda the next time you're talking politics around the office coffeepot. It certainly isn't difficult when the lousiest, least serious Republicans are among the most recognized and well-known politicians in America.

And that's why I have no problem with mocking and belittling the Republican Party and its leaders and members who make a mockery of America. Neither should you. I ridicule them. I call them names. Let's make fun of their conspiracy theories and their time-wasting probes into intentional distractions like Hunter Biden, or their inability to separate whatever "Jewish space lasers" are from actual climate change. This stuff is as laughable as it sounds, and it's fair game in politics. If Republicans want a serious debate about the future of America, they have to be serious first. Today's Republican Party has fallen far from that standard.

But, Rachel, why lower ourselves to their level? Why not go high when they go low?

Because, my friends, mocking the Republicans' lies, hateful legislation, gaslighting, and flimsy, vindictive congressional hearings is a demonstrably effective tactic for showing the rest of the country how ridiculous the Republican Party's agenda really is and how willing they are to abuse their power when they have it. If Democrats keep resorting to the familiar strategy of answering GOP lunacy on the high road with the same old facts, stats, and reason, we might all end up in "America First" reeducation camps because all we manage to do is legitimize their claims by treating them seriously.

Mocking Republican leaders relentlessly also reminds ordinary Americans that the Republican Party has decided to elevate their most embarrassing, least qualified, scandal-ridden members as leaders. Remember, because of confirmation bias, facts and explanations don't change minds in politics. But helping voters understand the choice between GOP absurdity and Democratic seriousness with mockery—and by making that contrast memorable with humor when possible—certainly can change minds. And it ultimately helps Democrats shore up their coalition while pushing swing voters away from Republicans . . . negative partisanship strategy!

PIVOT! BELITTLE! ATTACK!

Now that we're getting comfortable with landing punches, let's improve upon a fundamental GOP messaging tactic—a formula, really—in electoral war: *pivot and attack*. I heard a textbook example of this tactic from a prominent Republican in October 2022, a couple days after *The Daily Beast* published the first bombshell report of an ex-girlfriend claiming Republican U.S. Senate candidate Herschel Walker had paid for her abortion. That morning Ralph Reed, the conservative evangelical Christian founder of the Faith and Freedom Coalition, rushed to Walker's defense on NPR's *Morning Edition*.

"Why is the Republican Party still standing by this very flawed candidate whose scandals just seem to keep mounting?" the host Leila Fadel asked Reed.

"Well, I think in this particular case, we're dealing with a thirteen-year-old anonymous allegation that no other media organization has been able to independently verify," Reed answered. "Herschel denies this allegation. And I think voters are going to vote on the issues."

Then Fadel asked Reed whether Walker is "a man who lines up with conservative Christian values—with Republican values." It was a fair question given that Walker's Democratic opponent in Georgia, Senator Raphael Warnock, was an actual Baptist pastor. Here's how Reed used his airtime:

> I think what this really boils down to is we have an election in five weeks taking place when inflation is at a 40-year high. Gas prices are at the highest level in U.S. economic history. And people are voting on the failed policies of Joe Biden, whose job approval in Georgia is 37 percent. And among swing voters, Biden's job approval is 20 percent. And Raphael Warnock has voted with Joe Biden 96 percent of the time. He's tied to him. And so he's trying to change the subject to something that happened with Herschel Walker 13, 15, 20, 25 years ago.

Instead of answering a simple question about whether Walker lined up with conservative Christian values, Reed changed the subject and deployed counteroffensive attack messages (and brands) designed to push swing voters in Georgia away from supporting Warnock. And as if his response didn't feel gaslighty enough, Reed even changed the subject while criticizing *Warnock* for trying to change the subject!

Here's another example from one of the more polished experts in the art of pivoting and attacking. In April 2023, Mike Pence gave an interview to CBS's *Face the Nation*. The former vice president, then considering his own presidential run, was asked about the recent shootings of two people: one victim was shot after turning in to the wrong driveway in upstate New York; the other was a Black sixteen-year-old shot by a white homeowner in Kansas City after the teen accidentally rang the wrong doorbell. Pence began his response with a perfunctory "our hearts go out to the families," but note how quickly he pivoted away from the tragedies to go on *the attack:*

> I'm confident that local law enforcement will move forward and apply the law in a proper way, but I can't help but suspect that this

recent spate of tragedies is evidence of the fear that so many Americans are feeling about the crime wave besetting this country. I mean, look, we literally have lost control of the southern border. . . . Everywhere I go I hear about the avalanche of fentanyl in all of our cities that is tearing apart families, tearing apart lives, and driving a crime wave. Add to that liberal prosecutors that aren't putting people behind bars; add to that the Defund the Police movement.

This particular example might turn your stomach because it so callously skirts an important conversation about gun violence and race. It flips the script. It *whatabouts* the blame! But politically for Mike Pence, it was a perfect answer. Why talk about senseless gun violence and racism when blaming Democrats for crime is far more politically beneficial? Plus it *sounded* like a fair and proper response, right? Bingo!

As long as Democrats are dealing with a dishonest opposition party, they *must* get more comfortable with this tactic. They should pivot to stronger, more self-serving, counteroffensive messages that will help them win electorally whenever possible. They should especially pivot and attack whenever Republicans accuse them of off-message, made-up shit we'd rather not talk about—just as Republicans do to Democrats.

Republicans like Ralph Reed and Mike Pence understand that media interviews are one of the most powerful—and free—marketing platforms available to politicians. They recognize interviews not as opportunities to reflect public opinion, but rather as opportunities *to shape public opinion.* And while this tactic easily applies to media interviews, anyone on Team Blue can adopt this tactic for smaller-scale political messaging, from social media posts to carpool conversations.

But wait! There's an even more effective way to land punches by pivoting and attacking!

After decades of watching media interviews with Republican leaders, I worked with my friend Ceekay Tschudi, a political messaging expert who bills himself as a "professional 'alternative facts' destroyer," to improve on the tactic of pivot and attack by adding mockery to the mix.

Ceekay, by the way, is a former Idaho State debate champion with two degrees in communication. He's also a winning Democratic campaign strategist who helps candidates with debate prep.

Let's break down our three-step formula before we apply it to some real-world messaging:

1. Quickly pivot to change the subject from point A (politically harmful) to point B (politically beneficial);
2. Mock or belittle the opponent's argument; then
3. Use a counteroffensive attack to underscore point B. The more shocking or alarming this attack, the stronger and more memorable your argument will be for your intended audience.

Mocking point A legitimizes the pivot to point B, dismissing point A as unserious and making point B more plausible and more relatable to a wider audience. For a closer look on how to apply this formula, let's zoom into the feisty exchange in 2022 between Republican governor Greg Abbott of Texas and Democratic governor J. B. Pritzker of Illinois, after Abbott bused hundreds of migrants from Texas to Illinois. That year Abbott, DeSantis, and Republican governor Doug Ducey of Arizona sent thousands of migrants—mostly from Central and South America—to the blue cities of Chicago, New York, and Washington, D.C., as a headline-grabbing political stunt. Here's how Pritzker responded in a Twitter thread on September 14:

> Let me be clear: while other states may be treating people as pawns, here in Illinois, we are treating people as people. When someone comes running and seeking help, we will do the right thing and offer a hand. . . . The governor of the state of Texas is choosing not to notify us when he is sending busloads of families—we don't know how many are children or what they need before they arrive. Here in Illinois, we refuse to stoop to that man's level. We will provide food, shelter, and healthcare for the children, women, and men that need it.

A few days earlier, Pritzker said Abbott was treating migrants "like cattle," and called the stunt "disgusting." Sure, messages like this are appropriate from a Democratic governor in a "safe blue" state where many constituents were no doubt concerned about the situation as a humanitarian crisis. But Pritzker's message didn't really pivot away from playing defense. It didn't land a punch!

So let's imagine a stronger, more partisan response developed with the pivot-belittle-attack formula. Step 1? Identify a pivot *away* from point A (the unexpected arrival of immigrants in a big, blue city). As long as we know the state of Illinois is dealing with this stunt as an actual humanitarian crisis, why not serve a shitburger back to Abbott? How about pivoting to higher taxes on the middle class, since Abbott's own party proposed raising taxes by $4,500 for a family earning $50,000 per year? Our stronger statement might start like this:

> Pivot: *Busing migrants to blue states to "own the libs" on the taxpayer dime is just another distraction from the Republicans' embarrassing plan to raise your taxes, which they desperately want you to forget.*

There's plenty to mock in the GOP's middle-class tax increase plan, courtesy of Senator Rick Scott. But remember, most Americans don't know the names of U.S. senators the way they know their fantasy football leagues, so for the next part of our statement, let's keep the focus on Abbott and assign blame to the entire GOP:

> Belittle: *The Republican plan to increase taxes on middle-class families is as ridiculous as Donald Trump believing Mexico would pay for his border wall. My question for Governor Abbott: What are you doing to follow up on Trump's promise to make Mexico pay?*

By framing our mockery as a politically awkward question for a southern border state governor, we, at best, invite the media to ask Abbott about it. Coming from another sitting governor, the question itself would be newsworthy—a new headline—and fielding such a question would muddy up Abbott's messaging. At worst, the media are at least obligated to rehash Trump's promise to somehow make Mexico pay for his border wall, which is an embarrassing broken promise that all Republican leaders own—and want us all to forget. *See what we did there?* Assuming the media cover this statement, we just used bothsidesism to our advantage!

And now for the third act, *the attack*. Again, we have plenty to work with when it comes to Republicans and their long list of unpopular agenda items. So how about this?

> Attack: *And not only is the Republican Party planning to raise your taxes, they still want to yank away your Social Security and Medicare so they can pay for their worthless wall, because they know Mexico never will!*

Does it feel as if we were landing some punches? Good! Let's keep rollin'.

How can we pivot, belittle, and attack the issue of guns, specifically curbing gun violence and limiting gun ownership, which too many Democrats regrettably frame as "gun control"? The phrase "gun control" is an unfortunate one for us progressives because conservatives frame gun ownership as an untouchable right guaranteed through literal interpretation of the Second Amendment of the Constitution. That means Republicans talk about guns as a matter of freedom (our issue!), and they frame any effort to limit gun ownership as an infringement on that freedom as *government control*, the opposite of freedom. So how can we flip the script, in addition to banning "gun control" from our vocabulary?

First, let's find a pivot from point A (the "uninfringeable" right to own guns) to point B—one powerful and emotive enough to compete on the same plane as American freedom:

> Pivot: *I'm not talking about "gun control." I'm talking about grade-schoolers who get murdered by terrorists with assault weapons while learning their ABCs.*

In this example, we're pivoting from the right to own firearms to the right of innocent children not to get murdered in the safety of their schools. And it's important that we don't cede the value of freedom to Republicans. Ever. Remember, if a Republican claims preventing gun violence is a violation of his freedom, we have to *reframe* his rigid interpretation of the Second Amendment as a violation of your child's freedom to go to school without getting murdered by an assault weapon!

And now let's find a way to belittle point A. Democrats have actually been doing this pretty effectively in recent years, regularly mocking the standard "thoughts and prayers" response that so many politicians once used following mass shooting tragedies. Even President Biden mocked the phrase after a mass school shooting near Dallas in May 2023.

"Republican Members of Congress cannot continue to meet this epidemic with a shrug," the president said the following day. "Tweeted thoughts and prayers are not enough."

But let's dig a little deeper for another way to belittle the belief in unlimited gun ownership in America, and how that right, for too many, outweighs everyone else's right to live. Let's reframe that belief, accurately, as a deeply troubling moral priority among Second Amendment absolutists:

Belittle: *Republicans who still think this is an argument about the Second Amendment care more about the rights of mass murderers than protecting our children's lives.*

And now that we've put them on defense, let's land the punch with a shocking counteroffense:

Attack: *Republicans claim they want to protect kids, but not from getting slaughtered at school.*

See how we swatted down the hot potato, dipped it in boiling oil, then tossed it right back? That's exactly what pivot, belittle, and attack accomplishes: a hotter hot potato!

How about another pivot, belittle, and attack, this time on the issue of abortion? Remember, while Republicans have framed their opposition to abortion on the moral high ground of "life," Democrats have long framed it as "choice." So let's first pivot to point B by reframing the issue from choice to freedom:

> Pivot: *This is about one thing only: a woman's freedom to make her own decisions about what happens to her own body.*

As for step 2? Our message can claim the same moral high ground as the "pro-life" frame, belittling the argument by pointing out the clear hypocrisy of the GOP's rigidity on, well, the Second Amendment!

> Belittle: *I'll believe Republicans are "pro-life" when their party gets serious about preventing first graders from getting murdered at school with assault weapons.*

And as for an attack, let's go for the counteroffense again. Let's remind our audience of the brutal consequences of taking reproductive freedom away from women. Let's also remind them that the Supreme Court's MAGA-appointed majority already warned that they're just getting started, and we should take them at their word:

> Attack: *The Republican Party won't stop until they pass their national abortion ban, leaving American women nowhere to run.*

And here's an example of how to pivot, belittle, and attack the political brand Republicans have given to all Democrats thanks to the unfortunate slogan "Defund the Police." Did you notice, earlier in this very chapter, when Mike Pence referenced the "Defund the Police" movement as a sick, twisted justification for the shooting deaths of innocent people? That's a good sign Democrats need a powerful way to un-brand themselves from this messaging disaster, ASAP. So let's pivot to point B by using the GOP's official characterization of Donald Trump's failed, armed overthrow of the U.S. government *against them:*

> Pivot: *The Republican Party now justifies killing cops and rioting in the Capitol as "legitimate political discourse"—those are the GOP's actual words.*

> Belittle: *People died on January 6 and the GOP argues it was a Capitol "tour."*

> Attack: *To help Trump and his cronies get away with January 6th, Republicans plan to defund the FBI and let rapists and murderers have free rein in America.*

Does all this sound saltier and spicier than what we usually hear from Democrats? I hope so! That's because we're landing punches, baby.

The pivot-belittle-and-attack model is an effective tactic because it puts the target on the defense on terms set by their opponent's attack. It's a shameless tactic that ruins any chance of substantive debate but we have to do it anyway because we've got a democracy to save. Understand and adapt this formula, and don't be afraid to put it to the test as you become a no-more-bullshit brand ambassador for the Democratic Party. We need more of them!

YOUR WORDS ARE WEAPONS

By now I also hope you've noticed the language I've been using in these examples. In the art of electoral war, words are our most effective weapons; they're all we've got to land our punches. So every single one of them counts.

The most effective words in politics stir up emotions, resonate with our values, and paint vivid pictures of the future—the future we want

for ourselves and for our kids, and the much bleaker one envisioned by
MAGA Republicans. As Democrats find and use messages in the future, we have to employ simple, unflinching words to make sure all
Americans understand the consequences of the GOP and their plans
for our country.

Republicans have repeatedly tried to repeal Obamacare for as long as
it's existed. They persistently try to rob your Social Security money and
end Medicare as we know it. Political violence and instability appear to
be justifiable to them. So when I say Republicans are a threat to your
freedom, health, wealth, and safety, I mean every accurate word of it.
Those are simple, direct words, and I've landed punches with them. I've
weaponized them.

You may not be used to Democrats using language to kick some ass,
but we no longer have a choice. No more euphemisms. No more pussy-
footing around the consequences of bad ideas and dangerous leadership. No more giving Republicans the benefit of the doubt. *Play their
game.*

And now let's take what we've learned about landing punches with
words and use those words to give Republicans *wedgies.*

How to Give Wedgies

To anyone who calls President Biden "Sleepy Joe": *careful.* The man knows how to give a wedgie. In the middle of a State of the Union address, no less.

No political junkie will forget when Republicans in Congress jeered the president during his annual speech to Congress in February 2023. He had just criticized their plans to dismantle Social Security.

"All of you at home should know what those plans are," Biden said. "Instead of making the wealthy pay their fair share, some Republicans want Medicare and Social Security to sunset." Republicans loudly booed when Biden stated this fact, so he abandoned his teleprompter and flipped the script, off the cuff: "So, folks, as we all apparently agree, Social Security and Medicare is off the books now, right? Not to be stopped? All right! We got unanimity!"

The president's line even forced House Speaker Kevin McCarthy to clap. And that mattered, because four months later Biden and McCarthy hammered out a deal to get Republicans to avoid defaulting on national debt payments in exchange for ideologically based federal spending cuts. And while McCarthy forced cuts that threatened food security for poor adults, he agreed—at least that day—not to cut either Social Security or Medicare. And on the biggest political stage of the year.

Biden had successfully wedged the issue. He forced Republicans in

Congress into an awkward corner, calling them on the carpet, then using their own angry reaction to goad them—publicly, on live TV—into applauding for Social Security and Medicare. After that, any Republican who booed the president, then voted to cut either entitlement program, could be easily called to account.

In the art of electoral war, *wedging* is a tactic that messages a political issue—usually a complicated and controversial one—to divide a coalition, to further divide the electorate, and/or to forcefully frame the opposition party as a potential threat to something voters value or have. Wedge issues are like bunker-buster bombs—the opposite of finding common ground; they split people apart. When Republicans successfully give Democrats wedgies, they push us into defensive territory, often forcing us to do the politically uncomfortable work of defending or explaining hyperbolic claims, like "Democrats are coming for your guns" or "Democrats support murdering babies." Most important, wedge issues accomplish the two goals of negative partisanship: to turn out voters from your team and to disqualify the opposition in the eyes of swing voters.

It's rare, but even beyond Biden's State of the Union wedgie in 2023, Democrats sometimes give wedgies to Republicans. When liberal Democrats in Congress proposed national health insurance for all Americans, which Republicans generally oppose, some proponents switched from calling the idea "single-payer healthcare" to "Medicare for all." Why? Because "single-payer healthcare" is confusing and requires explanation. But Medicare is already a well-known single-payer (government) entitlement that sixty-five million Americans rely on for their health insurance, and GOP leaders know damn well how popular it is among voters. Using the term "Medicare for all" drives a wedge because it forces Republicans in Congress into an uncomfortable corner. It's easy for them to oppose "socialized medicine" and "government healthcare," but it's much more difficult for them, politically at least, to oppose something that already benefits millions of Americans—something as popular and straightforward as Medicare *for everyone*. This is pretty weak compared with the wedgies Republicans give us, but hey, even a weak wedge is still a wedge.

Today there are plenty of good opportunities for Democrats to harness the power of driving advantageous wedge issues against Republicans, and as we'll see below, every policy area is conducive to being wedged. Some Democrats in 2022 won elections by giving good wedgies on Roe but most campaigns have missed important opportunities to weaponize policy against Republicans. So let's take a deeper dive to understand what makes a good wedgie work and how to give more of them to Republicans.

THE GOP'S TWO MOST EFFECTIVE WEDGIES

The issues of abortion and gun ownership are the GOP's "original sins"—at least when it comes to messaging. Republicans wedged both issues for *decades* without an adequate counteroffense from Democrats. Until recently, Republicans have been so effective at wedging abortion and guns that many Democrats believed both issues naturally advantaged the GOP, that both were liabilities—losing issues—for Democrats. So, for a long time, Democrats avoided talking about them. Or at least they didn't talk about guns and abortion *strategically*.

Prior to the mid-1990s the abortion debate remained pretty straightforward: pro-abortion rights advocates, who'd had constitutional protection on their side since 1973, framed abortion as a "choice." Women should have a right to choose what happens to their bodies. Opponents framed their objection to abortion in the morally robust frame of protecting "life." But the issue really solidified as a wedge issue two decades after *Roe v. Wade,* thanks to three weaponized words.

In June 1995, Republican congressman Charles Canady of Florida introduced legislation in the U.S. House to outlaw a procedure known medically as a "dilation and extraction" abortion. In rare cases, doctors can use dilation and extraction to terminate a late-term pregnancy— often during a medical emergency. Canady, who became a Florida Supreme Court justice in 2008, named his bill after the National Right to Life Committee's inaccurate, nonmedical term for dilation and extraction abortions. He called his bill the Partial-Birth Abortion Ban Act. And that's when the ugly, dishonest, and extraordinarily effective phrase "partial-birth abortion" became mainstream, intensifying the national debate over abortion by *wedging* it.

"Partial-birth abortion" deliberately misleads people into believing that all abortions at all stages of gestation are gory, unthinkable acts of murder, performed on what the National Right to Life Committee calls "innocent human life." Of course, activists who deliberately use this term don't bother to mention the scarcity of late-term abortions and certainly leave out the fact that virtually all late-term abortions are due to terminal fetal defects. The Centers for Disease Control and Prevention reports that in 2020 less than 1 percent of abortions were performed after twenty-one weeks of gestation.

So what exactly makes the term "partial-birth abortion" a wedge message? Other people's abortions are none of my business, but I've never met anyone who wants to undergo unthinkable medical procedures, and I've never met a Democrat who's against protecting human life. But there's little room in this powerful message frame for explaining that the question of exactly *when life begins* is scientifically unanswerable, or for explaining how rare late-term abortions truly are. Certainly, it didn't serve the anti-abortion movement to admit that late-stage abortions are only done when medically necessary. Instead, they framed abortion around an image of selfish women aborting late-term fetuses because they changed their mind. Nuances, such as the truth about late-term abortions and their extreme rareness, don't matter in a wedge-issue debate. By design, wedge issues strip difficult political issues of all their complexities. They're meant to persuade voters with oversimplified, hyperbolic, and emotionally charged language and imagery. "Partial-birth abortion" is designed to further divide opponents and supporters, but it's also meant to change minds and divide abortion rights supporters against each other.

Wedge issues also force us to wrestle with and sort through our own values, which help us determine which political ideas we support and which we oppose. A staunch opponent of abortion might say his underlying values are protecting the lives of unborn children, preventing what he believes amounts to murder, and his literally interpreted religious beliefs. A supporter of abortion rights might say her underlying values are the ability to control what happens to her own body, her freedom to choose whether and when to have a baby, and the privacy to make those decisions without any government or religious influence. But this doesn't exclude her from caring about pregnancies and children! It doesn't mean she supports murder! And she very well may value her own deeply held religious beliefs.

The wedge of "partial-birth abortion" muddies these waters because it dishonestly associates abortion with violent murder. It creates a false, binary choice between (a) a woman's freedom to choose whether and when to be pregnant, and (b) protecting "innocent human life" from gory, unthinkable murder. This oversimplified false choice is what drives the wedge. Framed this way, someone who chooses to have an abortion is a baby killer.

As for guns? Republicans have wedged gun ownership in the frame of our beloved constitutional rights for decades. The most ardent defenders of unrestricted gun ownership in America, who now represent a lopsided minority, use and repeat untrue messages that rely on the psychology of loss aversion. That's why every response to every effort to regulate gun ownership *always* amounts, somehow, to Democrats wanting to "take away your guns!"

We can see how powerfully the Republican Party has wedged the issue of guns through the actions and messaging of the National Rifle Association, which has been an unabashed wing of the GOP since President Clinton signed the Assault Weapons Ban into law in 1994 (which Dubya Bush let expire a decade later). In the days following the massacre of twenty first graders and six adults by a gunman at Sandy Hook Elementary School in December 2012, the NRA stayed quiet. *Maybe, some of us thought, just maybe, twenty dead six- and seven-year-olds will finally bring the NRA and its Republican defenders to their senses. Maybe the*

NRA will finally support some basic legislation to stop people from taking their war weapons into elementary schools to slaughter children. But what message did the NRA end up pushing, just one week after the murders of children in Newtown? Maybe you remember what the NRA's executive vice president, Wayne LaPierre, said as clearly as I do:

> The only thing that stops a bad guy with a gun is a good guy with a gun. . . . I call on Congress today to act immediately, to appropriate whatever is necessary to put armed police officers in every school—and to do it now, to make sure that blanket of safety is in place when our children return to school in January.

LaPierre's carefully crafted message, delivered in the painful aftermath of the Sandy Hook massacre, didn't search for common ground; instead, the NRA further wedged the issue of guns by suggesting a wholly unfeasible option: *more fucking guns!* But to many in the GOP's coalition, the oversimplified, emotional "good guy with a gun" message sounded like a workable, commonsense solution: "Putting armed guards in schools—heck, *arming teachers themselves*—will protect children."

LaPierre's message drove a wedge because it introduced another solution, a terrible one, to the political narrative, thus giving policymakers a second option:

1. restrict ownership of assault weapons, which would violate a literally interpreted constitutional right (and hurt gun sales); or
2. *flood the zone* with more guns, and drive up gun sales, by turning teachers into armed cops.

Of course, the GOP responded with option 2, which allowed most Republicans to ignore even the tamest proposals to restrict gun ownership in America, like background checks and "red flag" laws. And it gave Republicans a way out; by demanding more guns in the frame of protecting children, they could appear to be responsive to the crisis without abandoning their loyalty to the Second Amendment.

And remember, the most effective wedge issues are also designed to deliver an awkward choice, or to force an uncomfortable examination of underlying values. This serves as a kind of ideology speed bump, requiring our opponents to consider the issue in a new frame that might just sound reasonable. LaPierre's "good guy with a gun" message did exactly that. Anti-gun-violence advocates had to defend themselves; to explain why protecting children by arming adults—something some schools and most museums and all airports already do—is worse than violating a right enshrined in the U.S. Constitution.

But most devastating of all, the GOP's "good guy with a gun" wedge has utterly failed America in the years since Sandy Hook because it led to a flurry of "good guy with a gun" loosening of gun safety laws in red states. It has turned our entire nation into an indifferent death zone where nobody is safe. We can't go anywhere without worrying about being gunned down: school, church, the movies, the shopping mall—even the wrong damn driveway—and it's all thanks to the GOP's embrace of the NRA's wedge. As for the killers who legally purchased their assault weapons and stocked up on countless rounds of ammo prior to their indiscriminate murder sprees? Well, they were all technically "good guys with guns," until they opened fire into crowds of strangers at malls, movie theaters, and elementary schools.

The fact that Republican gun ideology has turned America into a massive killing field gives Democrats an enormous opportunity to wedge the gun issue right back at them. In fact, we can yank up Republican Underoos on a whole bunch of other wedgeable issues, once we learn how.

A WEDGIE IN THREE SIMPLE STEPS

So how, exactly, can we turn important political issues into uncomfortable wedgies that push negative partisanship? I've boiled it down to three steps that require only a little bit of effort. But in our battle to save democracy, this is one of the more fun assignments. Before we get started, the trick, as you've heard me say before, is to **keep it simple**!

Too many progressives talk about complex issues like, say, climate change in wonky, Ivy League word salad that doesn't resonate with most people. When I hear a well-intentioned climate activist talk about "building sustainable, resilient communities" or "let's build a green energy future," my first response is this: *Nobody knows what that means, dude!* The earth is on fire! Entire cities are drinking poisoned water! Kids are literally choking on poisonous air! Republicans are sentencing our kids to live on a dying planet! *That's* the kind of emotive (and true!) language that connects with the people we need to connect with. Never forget that American electoral politics fires on all cylinders at a fifth-grade reading level!

Step 1: Identify the Strategic Goal and Underlying Rights and Freedoms

My first step in giving a good wedgie is to **identify the strategic goal.** For this example, let's stick with the issue of abortion. The goal of our wedgie is this: *to make all voters think about abortion as a matter of freedom and government control, not a question about the beginning and end of human life.* Now let's **identify the underlying rights and freedoms** in which to ground our message. How about:

- my right to control my own body;
- my economic freedom not to be forced into parenthood by the state;
- my freedom not to be medically tortured by the government for the "crime" of pregnancy complications.

Organizing our wedge message around a personal right is an important step because it uses the psychology of loss aversion—reframing the issue as a loss of freedom—to make the wedgie really hurt. It forces our opponents into defense on a core value shared by virtually all Americans. And that is right where we want them to be.

Step 2: Reframe the Stakes

The second step is to find and use powerful language that **reframes what's at stake in an us-versus-them frame** and **assigns blame to** them— Republicans. To do this, think about how best to **highlight the direct, immediate effects** on all of us if Republicans get their way: what they'll change, and what they'll take away.

Again, language is the most powerful weapon in our electoral war. So as Republicans do, we should use vivid, emotive words and loss-aversion messaging. Remember, loss-aversion language taps into the fact that ordinary people—conservatives, moderates, and liberals alike—fear and loathe losing what they already have, or *could* have.

Here's how to structure a message with loss aversion while assigning blame to Republicans, highlighting the immediate effects, and using vivid, emotive words:

- By forcing rape victims to give birth, the Republican Party gives rapists more rights than their victims.
- The Republican Party's extremist abortion laws torture women for the "crime" of pregnancy complication.
- The Republican Party's radical abortion policies won't stop until American women have nowhere left to run.

As you can see, I use extreme what's-at-stake scenarios. But don't get too hung up on the hypotheticals. Do all Democrats want to repeal the Second Amendment and take away every single gun in America? Of course not. America has made about *465 million* guns since the turn of the last century, for heaven's sake. But do Republicans tell their coalition and swing voters that *all* Democrats want to take away *all* their guns *all* the time? Why, yes, yes they do. They've repeatedly branded all Democrats as "gun grabbers" as they wedged the issue against us for decades. So let's play by their own rules.

An effective wedge issue is designed to frighten voters with worst-case scenarios. It is, by design, hyperbolic. Is the GOP really on the

verge of outlawing abortion in every state? Maybe not imminently . . .
for now. But that's exactly what the Republican Party's platform calls for,
and it's not our job to give them the benefit of the doubt, so *who cares?*
Let them get into the weeds! And we don't need to wait until Republicans in Congress introduce legislation first either. Our only responsibility is to make sure all voters know the GOP's vision for America:
"Republicans *everywhere* want to take away every woman's freedom to
control her own body."

I don't ever stoop to the Republicans' level of dishonesty, nor should
you, but we should never, ever mince words when it comes to saving
democracy. They have "pro-life." We have "pro-freedom."

Step 3: Drive the Wedge

The final step is to combine our inscrutable rights and freedoms with
our us-versus-them stakes-framing language to drive the wedge with a
single roundhouse kick of a message. A good wedge issue message
should make the debate uncomfortable. It should emphasize the GOP's
extremism. It should force Republicans to rethink their own values. It
should harness the power of negative partisanship. It should be *true.*
Here's mine:

> *Big government Republicans think they have more rights to your body
> than you do.*

Isn't that simple?! We've just wedged the issue of abortion against
Republicans. As we'll see soon, some Democrats in 2022 won their
elections by wedging this very issue with powerful, true, easy-to-
understand messages just like this.

Our wedgie forces squeamish swing voters to at least think about
their abortion beliefs in a new light: as a deliberate Republican attack on
personal freedom. No, you won't change every mind, especially on this
particular issue. But our wedgie forces all voters to ask themselves
which value is more important: "Protecting" the unborn? Or protecting

freedom for themselves, their wives, and their daughters? And even if this self-reflection never happens, you'll at least make voters think and talk about abortion rights in *our* frame, and you are still creating a powerful branding effect: Republicans hate freedom.

On the issue of abortion, by the way, Democrats have another added messaging advantage: Most Americans, despite their disinterest in politics, are well aware of the Supreme Court's 2022 unprecedented overturning of *Roe v. Wade.* A national survey by the Pew Research Center suggests an overwhelming 91 percent of Americans had heard about the decision just one week after the Supreme Court officially announced it. It's one of the rare political stories that immediately saturated the electorate. And that means it's much easier for us to wedge Republicans on their march to take away our freedom over our own bodies; the conservative supermajority the GOP muscled onto the Supreme Court has let the Republican Party "catch the car" of an issue that less than 20 percent of Americans support. Now we need to make them pay for it.

WEDGING GUNS AND GUN VIOLENCE

With our three-step formula, let's return to guns. Now that we're familiar with the way the GOP wedges unrestricted gun ownership in America, let's wedge 'em back. And let's begin with some important data, because again, the data don't lie.

According to an April 2023 survey commissioned by Fox News, of all outlets, 87 percent of respondents (with a +/− 3 percent margin of error) said they supported "requiring criminal background checks on all gun buyers." Sixty-one percent said they supported banning assault rifles and semiautomatic weapons. And only 45 percent said they supported "encouraging more citizens to carry guns to defend against attackers," compared with 52 percent who opposed Wayne LaPierre's "good guy with a gun" answer to gun violence. Many other surveys show similar results. The bottom line: a vast majority of Americans *support* restricting gun ownership for gun safety.

This flies in the face of the GOP's broad messaging on guns. The

Republican Party is now associated with trigger-happy zealots who believe the Second Amendment gives everyone in this country, even criminals and terrorists, carte blanche to own, carry, and use weapons of war, whenever and wherever they please. Some Republican lawmakers even take pictures with their spouses and kids, all clutching assault weapons, for their Christmas greeting cards (#Grooming).

Long gone are the days when the NRA focused more on firearm safety and responsible gun ownership. Way back then, the issue of gun ownership wasn't a particularly ideological one. Today, the Republican Party and the gun lobby work hand in hand to stop any sensible effort to curb gun violence, stomping out common sense at every turn. And that gives us an opportunity to reframe the gun debate into a wedgie.

So, let's walk through the steps one more time. Step 1: Identify a rights-and-freedoms-based strategic goal of the message. Don't overthink it! I'd suggest this: *To make all voters believe that the right to live—to not get killed by some mass murderer with an assault weapon—outweighs the right of Americans to own assault weapons designed for mass murder.*

Now let's illustrate our own version of a "right to life." Let's frame these in a way that resonates with most people so that if we strip away the controversial context, they'd be pretty difficult to disagree with:

- my right to send my first-grader to a school safe enough that she won't be shot to death;
- my freedom to go to a movie theater without wondering if a deranged murderer will open fire with his bump-stocked assault weapon that can spray seven bullets *per second* into the crowd;
- the public's "right to life."

Step 2: How can we reframe the stakes in an us-versus-them frame? Remember, "them" is the Republican Party, so we must assign blame to Republicans explicitly. We've got to emphasize the direct, immediate effects of the GOP's refusal to restrict gun ownership using emotive words. How about this?

- Extremist Republicans protect the rights of killers over the rights of our kids.
- With their "good guy with a gun" lies, extremist Republicans have turned America into a killing field.
- Extremist Republicans believe their right to own weapons of war outweighs your right to live.

Step 3: Use the ideas from the underlying rights and freedoms we identified, then combine them with our emotive, loss-aversion language to drive the wedge. There's more than one way to do this, by the way. Because we have several ideas to work with, we have options! But try this one on for size:

Republicans protect weapons of war instead of your kids.

Emotional? Check. Controversial and hyperbolic? Definitely. Simple? Absolutely. True? Yup. And the use of "your" is intentional because most humans, even liberals, are more motivated by things that affect them. Does this wedge flip the script and force voters to reexamine the issue in a new frame—one that pits the right to live against an unpopular, literal interpretation of the right in America to own any gun? Well, that's the idea.

WEDGING THE CLIMATE CRISIS

Let's walk through these three steps again, and this time let's return to the climate crisis. To wedge this issue, let's first cover a bit of background about how the sound science of our changing climate became a disputed, politically controversial issue in the first place. Spoiler alert: Republicans did it *intentionally.* Stupidly. Dangerously.

In 2006, former vice president Al Gore produced his Oscar-winning documentary, *An Inconvenient Truth,* warning of the dire dangers of climate breakdown. A year later, the Intergovernmental Panel on Climate

Change published a thousand-page report painstakingly researched, written, and reviewed by nearly four thousand scientists from around the world. The definitive scientific document, called *Climate Change 2007*, detailed clear, startling evidence that the crisis of a changing climate is real, urgent, rapidly getting worse, and caused by human activity. That year Gore and the IPCC shared the Nobel Peace Prize.

Back then, the climate crisis wasn't really a partisan issue. In fact, in 2008, Democratic House Speaker Nancy Pelosi and former Republican Speaker Newt Gingrich appeared in a TV ad sitting next to each other, urging Democrats and Republicans in Congress to "take action to address climate change."

"We need cleaner forms of energy," Pelosi says in the 2008 ad, "and we need them fast." "If enough of us demand action from our leaders," Gingrich adds, "we can spark the innovation we need."

But then, with Congress considering the possibility of implementing cap-and-trade policies to curb carbon dioxide emissions, Republicans in Congress responded by doing something catastrophic. According to the 2012 *Frontline* documentary "Climate of Doubt," a must-watch for any political junkie, special interests funded by oil and gas companies swooped in to change public opinion by casting fake doubt on real science. Why? It's hardly a secret. It's *all about the money*: about helping rich people and corporations who have no problem destroying the planet to make more moola.

Right-wing organizations, including Americans for Prosperity (funded by the oil billionaires Charles and David Koch), and secretive, conservative think tanks like the Competitive Enterprise Institute, the Heartland Institute, and the Science and Public Policy Institute worked alongside Republicans in Congress. These corporate-friendly organizations placed their own so-called scientists and experts in congressional hearings to dismiss the entire crisis as a *hoax*. Republican leaders told themselves that as long as enough of their voters believe the climate crisis is a hoax, they'll have no moral imperative to act on it.

"The right response to the non-problem of global warming . . . is to have the courage to do nothing," Christopher Monckton, an "adviser" to the Science and Public Policy Institute, told a House committee in 2009. Later that day he famously dismissed carbon dioxide as harmless "plant food." Monckton, by the way, is a conservative British hereditary peer who admitted "he has no scientific qualifications."

Still, these secretly funded, right-wing think tanks sent corporate activists posing as authorities all over the country to debunk the consensus of thousands of real climate scientists from every corner of the world. And, as the journalist Steve Coll told *Frontline*, their campaign borrowed tactics from the tobacco industry, which denied and dismissed the dangers of smoking for decades:

> The explicit goal that was written down as part of this campaign was, "Let's create doubt, create a sense of a balanced debate, and make sure that these lines of skepticism and dissent become routinely a part of public discussion about climate science." And in fact, they succeeded at that.

Yes they did. In 2022, more than a full decade later, Harvard University conducted a survey of more than twenty-six hundred American adults. Nineteen percent of them still believed "the climate in North America is not changing." And another 15 percent said "the climate in North America is changing, but not because of human activity." In other words, about one in three Americans still questions the reality of the climate crisis.

So, with this context in mind, let's wedge this issue. Our strategic goal: *to make all voters understand that Republican obstruction caused the climate crisis, and that they are preventing us from fixing it.* And now for a few simple, gut-punch, rights-and-freedoms-based statements associated with the crisis of climate obstructionism:

- freedom to live in a world that isn't burning up, drying out, blowing away, drowning us, starving us, overcrowding us, or suffocating us;
- the right to have a reliable supply of food and clean water that doesn't poison or sicken us;

- our national security, so we don't have to fight off violent invaders who want to steal our energy, clean water, and food;
- a planet our children's children can survive on.

Again, note how relatable these values are to most people, regardless of what they believe about the climate crisis. Who doesn't value reliable food and clean water? Who wants to starve or burn? This is why it's important to avoid unclear language like "climate action" and "resilient communities."

Now to step 2: framing the stakes, *us versus them*. Remember, we should highlight the direct, immediate effects of what's at stake in order to connect the issue to ordinary voters, and we must assign partisan blame. Unfortunately for much of America, many of the problems caused by the climate crisis feel too unsolvable or too counterintuitive to inspire urgency; we fail to show ordinary people how these problems affect them immediately and directly. Thawing permafrost, dying coral reefs, warming ocean currents—they are all disastrous for the future of the world's livability. But to give a wedgie, try staying closer to home when framing the stakes and assigning blame:

- Republican politicians are poisoning our air, polluting our water, and sentencing our kids to suffer a hostile planet to make their rich donors richer.
- The Republican Party turned climate change into a joke and now we're all paying the price.
- You cannot trust the Republican Party with your children's future.

And now for step 3: *driving the wedge*. Let's try to make it impossible for Republicans to defend their record of intentionally dismissing climate change as a hoax:

Republicans have a plan for climate change: let Earth burn.

WEDGING SOCIAL SECURITY AND MEDICARE

In terms of issue ownership, the Democratic Party inarguably "owns" the importance of protecting and strengthening both Social Security and Medicare. Democrats created both social safety net entitlements, and they've since remained steadfast in their support of them. But while Democrats regularly tout the need to sustain both of these popular programs, they usually don't *wedge* the issue against Republicans. Biden's State of the Union address was an exception, and that's unfortunate, because this is a target-rich environment for Democrats.

That's because, despite their claims of supporting Social Security and Medicare, the GOP has long tried to screw up both programs, or to do away with them altogether. George W. Bush made privatizing Social Security his top domestic issue in 2005, an idea that went nowhere because the American public quickly shot it down. In 2012, the Wisconsin Republican congressman Paul Ryan proposed severe changes to Medicare, including raising the eligibility age and hiking up the cost of prescription drugs. Ryan's plan didn't get very far either. And Republican senator Ron Johnson in 2022 publicly flirted with the idea of moving both programs into the government's discretionary budget. Under his dangerous proposal, millions of American seniors would no longer be able to rely on their guaranteed, automatic Social Security checks, and both programs could face drastic cuts every year.

And even Speaker McCarthy, in the aftermath of his 2023 debt ceiling deal with Biden, announced plans to form a congressional commission to reconsider the entire federal budget and "mandatory spending," the majority of which funds Social Security and Medicare. Whenever it's politically convenient for them (like during a live State of the Union address), Republican leaders will claim they want to "save" popular government initiatives, but then they'll keep threatening to cut the hell out of them. We should believe them when they tell us what they want to cut. Let *them* explain their own hypocrisy to voters. Our job is to drive the wedge.

Given all of this, are you already thinking about a rights-and-freedoms-based goal for our wedgie? Mine is this: *to convince voters that Republicans don't care about seniors or whether they starve on the streets.* Following our formula:

- the freedom of American seniors to never have to choose between medicine and food;
- the right of Americans to receive their earned benefits they spent a lifetime paying for in advance;
- the right of younger Americans not to be forced into being full-time caregivers for their ailing parents.

As for reframing the issue and assigning blame with emotive language, hopefully this process is becoming a bit more straightforward. The GOP's war on Social Security and Medicare is especially conditioned for loss-aversion messaging:

- After you've prepaid for Social Security all your life, extremist Republicans want to steal your money.
- Any Republican plan to cut Social Security and Medicare forces our seniors out on the streets.
- The GOP wants to give your retirement money to Wall Street fat cats to gamble away, leaving you with nothing.

And let's not forget this one, from President Biden himself:

- Instead of making the wealthy pay their fair share, Republicans want Medicare and Social Security to sunset.

And here's how I would give this wedgie:

The Republican Party's plan for Social Security is to force you to work till you die.

WEDGING RURAL AMERICA

With notable exceptions, most of rural America is now red America. Entire books have been written about how the Republican Party gained so much favor in our least populated states in recent years, so I won't spend much time on the how and why here. But it's important to note that not so long ago the Democratic Party *was* the party of rural America.

Franklin D. Roosevelt's New Deal transformed rural America by building and upgrading physical infrastructure, jump-starting commerce, improving access to hospitals and public schools, reforming agricultural practices, and creating economic safety nets to guarantee meaningful livelihoods for farmers and ranchers. Even today you'll come across old-timers in rural America who still proudly consider themselves FDR Democrats.

This is why I want to scream every time I hear a Democrat repeating the Republican Party's message that "Democrats left rural voters behind." Hardly. The GOP has increasingly controlled rural politics for more than two decades, and Republicans have overseen the decline of rural America. According to the Pew Research Center, in 1998, 45 percent of voters in rural America identified themselves as Republicans or Republican leaners, compared with 44 percent who identified with Team Blue. In 2017, that gap widened to 54 percent of rural voters who identified as Republican or Republican leaners, compared with 38 percent who identified with the other side (with a +/− 1.9 percent margin of error).

But the GOP's reign in rural America is marked by the decimation of entire economies and populations. The Republican Party's radical culture wars, their anti-working-class policies, their corruption, and their failure to govern have absolutely wiped out America's rural communities. And it's time for Democrats to make sure rural America hears all about it.

Democrats, and only Democrats, are delivering the only policy victories to rural America these days—like historic investments in physical

infrastructure and broadband technology; like social safety nets and robust publicly funded education. And we certainly need a much stronger
partisan credit-claiming campaign to make sure regular folks across the
interior of America hear about all the important work Democrats are
doing for them. But what we really need is good wedge messaging that
places blame for the woes of rural America *squarely* where it belongs—
on the Republican Party.

Now that we're familiar with the process for formulating wedgies,
I'm gonna fast-forward through some of the steps. But I don't want to
skip establishing a strategic goal: *to get all voters to understand that the
declining viability of rural America is directly correlated with the failed leadership of the Republican Party.*

On this particular issue, we can simply point to the Republican
Party's refusal to invest in basically *anything* in rural America, other
than tax cuts for millionaires and billionaires, most of whom don't even
live there. Instead of empowering communities across the heartland
by delivering the resources and infrastructure they need to grow and
thrive, as FDR and the New Deal Democrats did a little less than a century ago, most Republicans in Congress and in state legislatures across
rural America want to cut spending everywhere to the bloody bone
(only 13 House Republicans supported the 2021 infrastructure bill; 206
of them opposed it!).

Our wedgies for voters in rural America, then, should directly link
their setbacks and challenges to the Republicans who refuse to invest in
them, and to discredit the Reaganomics myth that making rich people
richer somehow means wealth "trickles down" to small, rural communities.

Well, that's pretty easy to do! Here are a few examples:

*Republicans steal from rural America to give more tax cuts to their
big-city donors.*

*Republicans said they made America great again, but now your kid's
school is open only four days a week.*

Extremist Republicans refused to expand Medicaid and now your community is losing its only hospital.

Our wedgies must make it crystal clear that the Republican Party's economic radicalism has left rural America holding the bag.

WEDGING WEED

Here's a *lighter issue*—pun intended: The recreational or medical use of cannabis is now legal in most American states. Turns out Americans love their weed, or at least a vast majority of them (upwards of 90 percent) want it to be legal for adults who medically need it or who want to consume it simply because they like it. The federal government still misclassifies marijuana as an illicit Schedule I drug, meaning Uncle Sam technically considers your stash of THC as dangerous as heroin, LSD, and ecstasy. But the prevalence of state-legalized cannabis suggests marijuana isn't nearly as dangerous as much of the country once believed.

In a comprehensive survey conducted by the Pew researchers in 2022, 73 percent of adult Democrats and Democratic leaners said cannabis "should be legal for medical *and* recreational use," whereas only 45 percent of Republicans and Republican leaners said the same. This means legalized recreational weed is another issue that Democrats should own. But how many voters associate legal weed with the Democratic Party? Not nearly enough.

To be clear: pot legalization became mainstream across America *because of Democrats*, over persistent opposition from Republicans. Just as nearly every American considers the GOP the party associated with unrestricted gun ownership, every American must also consider Democrats the party of legal pot, which Republicans take away. Remember, that's not pot you smell, it's freedom, and Republicans hate your freedom. But this mindset won't happen without a strategic shift in our messaging. That's because state after state has put citizen initiatives on their ballots to successfully decriminalize or legalize cannabis, and a significant portion of voters who said yes to legal weed also said yes to Republican candidates. Let me make an important point—a critical point: the Republican Party's own strategists would never let something like that happen on purpose.

By branding Democrats as the party *for* legal pot and Republicans as the party *against* it, Democrats can appeal to a segment of voters who don't even necessarily identify with a political party through an incredibly simple wedgie:

Republicans are coming for your pot.

As anyone with proximity to the pro-legal-weed community will tell you, folks love the stuff—as much as some Americans love their guns. In fact, I can envision a world where my apolitical budtender associates the Republican Party with taking away his entire livelihood. If we wedge the issue effectively, my budtender might even say, "I could NEVER vote for a Republican because they want to take away my weed!" Sound familiar?

WELL, NOW WHAT?

So now that we have good wedgies, how do we give them? What do we do with them? How do we make them stick?

I hope you've come this far along because you're as concerned about the dire state of American democracy as I am. And now you have a better understanding of how Republicans keep winning elections with dangerous ideas and ridiculously unqualified people, thanks to their ability to give effective wedgies. With your new understanding of how wedging works in the art of electoral war, you now have a sharp new tool in your kit to take with you into any political conversation—among friends, online, next to the office coffeepot, or around your family dinner table. You can also hold elected Democrats and Democratic candidates accountable to better, stronger, more effective messaging, as I do whenever I have the opportunity. Help them understand the power of a good wedgie. Lord knows they need it. Once you find a good way to wedge a sticky issue, repeat it. Repeat it. Repeat it.

More important, pass it on to other Democrats so they can do the same. Democracy needs you to get to work helping us give wedgies *yesterday*. Why tell people that Biden and Democrats passed the largest infrastructure package since Eisenhower when you could tell them something that evokes imagery and emotion like: *Thanks to President Biden's massive infrastructure bill, your friends and family will arrive alive?*

Through effective wedge issue messaging on issues that matter the most to the electorate, we can pull them into our coalition to vote for Democrats who share their values and priorities. And for the independent, single-issue swing voters? With a good wedgie, we can push them away from voting for Republicans, just as several Democrats did, quite successfully, in 2022.

The Proof Is in the Pudding

Let's start with the good news: Democrats can win the toughest of elections when they put the power of negative partisanship strategy to work. They already have! In 2022, the midterm election that was supposed to screw us all with a "Red Tsunami" of Republican victories nationwide, Democrats in several key swing states rebuffed expectations and proved a whole lot of pundits wrong. These candidates won despite the trend of the Midterm Effect, when swing voters tend to vote against the in party—the one that holds the presidency—between presidential elections.

Victorious Democrats succeeded in getting their voters (reliable base voters and motivated leaners) to the polls and made a powerful case to swing voters that Republican candidates are too extreme for America. The result? Democrats unexpectedly picked up a seat in the U.S. Senate and limited the Republican majority in the House to a mere five seats. Despite winning back control of the House on election night, 2022 *sucked* for the Republican Party, and the still-sane Republicans know it. That's because the Democrats who won in 2022 controlled the narrative, gave wedgies, and made clear and convincing cases about Republicans to voters. They won by dipping their toes into negative partisanship and beating Republicans at their own game. But not all Democrats did this in 2022. In fact, some Democrats that year lost some of the most consequential elections in the country because they played by the old rules, and now we get to learn the lessons from their mistakes.

WINNING ELECTIONS WITH NEGATIVE PARTISANSHIP STRATEGY

For Democrats, it helped that Arizona Republicans chose a slate of Trump-like, ultraconservative insurrectionists and fascists to run for statewide offices in 2022. All of them redefined "radical extremist," and if that happens among GOP candidates in a purple state like Arizona in 2022, you know it's bad in red America. Democrats saw a political opportunity as wide as a certain canyon, and they seized it. They turned democracy and *freedom itself* into wedge issues.

In her race for governor, Democrat Katie Hobbs—then Arizona's secretary of state—painted a terrifying picture of what would happen to their state if voters elected her opponent, Kari Lake. Lake, a former TV personality, was not only an unhinged election denier; she even went so far as to suggest that elections officials in Maricopa County (Phoenix and its suburbs) be "locked up" for doing their jobs.

In June, Hobbs's campaign ran a TV ad featuring news coverage of the violent threats that she and her family had been getting from anonymous MAGA mouth-foamers. Over the news clips, these words appeared on-screen: "Katie Hobbs faced death threats and violence, but Katie Hobbs protected our democracy." Then Hobbs says directly into the camera, "As your secretary of state, I knew I'd face attacks. But when they came after my family, our state, our *freedom*—that's where I draw the line."

A few months later, Hobbs told MSNBC what she had been telling Arizona voters: that Kari Lake was "too dangerous and too extreme."

"Democracy is on the ballot in 2022, and that is certainly the case in Arizona," Hobbs said to Lawrence O'Donnell. "[Lake] has centered her whole campaign around Trump's Big Lie and is running for office so that she can change the rules and overturn the will of the voters in future elections . . . and she would create untold levels of chaos in the state of Arizona if she were elected governor."

Other Democrats in Arizona leaned into similar messaging in their

statewide races. My buddy Adrian Fontes, who succeeded Hobbs as secretary of state, ran his own gut punch of an ad. "We have a decision to
make," Fontes told voters. "Our elections should not be controlled by
extremists. Vote Fontes for secretary of state because democracy *is* a
decision."

On Election Day, Fontes handily beat his Republican opponent,
Mark Finchem, by more than 120,000 votes. Hobbs beat Lake by more
than 17,000 votes (though Lake falsely claimed otherwise *for months*).
Attorney General Kris Mayes eked out a win over Republican Abe
Hamadeh by a few hundred votes. And U.S. senator Mark Kelly beat the
far-right conspiracy theorist Blake Masters by more than 125,000 votes
to keep serving in the Senate. All of these Democrats leaned into negative partisanship strategy by *disqualifying the other option* with powerful,
emotive messages like "chaos," "danger," "changing the rules," and
"overturning the will of voters."

The threats to law and order, majority rule, democracy, and freedom
under Republican control of the government in Arizona were singular
messages that gave Democratic voters good reason to get out and vote
for Democratic candidates, and they gave lots of reasons to swing voters
who value democracy and freedom to *not vote* for the GOP's slate of
dangerous weirdos. That's how Democrats pulled off negative partisanship strategy in Arizona, and they won comfortably.

But we saw one of the biggest negative partisanship success stories
of 2022 in Michigan. Governor Gretchen Whitmer made the issue of
abortion her central reelection message even before the Supreme
Court's 2022 ruling on *Dobbs v. Jackson Women's Health Organization*,
which overturned *Roe v. Wade.* The controversial decision simply
heaped a whole lot more fuel onto Whitmer's fire, delivering one hell of
a proof point.

Prior to the *Roe v. Wade* decision in 1973, Michigan had an extreme
state law on the books banning all abortions, without exception. If the
court overturned *Roe*, Whitmer argued, the old, draconian state law
would go back into effect and would, in her words, "criminalize abor-

tion and impact nearly 2.2 million Michigan women." Weeks before the American public even got word of *Dobbs,* Whitmer filed a lawsuit asking the Michigan Supreme Court "to immediately resolve whether Michigan's constitution protects the right to abortion."

While running for reelection, Whitmer continued branding herself as a tough champion of women's rights and reproductive freedom, reminding Michiganders exactly how she was fighting for them—going high—as their governor. She filed motions in court, wrote national op-eds, launched websites, and signed executive orders aimed at protecting reproductive freedom in her state. Abortion rights activists, meanwhile, gathered enough signatures to put a "Reproductive Freedom for All" initiative on November's general election ballot asking voters whether to enshrine the right to an abortion in Michigan's constitution (did you notice that f-word again?).

Whitmer's Republican opponent, another Trump-endorsed TV personality named Tudor Dixon, opposed all abortions, except to save "the life of the mother." And in July 2022 a podcaster asked her whether Michigan's reinstated abortion ban should apply, hypothetically, to a fourteen-year-old girl impregnated by her uncle.

"Yeah, perfect example," Dixon replied.

"You're saying *carry that* [pregnancy to term]?" the podcaster, Charlie LeDuff, followed up. "Yes or no?"

"A life is a life for me," she answered. "That's how it is."

"You heard it," LeDuff said. "No exception except for the health of the mother."

Democrats and their allies pounced, using Dixon's response in hard-hitting TV ads that hammered home the Republican candidate's extreme position on abortion. Their message echoed the wedgie the Michigan Democratic Party gave in response to Dixon's alarming interview:

Tudor Dixon has now gone so far in her radical anti-choice crusade as to say that a child who is the victim of incestual rape is the "perfect example" of why abortion should be banned outright in Michigan. Her callous remarks are the perfect example of how dangerous Tudor Dixon would be for Michigan families.

Now *that* is negative partisanship, and it worked beautifully in Michigan following the overturn of *Roe v. Wade*. On Election Day, voters overwhelmingly reelected Whitmer as governor and Democrat Garlin Gilchrist as lieutenant governor (by almost eleven points!), flipped both chambers of the state legislature to Democratic control, and amended their constitution to protect abortion rights—shitcanning the old, extreme antiabortion law.

Through it all, nobody really accused Gretchen Whitmer or her campaign of "going low." There was no impression that she was punching below the belt, slinging mud, or calling names. She simply took the rage and turned it into a *strategy*, wedging a message that drove Democratic voters to the polls and reminded everyone else of the freedoms they'd lose under Republican control of their government.

APOLOGETIC DEMOCRATS

But now it's time to take some medicine. Let's pull the curtain back a little further to look at another high-profile campaign that didn't fare as well for Democrats in 2022: the U.S. Senate race in Ohio. That election pitted Republican author/investor J. D. Vance against the ten-term Democratic congressman Tim Ryan. Despite the Beltway's fawning over the Ryan campaign, Vance won comfortably by a quarter of a million votes—just over six percentage points.

But *why*, exactly, especially given the Democratic upsets elsewhere? Tim Ryan had decades of experience, for crying out loud. He was likable, well known across his state for his moderate record in Congress. He was an effective speaker with good ideas and a well-funded campaign. And he was up against a thirty-eight-year-old, Trump-endorsed, Yale-educated Republican known for little more than writing a book about hillbillies.

For an answer, let's turn to hard numbers once again. They paint a pretty compelling picture of the effectiveness of negative partisanship and why Ryan lost. The data come from a strategy-oriented progressive organization called Way to Win, which meticulously tracks and analyzes TV advertising for U.S. Senate and House elections across the country—publicly available information that gives us a revealing look inside the playbooks of both Democratic and Republican campaigns.

According to Way to Win, Ryan outspent Vance on broadcast TV ads by about $4 million in 2022 (Ryan's campaign spent $20 million on TV advertising in Ohio; Vance's spent $16 million). Contrary to conventional wisdom, Ryan's campaign didn't fail for lack of investment. But here's the key to understanding why Tim Ryan lost a race Washington pundits and political reporters thought was pitch-perfect: not a single TV ad from Ryan's campaign mentioned abortion or, more important for swing voters, the *threat to American freedom* that the overturning of *Roe v. Wade* signals.

Instead, Ryan's campaign figured he could optimize his chances by running the traditional Democratic campaign strategy of "but I'm not THAT kind of Democrat!" You might recognize this "apologetic Democrat" strategy from races we lost but should have won in 2020, 2018, 2016, 2014, 2012, 2010 . . . you get the point. Despite the media gushing over Tim Ryan's strategy of "running against his own party," there was nothing innovative about it. It is the strategy this book is designed to finally kill off. Ryan's campaign even aired a TV ad on Fox News, titled "Fox News Friends," featuring clips of various Fox hosts interviewing the congressman, calling him a "very moderate" "jobs creator," and praising him for opposing open borders.

Though none of Ryan's ads mentioned President Biden, his campaign did spend nearly $1 million on a TV spot criticizing Barack Obama. In that ad, Ryan speaks directly into the camera as he strolls through a neighborhood in Youngstown.

"When Obama's trade deal threatened jobs here, I voted against it," Ryan says in the thirty-second ad. "And I voted with Trump on trade. I don't answer to any political party. I answer to the folks I grew up with, and the families like yours all across Ohio."

Ryan's Senate campaign strategy, for whatever reason, was to skip the wedge issues and avoid partisan blaming to run as an apologetic Democrat. His message might have *sounded* reasonable to moderates in a swing state. But this kind of messaging no longer cuts the mustard with a dishonest opposition party that cares only about winning power for Republicans so they can destroy democracy and replace it with fascism. Democrats who apologize for being Democrats only reinforce to swing voters exactly what Republicans want everyone to believe: that the Democratic brand isn't worth buying!

Democrats in swing and red states often force a similar error by leaning heavily into messaging *bipartisanship*—their ability and willingness to "work with" Republicans. In fact, Democratic House candidates in 2022 spent nearly $17 million on ads mentioning bipartisanship. Working across party lines is a quaint notion that might have worked in the past as a winning message and no doubt still "tests well" in political polling. But that was before Donald Trump radicalized the entire GOP. Bipartisanship certainly appeals to plenty of voters, abstractly. Hell, even I love bipartisanship!

But when we Democrats focus our messaging strategy on ideological bipartisanship, we give even the most extreme Republicans credibility and benefit of the doubt; we blur the lines and step on our own argument that the Republican Party is the greatest threat to the health, wealth, and safety of every American! We also presume, wrongly, that Republicans care to reciprocate. Another spoiler alert: They don't. GOP candidates running for Congress spent less than $3 million touting bipartisanship in 2022, by the way.

Other Democrats who lost in 2022 made other mistakes to learn from. In Florida, the U.S. Senate candidate Val Demings, a congresswoman who formerly served as Orlando's police chief, challenged Senator Marco Rubio by answering the GOP message accusing Democrats of being weak on crime. Demings's campaign made her support of police one of its central themes, certain that *this time* biography would trump partisan attacks from the GOP. While Rubio's campaign spent millions on TV ads hammering home the GOP brand that *all* Democrats love criminals, the Demings campaign countered by promising bipartisanship and showing off biographical qualifications.

Demings's campaign did run a TV ad about abortion, but not until three months after the *Dobbs* decision, and that spot focused on Rubio's desire "to criminalize abortions with no exceptions for victims of rape or incest."

"I know something about fighting crime, Senator Rubio," Demings says in her ad. "Rape is a crime. Incest is a crime. Abortion is not."

Of course that's an important message, but it doesn't keep the strategic focus on the broader threat: that the Republican Party is trying to *take away your freedom.* And one negative TV ad does not a wedge campaign make. Like in Michigan, it needs to be the central theme— one that gets repeated until voters are nauseated. And, as Way to Win notes, focusing on exceptions for rape and incest can stigmatize abortions for people who may need them for other reasons, and it shies away from the Democrats' most persuasive argument: "Government shouldn't play a role in regulating these kinds of deeply personal decisions at all."

Democrats running for Congress in 2022 spent a combined $168.4 million on TV ads that mentioned abortion. The overturn of *Roe v. Wade* was, by far, the top issue for Democrats running for both House and Senate seats, and many of them turned the issue into a wedgie. They used the Republican Party's attack on freedom to make a convincing case to their coalition, and to swing voters, that freedom and democracy were on the ballot in 2022. And they kept the dreaded Red Tsunami at bay. Democrats who didn't lean into the overturn of *Roe* as their top messaging opportunity lost on Election Day.

As for Republican candidates? In 2022 they kept their sights set on the issues of crime and the economy—specifically taxes and inflation, which most of them blamed directly on President Biden. In fact, GOP candidates for House and Senate spent an eye-popping $135 million on ads that mentioned Biden (and only $1.4 million on ads that mentioned Trump).

But here again, too many Democrats missed an important political opportunity. Remember, Democrats are poised to reclaim the health of the American economy as *our* issue. Republicans only own it because they've branded themselves successfully. That allowed the GOP to persistently attack Democrats on taxes, inflation, gas prices, and trade in 2022. Most Democrats, however, left those attacks unanswered.

"When talking about jobs and the economy," Way to Win's analysis found, "Democrats did not focus on their economic accomplishments." Democratic economic policies enacted since Biden's victory in 2020, Way to Win adds, "led to the fastest recovery from a recession ever, record job growth, the lowest unemployment since humans walked on the moon, and some of the lowest post-COVID inflation across the globe. Democrats also cut child poverty in half for a year."

Democrats didn't talk about any of these accomplishments on the campaign trail, at least in their TV ad campaigns. To date, the only Democrat really making an effective argument on the strength of America's economy under the presidency of Joe Biden is California's governor, Gavin Newsom. Newsom sat down for an hour-long interview with Fox's Sean Hannity in June 2023 and gave Democrats a master class in how to challenge Republican messaging. Newsom ran circles around Hannity, leaving the Fox host speechless on numerous divisive issues, like immigration reform and Biden's record.

But Newsom cleaned Hannity's clock when he was pressed about the economy. The governor had his facts down pat, but remember, rebutting political messages by simply citing facts and figures doesn't alone win arguments. The reason Newsom steamrolled Hannity was that he showed viewers that Hannity's premise—that America's economy was suffering under Democratic leadership—was ridiculously wrong to begin with and that Hannity hadn't even done his homework. And Newsom didn't allow Hannity to breeze through any of his oversimplified talking points, though he tried:

NEWSOM: You said the economy? Thirteen-point-one million jobs, [Biden's] created.

HANNITY: These are post-COVID jobs. You know that. I mean, that's an artificial number.

NEWSOM: Then let me stipulate this as an opportunity to engage civilly on this—

HANNITY: —okay.

NEWSOM: Fair point, your president, Donald Trump, lost 2.6 million jobs during his four years. We've created 13.1 million. Fine, you can maintain a COVID frame. How about the fact that Joe Biden's created more jobs—six times more jobs—than the previous three Republican presidents combined—*combined*, Sean!

HANNITY: Are you gonna tell me that the average family, where we have two-thirds of Americans now living paycheck to paycheck—

NEWSOM: —it was 70 percent under Trump! It was *70 percent* under Donald Trump, living paycheck to paycheck. . . . You and I are living with the lowest unemployment in our lifetime, Sean. You can't make that up.

And that's where Hannity changed the subject—something that happened frequently during his interview with Newsom. Hannity simply wasn't used to a Democrat winning an argument about an issue that Democrats can no longer afford to lose.

CHARACTER MATTERS, BUT . . .

One more thing while we're on the topic of lessons learned in 2022: The Democrats who won U.S. Senate seats in the swing states of Pennsylvania and Georgia used negative partisanship strategy a bit differently. They both made their elections a referendum on *the characters* of their opponents—very effectively.

John Fetterman, Pennsylvania's six-foot-eight, hoodie-sporting lieutenant governor, framed his entire campaign around the Trump-endorsed Republican running against him: the celebrity doctor Mehmet Oz. For Democratic voters, Fetterman easily made the case that he was better qualified to serve in the Senate—that he had a better temperament for the job, that he was the only candidate born and raised in

Pennsylvania, and that his long record of experience and public service mattered more than celebrity.

But for the swing voters, Fetterman's objective was to disqualify Oz, a politically inexperienced, wealthy daytime TV personality who didn't even live in Pennsylvania. When Oz starred in a poorly planned social media video meant to blame President Biden for the high cost of groceries, he bemoaned the prices of the raw veggies he needed to make "crudités." Fetterman immediately pounced on his opponent's use of the fancy-pants word for "vegetable tray" to brand Oz as an out-of-touch carpetbagger who had no clue how to relate to workaday rust-belt Pennsylvanians. Then, just when it couldn't get much worse for Oz, the Fetterman campaign branded him a puppy killer, because it turns out he was! Fetterman and his campaign kept twisting the knife at every turn to convince swing voters that Mehmet Oz had no business butting into Pennsylvania politics, and it worked. Fetterman beat Oz by a decisive 263,752 votes on Election Day.

And then there's Herschel Walker's 2022 Senate bid in Georgia. Personally courted by Donald Trump and usually flanked, oddly, by Republican Party "minders" during TV interviews, the former football star—who lived in Texas—mounted an expensive campaign to unseat the Democratic incumbent, Raphael Warnock. Walker came within just a few percentage points of winning that seat despite plenty of evidence that he had no clue how Congress worked. He could not speak in coherent sentences, he had a documented history of domestic violence, and—as we've discussed—he faced more than one credible accusation that he paid for his girlfriends' abortions, even though he claimed to vehemently oppose abortion. Warnock ended up narrowly beating Walker by just under 100,000 votes.

Man, it was easy to make fun of Herschel Walker. *Saturday Night Live* roasted him as a clueless rube. In a viral speech before Georgia's runoff election, even Barack Obama ridiculed Walker's bizarre diatribe about how he'd rather be a werewolf than a vampire.

As we were all reminded in 2022, *candidate quality matters*. Democrats held on to the U.S. Senate because Trump's Republican Party elevated some of the lowest-quality candidates it had to offer. But here's the thing: most rank-and-file Republican voters don't lose much sleep over candidate quality. More than 1.7 million Georgians either didn't know or didn't care that Herschel Walker did not have a résumé or an intellect that qualified him to serve in the U.S. Senate. They voted for him anyway because, well, he was the *Republican* candidate endorsed by the Republican Party. He had a familiar, famous name. And for most of those voters, electing a Republican to the Senate, even a derpy one accused of having double standards and shameful personal baggage, was *still* better than a Democrat.

"We're in a post-shame world, a post-hypocrisy environment," the Lincoln Project's co-founder Rick Wilson said in 2022. "You can't shame Republicans anymore. You have to show people that you're better for them [as a candidate]. That takes a lot of work."

Sure, showing voters the personalities and intellectual qualities of candidates is necessary. Sometimes it's deliciously fun to lampoon high-profile candidates like Herschel Walker, Kari Lake, and Dr. Oz. And as I said earlier, mocking the work of unserious people who want power is an important responsibility of serious ones. But remember that American voters and media consumers are told round the clock that all politicians are dumb, dysfunctional, and dishonest, so ridiculing and shaming Republicans *alone* is usually insufficient to win elections.

To win political power, it's more important for Democrats to show voters *how* a candidate's optimal or subpar character, values, and intellect *matter to them*—as Democrats did with so much success in Arizona and in Michigan in 2022. Calling a Republican candidate a bumbling hypocrite doesn't always push swing voters away from supporting that Republican. But showing those voters that that Republican candidate is "hijacking your freedom so he can turn America into a rogue nation, making you sicker, poorer, and less secure as he does"—now we're talkin'!

How best to do that? Well, we have to do better at meeting voters where they are. And that's another thing Democrats could use a little help with.

Voters Are Just Not That into You

How many times have you checked your mailbox after work, only to find a stack of junk you're never really gonna read: a couple credit card offers, maybe something announcing a furniture store liquidation sale, and the occasional political mailer—those flyers printed on glossy paper urging us to vote for or against a candidate or a ballot initiative? Some of these mailers come from candidates' campaigns; others come from independent organizations that want to influence elections, like super PACs, labor unions, or nonprofits.

These pieces of "direct mail" serve a single, fleeting purpose in electoral politics: to make direct contact with voters to either change their minds with a message or remind committed partisans to show up and vote. Contacting voters by mail is just one part of the challenge of *message distribution*—making sure the right people hear, see, and *feel* our campaign messages.

Message distribution is a tough nut to crack for both parties, especially with the ever-changing ways that Americans consume their news and information. Messages, whether they be for products or politicians, must find their way in front of people. This requires a distribution strategy usually involving a mix of TV and digital ads, direct mailers, billboards, and direct contact with voters at their homes, "in the field."

Message distribution via paid media costs big bucks. TV ads cost large, statewide campaigns *millions*. But every aspect of message distribution is expensive. Sending two or three pieces of direct mail targeting only a small subset of voters can cost $25,000 or more. Though much cheaper than TV commercials, digital ads (ads that run on social media or within streaming services like YouTube and Hulu) need tens, even hundreds of thousands of dollars to air enough times to have any effect on voter behavior.

Beyond their prohibitive costs, there are other pitfalls that pervade message distribution. Imagine spending $25,000 on political mailers, only to find out few recipients even bothered to read them. Remember, most ordinary Americans have little or no interest in politics, which means they aren't paying attention to what we have to say. Politics is a product few people want to buy. If we want American voters to know the Republican Party has collapsed into a dangerous cult hell-bent on destroying democracy and the rule of law, we have to tell them, and we have to make sure they actually receive the message.

The combined goal of all these efforts, which can add up to tens, even *hundreds* of millions of dollars for the biggest campaigns, is simply to get their voters to the polls (or to vote by mail on time) and to earn the support of a handful of persuadable swing voters who, as much as we'd like to believe, are not staying up at night angsting over which party to vote for.

So how can Democrats optimize our message distribution to make sure we win more elections in a political environment paralyzed by disinterest and disdain for politics? How can we calibrate our strategy so that we can capture the time and attention of voters who probably would care much more deeply about saving democracy if they understood how sick and endangered it truly is? How do we prosecute the Republican Party for intentionally putting American democracy on its deathbed?

The good news: the solution isn't difficult; it's a matter of *uncomplicating* the way Democrats and progressives currently communicate with voters. We do it by meeting voters *where they are*.

THE MESSAGE-IN-A-GLANCE TEST

Let's keep picking on those ubiquitous campaign mailers for a moment, because I can't even count the number of times I've given the same advice to campaigns that spend way too much time fretting over details like which politically correct stock photos to use, how many policy positions we can explain in the little bit of space or time we have, and how exactly to describe those policy positions without offending anyone.

One recent mailer from a progressive organization included not one, not two, but *five* wordy reasons for voters to oppose a local sales tax, in tiny print. All five reasons were crammed between an endorsement by the local Democratic Party and a picture of some *former* city official no one knows and his seventy-five-word quotation giving even more reasons to oppose the measure.

I don't know how to say this gently, but all campaigns need to remember: *voters are just not that into you.* It's not as if they were eagerly checking their mailboxes for your mailer like Ralphie Parker waiting for his Little Orphan Annie decoder pin in *A Christmas Story*. Folks aren't clamoring for the opportunity to spend their precious time educating themselves with your *junk mail*. We've got *one glance* to deliver our message in the time it takes to carry this mailer from the mailbox to the recycling bin. Ten seconds. That's all we get to make our message stick.

Instead of giving voters wordy reasons they'll never read to be against higher taxes, this wordy mailer should have taken the opportunity to effectively deliver its main message on its brief journey to the recycling bin:

Three reasons to vote NO:
1. Republican. 2. Tax. 3. Hike.

My revised version, unlike the original, passes what I call the Message-in-a-Glance test. It delivers a simple message in the brief amount of time we have if we're lucky enough to capture the voter's attention. It assigns blame. It uses loss-aversion language. It's simple and memorable. It brands the Republican Party as trying to raise your taxes. And the best part of all? It's a message that is delivered in a glance.

If you've ever glanced at a MAGA mailer, you know Republicans are particularly skilled in creating messages that pass this test. Their mailers often deliver one hyperbolic, partisan headline like "Joe Biden's Socialist America" or "Democrats: Grooming Your Children" and rely on images more than fine print. While the bold-print headlines on mailers carry most of the weight, Republican mailers also rely heavily on imagery and association, which is why so many of them include the sinister-looking faces of familiar Democrats they've vilified, like Chuck Schumer and Nancy Pelosi, even in state-level elections where Schumer and Pelosi have nothing to do with the message. In one glance at a GOP mailer, I see a negative political message about someone I've likely never heard of, and now I associate him with the Democrats whose faces I already know and have been told to fear. And that core message got delivered in the time it took me to throw the whole thing away. I didn't even get a chance to "opt out" of seeing it.

This challenge certainly isn't limited to political mailers, of course. Online political ads are basically unavoidable, digital versions of junk mail flyers. So are the political memes all over Instagram, Facebook, and Twitter. Even political TV and radio commercials go sideways when they try to cover more than one simple message in a few precious seconds. And when these ads are designed for disinterested people who need to be reminded to vote, our messages need to stick like glue the first time. Save the details for another day! You need one bold-print message that can't be missed.

ONE MESSAGE TO RULE THEM ALL

Aside from a few notable exceptions, like Gretchen Whitmer's and Katie Hobbs's 2022 campaigns, remember that Democrats still tend to orbit around an outdated, complicated electoral strategy. The goal of that old strategy: to turn out coalitional voters to vote for Democrats with one set of messages to excite and motivate the progressive base, then use a different set of messages to persuade swing voters to vote for Democrats.

And now that political campaigns have access to data about virtually every American with a cellphone, a social media account, or a credit card, they have become much more sophisticated in their ability to narrow the audiences of their message distribution—to *microtarget* specific messages to precise groups of voters—the same way social media platforms deliver us ads tailored to our individual likes and interests. *Especially given how much value the Democratic Party places on identity in politics,* the thinking goes, *why not deliver separate, unique messages directly to each faction of our coalition and swing voters?* Why not microtarget an ad about women's rights to play right before a TV show that we know women's rights activists watch, like *Grey's Anatomy?* Why not deliver messages in support of organized labor straight to union workers' Facebook feeds?

Though this type of microtargeting makes sense, many modern Democratic campaigns are jumping into an overcomplicated rabbit hole of developing and microtargeting different policy messages that resonate with different groups of voters. Why is this strategy so appealing to Democrats? It goes back to the differences between the two parties. While the GOP largely represents a diminishing slice of the electorate (mainly wealthy, straight/closeted, mostly Christian, mostly white Americans), the Democratic Party has a much bigger, more diverse tent: women's rights activists, the LGBTQ community, people of color, climate crisis activists, immigrants, the poor, union workers, gun safety activists—you get the idea. All these factions care about different things, so why not saturate each of them with messages they care more about?

Well, because with negative partisanship strategy, we don't need to get down into policy weeds!

Negative partisanship strategy relies on *broad, overarching messages* to accomplish its two goals: to freak the hell out of *all factions* of coalitional voters so much that they'll go out of their way to show up to vote for Democrats, and to freak the hell out of swing voters so much that they'll vote against Republicans and for Democrats, even if it's by default. In other words, we can win elections by tying our various interests under one branding umbrella messaging theme to rule them all—one powerful enough to appeal to, to motivate, and to persuade a majority of the entire electorate:

Republicans are a threat to your freedom, health, wealth, and safety.

With a single hard-hitting, partisan, stakes-framing umbrella message framework, campaigns—especially smaller, thriftier ones—don't need to choose between spending money on mobilizing base voters and persuading swing voters. They can kill both birds with a single contrasting message, and they can use the money they save for the far more important priority of *distributing* that message. We should be broadcasting big, brand-centric messages that assail the whole of the Republican Party, firing up our coalition while scaring swing voters away from the GOP. We should do what Republicans all but perfected a decade ago: We should rely on our improved, simpler, wedgier messaging to achieve the two goals of negative partisanship strategy.

Republicans, after all, didn't steal South Florida from Democrats by using twenty different messages targeting twenty different Latino subgroups. No, they won South Florida by investing millions of dollars into a decades-long Latino outreach operation that targets Latinos with culture war negative partisanship messaging that brands Democrats as dangerous socialists, and more recently, as groomer pedophiles that want to mutilate children's genitalia. Who would ever vote for a party like that?!

The fact that moderate Democrats keep losing to radical, far-right Republicans should be a clue that we're not in Kansas anymore; negative partisanship messaging is already a winning strategy for the GOP.

I WANNA GO WHERE THE PEOPLE ARE . . .

On April 18, 2023, moments before opening statements were set to begin, Fox News settled its defamation lawsuit from Dominion Voting Systems for a staggering $787.5 million. The settlement meant Fox News wouldn't have to further embarrass itself in court, amid mountains of damning evidence. It would no longer have to explain and defend all the lies Fox viewers heard about Dominion in the aftermath of the 2020 presidential election. As the Republican Party happily excused Donald Trump's claims—with no evidence—that his election was the first in U.S. history to be "stolen," Fox hosts and guests entertained lies that Dominion's electronic voting machines somehow switched votes from Trump to Biden. Dominion initially sued Fox News for $1.6 billion, claiming "reckless disregard" for the truth.

Though the Dominion settlement was a huge blow to Fox, and a major news story that millions of Americans saw, there's a good chance millions more loyal Fox viewers had no idea it ever happened. They had no clue that Fox News would rather fork over three-quarters of a billion dollars than admit, under oath, that it lied to its viewers about election fraud. That's because the network banned the Dominion settlement story from its own airwaves.

So, if Fox News builds an impenetrable propaganda wall around its own viewers, how can we reach them? You target them on ESPN, on the Golf Channel, in NFL RedZone, on sports streaming services, and maybe most of all on sports radio. You target the stuff average Americans actually watch, and it ain't PBS or MSNBC. You run ads on *America's Got Talent*. You buy airtime on TLC. You can tell women that Republicans have turned them into chattel during episodes of *The Bachelor*. You can de-radicalize men with ads during NASCAR. The last people who need to see your ads are the ones watching CNN and MSNBC.

AND SPEAKING OF POLITICAL ADS

The best message in the world is useless if no one sees it. And no one who needs to see your message is going to watch your three-minute biographical ad. Now, don't get me wrong, I get the appeal. These longer ads, which can cost as much as $30,000 just to produce, make us political junkies swoon. We love to see our candidates exiting fighter jets, riding motorcycles, running their tractors, and telling us all about the credentials that qualify them for office. But I'm here to tell you, at best—AT BEST—you have only thirty seconds to make your point.

And I get it—it's hard to make your point in thirty seconds. You have to be succinct. You have to leave out nuance. You have to pick one message and make it the focal point of the ad. How about a few examples?

Here is the copy of one thirty-second ad I co-created with the People PAC:

Scandals. Corruption. Lies. Insurrection. Radical Republicans are willing to do *anything* to protect Donald Trump from accountability for his own actions. Left unchecked, Republican politicians will plunge America into chaos, allowing criminals free rein and leaving our children unprotected. This November, send the Republican Party a clear message about their radical agenda. Vote Democrat.

And this one, which I produced with Way to Win, modeled off the GOP's famous "Harry and Louise" political ads from the 1990s:

WIFE: Did you see this? (Shows husband a headline on her tablet.)
HUSBAND: "Republicans Release Plan to Raise Taxes on Most Americans."
WIFE: It's not enough that Republicans ended the child tax credit!
HUSBAND: Six hundred dollars a month. Could've really used that.
WIFE: And they want us to vote for them to take Congress back. More chaos and less security for families like ours.

HUSBAND: Well, they clearly don't care about people like us. It's just all
    about power for them.
WIFE: If these Republicans win . . .
HUSBAND: . . . we all lose.

Or this thirty-second ad I made with my Strike PAC colleagues for
Virginia's 2021 gubernatorial race:

Let's connect the dots on the Republicans' scheme to try to steal
our elections. First, they tried to hijack the presidency. But when
that failed, they started passing laws across the country to rig future elections. And if Trump ally Glenn Youngkin and Republicans win here in Virginia, they'll come for your vote too, putting
power and party over free and fair elections. So this November,
don't waste your one chance to stop them.

Nuance is the enemy of the thirty-second ad. Try reading these
scripts at a narrator's pace and you'll see why they need to milk every
single second. You'll also find that the most important point the ad is
trying to convey is right up front. Why? Because even at thirty seconds,
many people who see these ads on connected TV or streaming services
like YouTube will give you exactly the *six* seconds they have to watch it
before they can hit the Skip button. You need to hook 'em right off the
top of the ad and accept the fact they may never watch the rest. Make
your main point right out of the gate in that first six seconds.

EVERYONE'S AN INFLUENCER

Okay, okay. I know. Most of you will never design a direct mailer or
write a thirty-second political ad. But has anyone ever told you that *you*
are an influencer? If not, allow me to be the first.

Sure, your social networks might feel small. Not all of us can be a
Kardashian. But whatever the size of your following, your influence is
mighty! All those silly memes you see on Facebook, Twitter, and Insta-

gram might seem like sometimes fun and sometimes irreverent distractions, but each and every one of them has the power to deliver the Message. You have power and influence whether you have 100,000 followers on Instagram or 100. *Are you using that power?* Are you doing everything you can to make sure your followers see messages that remind them their freedoms are at stake from a dangerous Republican Party? Are you utilizing every chance you get to use that RT or Share button to lift the Democratic Party's brand within your own network?

The fact is, memes and GIFs serve the exact same purpose as an expensive direct mail campaign or a prime-time TV ad. They're designed to deliver messages directly to voters, which means the entire online world is a "digital field" where the electoral wars are fought and won or lost. Republicans wised up to the power of leveraging the digital field back in 2016, when Trump's "digital-media director," Brad Parscale, designed and deployed a strategy to essentially use Facebook as a nontraditional, out-of-the-box, cost-efficient direct mail vendor, helping Donald Trump thread the needle to win the Electoral College (Parscale also managed Trump's unsuccessful reelection campaign four years later).

When you see effective messaging—messaging that brands Democrats as good and Republicans as bad, messages that pass the "glance test," messages that give Republicans wedgies—*share it* on your networks. One of the most important messaging resources Democrats have is YOU.

Remember, saving democracy takes a village. So because voters are just not that into us, let's play the GOP's game. And let's play it to win. Winning requires guts and grit. It requires us to move quickly—at the speed of modern politics. It will no doubt require breaking a few eggs for the sake of saving democracy—*your* democracy.

Conclusion

Democracy, If We Can Keep It

On the evening of October 2, 1930, Will Rogers attended the star-studded premiere of a John Wayne western called *The Big Trail* at Grauman's Chinese Theatre. The famed humorist showed up to introduce the crowd of Hollywood elites to his friend the San Francisco Mayor James Rolph, then a *Republican* candidate running for governor of California. According to an account by the Chicago Tribune Press Service, Rogers brought the house down with laughter and described himself as a "contact man between art and politics." Then he said something that became far more famous than *The Big Trail* ever did—a quip both Democrats and Republicans love to quote (and innocently misquote) to this day:

> I am of no political faith. I belong to no organized party—that is,
> I am a Democrat and nobody can accuse the Democrats of being
> organized.

The more familiar version of this quote, "I'm not a member of an organized party, I'm a Democrat," has so much staying power because it still strikes a chord nearly a century later. It forms the underlying basis for the media's "Democrats in Disarray" narrative. We all know the Democratic Party, like anything or anyone else, is far from perfect. But after nearly a century of accepting the brand that Democrats are destined to be disorganized, we need to get our shit together now. We are out of time.

By now you know I don't waste time sugarcoating my observations or political opinions. Partisan politics is sticky enough as it is. I dish out lots of tough love for the party of the people because we're way past the point of gentle nudges and polite suggestions. This isn't *The Great British Baking Show* or *Survivor: Red Versus Blue*. The Republicans are playing the political equivalent of *The Hunger Games,* and we're their tributes. The fact is, we're outmatched and out-resourced here in District 12. America's democracy is circling the drain after a decade of assault by the Republican Party. If you love America despite all its faults and scars as much as I do, then you're playing this game whether you like it or not.

But it's not really you, fellow player, I worry about. *You* are at the end of an entire book about how to win back democracy by strengthening the strategies and messages of the Democratic Party. No, I worry about the hundred million Americans who can vote and should vote, but don't. I worry about the countless folks who shrug off politics as a dirty word, or worse, as someone else's problem without even *wanting* to understand how good we've got it, or how easily we can lose it. I worry about what'll happen to our ability to self-govern this country when nearly half its citizens refuse to believe objective truths despite plain evidence, common sense, and basic human decency. I worry a great deal about MAGA's march toward fascism and the horrifying loss of freedom, peace, and security that will come with it.

But what good is worrying gonna do? *None.* In politics, only action matters.

And that's why I want to end this book with an urgent assignment. Your grade is either pass or fail. My assignment for you is to *put some of your own skin into this game.* It is, after all, *your democracy.*

IF NOT YOU, WHO?

Whatever that "skin" looks like is entirely up to you. Maybe you commit to doing something minor and regular, like making it a point to switch any community TV tuned to Fox News (which seems to be omnipresent in gyms, motel lobbies, and waiting rooms across America) to something—*anything*—else. But I hope you put more skin into this game than just that.

If your state allows it, maybe your involvement is as simple as signing yourself (and your spouse, if you have one) up for absentee voting, so you can vote by mail weeks before Election Day. But I hope you and your spouse commit to doing more than that too.

Maybe your role in defending American democracy is to run for your local school board so you can personally hold public schools accountable for teaching basic civics to our kids, or so you can show Moms for Liberty that other parents have rights too.

Maybe you'd like to see who else shows up at the next meeting of your local Democratic Party? You, even *you*, probably aren't a regular! In fact, I'm guessing most of you don't even belong to your county Democratic Party! I'll never forget what a political mentor once told me: that in politics the real power belongs to the volunteers who set up the folding chairs and make the coffee before everyone else arrives. Maybe your role, when in this meeting, is to assess the strength of their messaging, or to offer punchier messages; maybe it's to show 'em how to come up with a good wedgie! Or maybe your role is to help them come up with a specific plan of action for winning Democrats more power on Election Day.

Maybe you commit to reading the political news section of whichever website you log on to before checking your emails at the office, even when the headlines seem dull. Political news coverage may be frustrating, but again, you can't be outraged about things you don't know are happening. Does your source of news gloss over political coverage? Find another one. Did your favorite radio reporter just commit bothsidesism by giving the Republican an opportunity to push false propaganda? Let that reporter or his editor know (respectfully) that America can no longer afford that kind of political coverage if they value American democracy.

If you start paying attention to a particular Democrat running for office, maybe you send her campaign a few bucks. Are you liking what you see? Maybe you write a bigger check next month. Hell, maybe you can volunteer to spend a Saturday or two in the fall knocking on doors or making phone calls on her behalf. Can you bring a hot, home-cooked meal to her team of young, underpaid campaign staffers? They've been consuming nothing but frozen burritos, Tootsie Pops, and Mountain Dew for the past three months!

Helping a political campaign financially doesn't have to stay local. In fact, most high-profile Democratic campaigns rely on "small dollar" campaign contributions—to the tune of $5 or $10 at a time, from donors all over America. This adds up! Pitching in just a few dollars gives you skin in the game. Just don't forget what I pointed out in the last chapter, though; as big, high-profile campaigns rake in cash from across the country, smaller campaigns always struggle to stay funded and relevant—so maybe your skin in the game is contributing to the unknown guy running for secretary of state while everyone else is sending money to the U.S. Senate candidate.

Or maybe you throw your whole hide into the game by running for office yourself. I don't really care where you start, but Democrats desperately need to field more candidates at the local and state levels—especially in races considered "nonpartisan." If running for office sparks any interest, the best advice I can give, in addition to the advice you've read so far, is to remain *true to yourself;* most voters know exactly when candidates pretend to be someone they're not, so don't even bother. And remember, if their message is "Democrats suck," your message needs to be "Democrats rock." The "apologetic Democrat" model is a loser. Be ruthless. *Campaign as if our very future depends on it,* because it does. And if you run, *run to win.*

WALKING ON EGGSHELLS

As you think about how to put your own skin in the game, consider this: Too many Democrats have a destructive habit of vilifying our well-intentioned allies who may not always use the most politically correct language, or who may not share our exact same worldview. Rather than moving the ball down the field, we end up dividing ourselves by reprimanding and cutting down imperfect people who also want a better America. I'm certainly not suggesting we excuse intolerance, hate, or hateful language, but I am suggesting that we don't cut off our own noses to spite our own faces.

"I think where [Democrats] get into trouble sometimes is when we try to suggest that some groups are more—because they historically have been victimized more—that somehow they have a status that's different than other people, and that we're going around scolding folks if they don't use exactly the right phrase," President Obama told the *Pod Save America* dudes in the fall of 2022. "Identity politics becomes the principal lens through which we view our various political challenges."

> I think that that, for a lot of average folks, ends up feeling as if you're not speaking to me and my concerns, or for that matter, my kids' concerns and their future. It feels as if I'm being excluded from that conversation rather than brought into the conversation. So that's something that we all have to be mindful of and cautious about.

Sometimes, President Obama added, "people just want to not feel as if they are walking on eggshells, and they want some acknowledgment that life is messy."

That's important advice from one of the Democratic Party's more successful messengers. If our friends have the right intentions, make room for them. Try to understand where they're coming from, and understand that our fellow Democrats are and should be as diverse in their worldviews as America itself. So let's lay off a little. We've got to give our friends and allies some space, because it's their democracy too. As Benjamin Franklin reportedly said upon signing the Declaration of Independence, "We must all hang together, or most assuredly we shall all hang separately."

YOU CANNOT GOVERN IF YOU DO NOT WIN

The Democratic Party and the progressive movement are full of good people who care deeply about the future but who have forgotten that in modern American democracy winning political power has to happen before anything else can. There is a difference between politics and governing. We run on governing while they destroy us with politics. Nothing can or will happen—we will see no progress or change—if Democrats don't win elections first.

Of course we'll have disagreements along the way. Of course Democrats are entitled to different ideas and strategies for how to make our nation better for all who live here. Of course there will be times when we have to elevate some ideas or candidates over others, and to compare and contrast the differences. We can do this while folding in as many people as possible, while respecting beliefs, cultures, identities, abilities, and perspectives from every corner of America. But if Democrats lose elections, none of what we stand for matters. We cannot govern when we do not have political power, so our top priority as a party must be to win that political power in elections.

When did so many Democrats lose sight of this fundamental truth of American politics? Why did other noble endeavors push *winning* out of the top of anyone's list of priorities? I'm certainly not saying our ideals aren't worthy and worth fighting for—of course they are. But I'll never be able to wrap my brain around idealists and activists who are so rigid in their beliefs that they undermine our ability to win elections. In our political system, *fighting for* the change we need and actually delivering that change is literally the difference between losing and winning.

Here's a hypothetical example of where we lose sight of victory, one lifted from my actual experience with Democratic campaigns across the country. Let's say our campaign is developing one of those glossy mailers—the ones that Democrats love to overcomplicate with data and facts that won't change any minds because no one who needs to will ever take two minutes to read it. Let's say our mailer is about Republican efforts to take away women's freedom by outlawing abortion.

"There aren't enough people of color in the stock photo," someone says. "We need different photos that show more diversity." Great feedback! *Yes, Democrats value representation and racial and cultural diversity.*

"Is a unionized print shop producing this mailer?" someone else asks. "And are we using recycled paper and soy-based ink?" Yes and yes. *Democrats patronize unionized businesses because we honor and respect organized labor. And of course we're using materials that have less effect on the environment.* But they also cost a lot more, which means we hit fewer voters with our message.

"The copy should say 'pregnant people,' not 'pregnant women,'" some dude pipes in.

Okay, stop. Yes, some people who don't identify as women can get pregnant, but the goal here isn't to win a ribbon for inclusivity. It's to win a messaging war to win elections. Using terms like "pregnant people" creates mission creep by prioritizing competing objectives (in this case, promoting inclusivity)—language that doesn't resonate with everyone or that dilutes the main message and detracts from our main objective: winning political power.

So let's produce the most effective mailer possible, even if the handful of words we use aren't as considerate and inclusive as they can possibly be and even if the focus of the mailer isn't on the issue that matters to you, or your group, the most. The means justify the end because marginalized people we care about—including pregnant people who may not identify as women—will pay the highest price if we lose our democracy to Republicans who dehumanize them and who are using the political power *they won* to legislate them out of existence.

At the end of the day, we will all suffer if the Republican Party succeeds in upending American democracy and replacing it with fascism and authoritarianism. With millions of Americans tuning out, and millions more falling for lies and wild conspiracy theories, *winning* is all that matters, whether we like it or not. It *has to be,* because for Republicans winning is the be-all and end-all. The Democratic Party has to fight to win with everything it's got—smarter, harder, and quicker—as the GOP throws out rights and freedoms for countless people who don't conform with whatever Republicans stand for.

When they go low, we need to hit 'em where it hurts.

Acknowledgments

Prior to the white nationalist "Unite the Right" rally in Charlottesville in August of 2017, I had never even heard the word *antifa*, an abbreviation of anti-fascism. I remember being surprised there were people still devoting their lives to countering neo-Nazis.

Now we are all antifa.

There are so many people who played pivotal roles in helping me make this book a reality. Lawrence O'Donnell and Joe Scarborough did so much to help legitimize me and put negative partisanship on the radar.

Jaime Harrison has done more than anyone to help me turn negative partisanship into an articulated electioneering strategy.

Laurie Spivak and Ashley Jacobs selflessly co-created and ran Strike PAC, so we could show other content creators what negative partisanship looks like in the form of political advertising. The donors to Strike PAC believed in our mission and put their money where their mouths were.

Several creators have donated their time and energy to create negative partisanship content: Doug Haddix, Thomas Santoriello, Rick Peterson, Ceekay Tschudi, and Yuval King. You made me look good and seem smarter than I am.

Thank you to the hundreds of folks who shared their social media audiences to grow mine by reposting ads and tweets and telling others to follow my work. There is no me without you, you selfless defenders of democracy. I love my Twitter family.

There are people who have contributed greatly to spreading the word about negative partisanship strategy: Joy-Ann Reid, Jonathan Capehart, Stephanie Ruhle, Paul Rosenberg, Bob Cesca, and David Pepper, all of whom selflessly shared their audiences with me.

Thank you is also due to Adrian Fontes, Aaron Black, John "Bowser" Bauman, Jennifer Fernandez Ancona, Dan Ancona, Kurt Bardella, Christine Jenkins, Lavora Barnes, Michael Hirschorn, Hannah Rosenzweig, and Matt Grodsky for embracing negative partisanship strategy in their own work.

And then there's the team who literally made this book possible. First, a big thanks to Ryan Busse (author of a book you should read titled *Gunfight: My Battle Against the Industry that Radicalized America*) who, of his own accord, told Julie Stevenson, the G.O.A.T. of literary agents at Massie McQuilkin, about my work and my burning need to publish it.

My editorial team at Crown: Kevin Doughten and Amy Li, who made this book better with every read and most important, believed in its central mission from Day One. Kevin, thank you for rolling the dice on me.

And now, most especially, a huge thank-you to my long-suffering co-writer Aaron Murphy, who deserves a Golden Keyboard Award for what he's done to turn the collection of facts, strategies, theories, ideas, data, and political science mashed up in my head into what I hope you'll agree is literary gold. Aaron, working with you was the best decision I've ever made and I'm already old AF!

I'll never forget the folks who brought me to the dance. Thank you all.

Notes

Introduction: The Dirtiest Word in America

x **In a typical midterm election** Geoffrey Skelley and Nathaniel Rakich, "Why the President's Party Almost Always Has a Bad Midterm," FiveThirtyEight .com, Jan. 3, 2022, fivethirtyeight.com/features/why-the-presidents-party -almost-always-has-a-bad-midterm/.

Chapter 1: Democracy on Its Deathbed

4 **In fact, the American Political** American Political Science Association, "Toward a More Responsible Two-Party System: A Report of the Committee on Political Parties," *American Political Science Review* 44, no. 3, pt. 2, supplement (Sept. 1950), www.jstor.org/stable/1950996.

5 **First, consider this** "Americans' Civic Knowledge Drops on First Amendment and Branches of Government," Annenberg Center for Public Policy, University of Pennsylvania, Sept. 13, 2022, www.annenbergpublicpolicycenter .org/americans-civics-knowledge-drops-on-first-amendment-and-branches -of-government/.

5 **Another respected nonpartisan** Meredith Dost, "Dim Public Awareness of Supreme Court as Major Rulings Loom," Pew Research Center, May 14, 2015, www.pewresearch.org/fact-tank/2015/05/14/dim-public-awareness -of-supreme-court-as-major-rulings-loom/.

5 **And a 2020 survey** Jodi Goldberg, "Study: Up to 80% of Americans Follow Politics Casually or Not At All," Fox 5 New York, Oct. 23, 2020, www.fox5ny .com/news/study-up-to-80-of-americans-follow-politics-casually-or-not-at-all.

6 **Google's five most searched** "Year in Search 2022," Top Search Trends, Google, accessed Jun. 16, 2023, trends.google.com/trends/yis/2022/US/?hl =en-US.

8 **In 2022, 53.4 percent** U.S. Elections Project, "2022 November General Election Turnout Rates," accessed Jun. 16, 2023, www.electproject.org/2022g.

8 **"[Nonvoters] come from"** "The Untold Story of American Non-voters," The 100 Million Project: A Knight Foundation Study, 2020, 47, knightfoundation.org/ wp-content/uploads/2020/02/The-100-Million-Project_KF_Report_2020.pdf.

8 **"Many non-voters cite"** Ibid., 15.

9 **There are twenty such nations** Central Intelligence Agency, "CIA World Factbook—Suffrage," accessed Jun. 16, 2023, www.cia.gov/the-world-factbook/field/suffrage/.

9 **Australia has had compulsory** Commonwealth of Australia, Parliamentary Education Office, "How Many People Voted in the Last Election?," accessed Jun. 16, 2023, peo.gov.au/understand-our-parliament/your-questions-on-notice/questions/how-many-people-voted-in-the-last-election.

10 **In 2021, a year that began** Brennan Center for Justice, New York University School of Law, "Voting Laws Roundup: December 2021," Dec. 21, 2021, www.brennancenter.org/our-work/research-reports/voting-laws-roundup-december-2021.

11 **First, there's a party-wide** Daron R. Shaw and John R. Petrocik, "Does High Voter Turnout Help One Party?," *National Affairs*, no. 53 (Fall 2021), www.nationalaffairs.com/publications/detail/does-high-voter-turnout-help-one-party.

11 **Oregon saw a 62.4 percent** U.S. Elections Project, "2022 November General Election Turnout Rates."

12 **Georgia made it a crime** Kate Brumback, "Judge Declines to Block Ban on Giving Food, Water to Voters," Associated Press, Aug. 19, 2022, apnews.com/article/2022-midterm-elections-voting-rights-georgia-stacey-abrams-general-c1c7c7103c4757c46f266afde514fd59.

12 **Voters of color also** Brennan Center for Justice, New York University School of Law, "The Impact of Voter Suppression on Communities of Color," Jan. 10, 2022, www.brennancenter.org/our-work/research-reports/impact-voter-suppression-communities-color.

12 **In Mississippi, turnout** German Lopez, "How the Voting Rights Act Transformed Black Voting Rights in the South, in One Chart," *Vox*, Aug. 6, 2015, www.vox.com/2015/3/6/8163229/voting-rights-act-1965.

13 **But counterintuitively** Shaw and Petrocik, "Does High Voter Turnout Help One Party?"

13 **The late Christopher Joyner** Christopher C. Joyner, "The Impact of Political Socialization upon Partisan Identification: An Assessment," *Journal of Political Science* 1, no. 1 (Nov. 1973): 37–48, digitalcommons.coastal.edu/jops/vol1/iss1/3.

13 **No, the most important socialization** Elizabeth Theiss-Morse et al., *Political Behavior of the American Electorate* (Thousand Oaks, Calif.: Sage/CQ Press, 2018).

15 **That these three countries** Marnie Hunter, "The World's Happiest Countries for 2023," CNN, Mar. 20, 2023, www.cnn.com/travel/article/world-happiest-countries-2023-wellness/index.html.

Chapter 2: Partisanship Is a Helluva Drug

17 **"by which cunning, ambitious"** George Washington, "Farewell Address," Sept. 19, 1796, U.S. National Archives, Founders Online, founders.archives .gov/documents/Washington/05-20-02-0440-0002.

17 **Although a majority** "Political Polarization in the American Public: How Increasing Ideological Uniformity and Partisan Antipathy Affect Politics, Compromise and Everyday Life," Pew Research Center, Jun. 12, 2014, www .pewresearch.org/wp-content/uploads/sites/4/2014/06/6-12-2014 -Political-Polarization-Release.pdf.

19 **But even worse for Walker** Maya King, Lisa Lerer, and Jonah E. Bromwich, "Herschel Walker Urged Woman to Have a 2nd Abortion, She Says," *The New York Times*, Oct. 7, 2022, www.nytimes.com/2022/10/07/us/politics/ herschel-walker-abortion.html.

19 **CNN exit poll data** 2022 Exit Poll Data, U.S. Senate—Georgia, by Party ID, CNN, accessed Jun. 16, 2023, www.cnn.com/election/2022/exit-polls/ georgia/senate/0; 2022 Exit Poll Data, Governor—Georgia, by Party ID, CNN, accessed Jun. 16, 2023, www.cnn.com/election/2022/exit-polls/ georgia/governor/0.

21 **Even the Super Bowl** U.S. Elections Project, "2020 Presidential Nomination Contest Turnout Rates," accessed Jun. 16, 2023, www.electproject.org/ 2020p.

21 **When Colorado held its primary** State of Colorado Secretary of State, "2020 Voter Registration Statistics," Jun. 2020, www.sos.state.co.us/pubs/elections/ VoterRegNumbers/2020/June/VotersByCongrsnlDist.pdf.

21 **And that meant thirty-three-year-old** State of Colorado Secretary of State, "2020 Primary Election Results," Jun. 30, 2020, 13–16, www.coloradosos .gov/pubs/elections/files/2020StatePrimaryResultsCert.pdf.

22 **For a majority of Republican** American Bar Association, "Ratings of Article III and Article IV Judicial Nominees," 115th Cong. and 116th Cong., accessed Jun. 16, 2023, www.americanbar.org/groups/committees/federal _judiciary/ratings/.

26 *The Daily Show's* **Desi Lydic** "Understanding the Undecided Voter," *Daily Show with Trevor Noah*, Comedy Central, Oct. 27, 2020, video, www.cc.com/video/ 09zebh/the-daily-show-with-trevor-noah-understanding-the-undecided-voter.

27 **On October 17, 2022** Shane Goldmacher, "Republicans Gain Edge as Voters Worry About Economy, Times/Siena Poll Finds," *The New York Times*, Oct. 17, 2022, www.nytimes.com/2022/10/17/us/politics/republicans-economy-nyt -siena-poll.html.

27 **A link to a page** "Cross-Tabs for October 2022 Times/Siena Poll of Likely Voters," *The New York Times*, Oct. 17, 2022, www.nytimes.com/interactive/ 2022/10/17/upshot/times-siena-poll-likely-voters-crosstabs.html.

29 **In 2004, Rove worked behind** Wayne Slater, "Karl Rove Says He Didn't Engineer Anti-gay Marriage Amendments. He Did," *Dallas Morning News*, Aug. 26, 2010, www.dallasnews.com/news/politics/2010/08/26/karl-rove -says-he-didn-t-engineer-anti-gay-marriage-amendments-he-did.

29 **Even in my bright blue** State of Oregon Secretary of State, "2004 November General Election Official Results," State Measure No. 36, Nov. 2, 2004, 58, records.sos.state.or.us/ORSOSWebDrawer/Record/8411085.

30 **Research from Chapman** Juhi Doshi, "How Conservative Media Influences Views on Illegal Immigration," Center for Undergraduate Excellence, Chapman University, Spring 2022, digitalcommons.chapman.edu/cgi/viewcontent .cgi?article=1539&context=cusrd_abstracts.

30 **"When Mexico sends its people"** Donald J. Trump, "Full Text: Donald Trump Announces a Presidential Bid," Jun. 16, 2015, *The Washington Post*, Jul. 20, 2022, www.washingtonpost.com/news/post-politics/wp/2015/06/ 16/full-text-donald-trump-announces-a-presidential-bid/.

Chapter 3: You Are What You Eat

33 **And while Stephen Colbert** "America's Bizarro Weather | Buttigieg Finally Visits Ohio | Fox Frets over 'Woke' Legos," YouTube video, posted by *The Late Show with Stephen Colbert*, Feb. 23, 2023, youtu.be/Bwg-HPKgj-o?t=299.

34 **"Fox has retained its influence"** Matt Gertz, "Fox News Is the Republican Party. Here Are over 400 Examples Proving It," Media Matters for America, May 16, 2022, www.mediamatters.org/fox-news/fox-news-republican-party -here-are-over-400-examples-proving-it.

35 **Algorithms make clear** Aaron Smith, "Public Attitudes Toward Computer Algorithms," Pew Research Center, Nov. 16, 2018, www.pewresearch.org/ internet/2018/11/16/public-attitudes-toward-computer-algorithms/.

35 **This is known as** Jihii Jolly, "How Algorithms Decide the News You See," *Columbia Journalism Review*, May 14, 2014, archives.cjr.org/news_literacy/ algorithms_filter_bubble.php.

35 **The Pew Research Center found** Smith, "Public Attitudes Toward Computer Algorithms."

36 **The new algorithm** Adam Mosseri, "Facebook Recently Announced a Major Update to News Feed; Here's What's Changing," Facebook (Meta), Apr. 8, 2018, about.fb.com/news/2018/04/inside-feed-meaningful-interactions/.

36 **"A like, comment, or share"** "News Feed FYI: Bringing People Closer Together," Facebook, video, Jan. 11, 2018, www.facebook.com/facebook/videos/ 10156988765141729/.

36 **Facebook's news feed** Tobias Rose-Stockwell, "This Is How Your Fear and Outrage Are Being Sold for Profit," *Quartz*, Jul. 28, 2017, qz.com/1039910/ how-facebooks-news-feed-algorithm-sells-our-fear-and-outrage-for-profit/.

37 **They're paid big bucks** Sara Fischer, "The Daily Wire Is Profitable, and Eyeing Entertainment," *Axios*, Jan. 19, 2021, www.axios.com/2021/01/19/daily-wire -ben-shapiro-revenue-movies-podcasts; Roger Sollenberger, "Revealed: The Donors to Tucker Carlson's News Org—and Their Ethical Conflicts," *Daily Beast*, Dec. 20, 2022, www.thedailybeast.com/donors-to-tucker-carlsons-daily -caller-news-foundation-revealed.

37 **A third of adults** Naomi Forman-Katz and Katerina Eva Matsa, "News Plat-

form Fact Sheet," Pew Research Center, Sept. 20, 2022, www.pewresearch .org/journalism/fact-sheet/news-platform-fact-sheet/.

38 **On October 6, 2022** "Vice President Kamala Harris Involved in Motorcade Accident," YouTube video, posted by *Today*, NBC, Oct. 6, 2022, youtube/ watch?v=c1bYaChsdsc.

38 **The *Post*'s nearly thousand-word story** Carol D. Leonnig, "VP Was in Car Accident, Secret Service First Called It 'Mechanical Failure,'" *The Washington Post*, Oct. 5, 2022, www.washingtonpost.com/nation/2022/10/05/harris -motorcade-accident-secret-service/.

39 **According to Pew** Pew Research Center, "Cable News Fact Sheet (2020)," Jul. 13, 2021, www.pewresearch.org/journalism/fact-sheet/cable-news.

40 **Vilifying the "mainstream media"** Andy Barr, "Palin Trashes 'Lamestream Media,'" *Politico*, Nov. 18, 2009, www.politico.com/story/2009/11/palin-trashes -lamestream-media-029693.

40 ***The Independent* reported** Alex Woodward, "'Fake News': A Guide to Trump's Favourite Phrase—and the Dangers It Obscures," *Independent*, Oct. 2, 2020, www.independent.co.uk/news/world/americas/us-election/trump-fake-news -counter-history-b732873.html.

41 **In fact, data analysts** Kalev Leetaru, "Fox News Has Covered Portland 6.7 Times More Than CNN and MSNBC Combined This Year," RealClearWire, Jan. 31, 2021, realclearwire.com/video/2021/01/31/fox_news_has_covered_portland _67_times_more_than_cnn_and_msnbc_combined_this_year_658595.html.

42 **But the most dangerous example** Federal Election Commission, "Federal Elections 2020: Election Results for the U.S. President, the U.S. Senate, and the U.S. House of Representatives," Oct. 2022, 5, www.fec.gov/resources/ cms-content/documents/federalelections2020.pdf.

42 **In the court filings** Superior Court of the State of Delaware, "Dominion's Brief in Support of Its Motion for Summary Judgment on Liability of Fox News Network LLC and Fox Corporation," Public Version (Redacted), Feb. 16, 2023, *The New York Times*, 34, int.nyt.com/data/documenttools/redacted -documents-in-dominion-fox-news-case/dca5e3880422426f/full.pdf.

42 **Let the record show** Ibid., 35.

42 **Former congressman Adam Kinzinger** "Adam Kinzinger: Tucker Carlson Lies to His Audience 'Because He Wants People's Money,'" Media Matters for America, Mar. 7, 2023, www.mediamatters.org/january-6-insurrection/ adam-kinzinger-tucker-carlson-lies-his-audience-because-he-wants-peoples.

43 **So, in a brief letter** William P. Barr, "Attorney General's Letter to House and Senate Judiciary Committee," U.S. Department of Justice, Mar. 24, 2019, www.justice.gov/archives/ag/page/file/1147981/download.

44 **A few days after Barr** Robert S. Mueller III, "Special Counsel Robert Mueller's Letter to Attorney General William P. Barr," *The Washington Post*, Mar. 27, 2019, games-cdn.washingtonpost.com/notes/prod/default/ documents/72509902-0d00-41e8-9795-908605cdcc03/note/d644607b-38f4 -4b89-9408-a25e25c588a4.pdf#page=1.

46 **The train that derailed** Sarah Swann, "Obama-Era Safety Rule for High-Hazard Cargo Trains Was Repealed Under Trump," PolitiFact, Feb. 15,

2023, www.politifact.com/factchecks/2023/feb/17/occupy-democrats/obama
-era-safety-rule-high-hazard-trains-was-repea/.

46 **But when *The New York Times*** Jonathan Weisman, "In Fog of East Palestine's Crisis, Politicians Write Their Own Stories," *The New York Times*, Feb. 23,
2023, www.nytimes.com/2023/02/23/us/politics/east-palestine-politics.html.

47 **"Fox News has played"** Ari Shapiro, "Former Australian Prime Minister Blames
Fox News for America's Polarized Politics," *All Things Considered*, NPR, Aug. 31,
2022, www.npr.org/2022/08/31/1120355466/former-australian-prime-minister
-blames-fox-news-for-americas-polarized-politics.

48 **It's "a loaded word"** David Bauder, "News Media Hesitate to Use 'Lie' for
Trump's Misstatements," Associated Press, Aug. 29, 2018, https://www
.apnews.com/88675d3fdd674c7c9ec70f170f6e4a1a/News-media-hesitate
-to-use-'lie'-for-Trump's-misstatements.

48 **Yet Republican House Speaker** Cameron Sexton, interview by Hallerin Hill,
"TN Speaker Says Protests in Nashville Was an 'Insurrection,'" *The Hal
Show Podcast*, Mar. 30, 2023, omny.fm/shows/the-hal-show-podcast/tn-house
-speaker-says-protests-in-nashville-was-an?fbclid=IwAR0lilxBtFqbFMJAE
MCxJv7iI_pxvMcYV8n_zd3Dxl520GkWKHPjXyuyvMM.

49 **My trench buddy Rick Wilson** Chauncey Devega, "NeverTrumper Rick Wilson on the Midterms: 'Democrats Are About to Pay a Terrible Price,'" *Salon*,
Oct. 27, 2022, www.salon.com/2022/10/27/nevertrumper-rick-wilson-on
-the-midterms-democrats-are-about-to-pay-a-terrible-price/.

50 **This overcorrection is why** Rob Savillo, "Report: Diversity on the Sunday
Shows in 2015," Media Matters for America, Mar. 15, 2016, www.mediamatters
.org/fox-nation/report-diversity-sunday-shows-2015.

50 **In 2021, only 35 percent** Jeffrey Gottfried and Jacob Liedke, "Partisan Di-
vides in Media Trust Widen, Driven by a Decline Among Republicans," Pew
Research Center, Aug. 30, 2021, www.pewresearch.org/fact-tank/2021/08/
30/partisan-divides-in-media-trust-widen-by-a-decline-among-republicans/.

50 **It's because many politically** John Gramlich, "5 Facts About Fox News," Pew
Research Center, Apr. 8, 2020, www.pewresearch.org/fact-tank/2020/04/
08/five-facts-about-fox-news/.

Chapter 4: A Critical Culture War

54 **With millions of people watching** "Critical Race Theory Has Infiltrated the
Federal Government | Christopher Rufo on Fox News," YouTube video,
posted by Heritage Foundation, Sept. 2, 2020, youtu.be/rBXRdWflV7M.

54 **Earlier in 2020** Benjamin Wallace-Wells, "How a Conservative Activist Invented the Conflict over Critical Race Theory," *The New Yorker*, Jun. 18, 2021,
www.newyorker.com/news/annals-of-inquiry/how-a-conservative-activist
-invented-the-conflict-over-critical-race-theory.

54 **The documents, which Rufo shared** Christopher F. Rufo, "City of Seattle
Holds Racially Segregated Civil Rights Training—in the Name of Social Justice," christopherrufo.com, Jul. 29, 2020, christopherrufo.com/separate
-but-equal/.

54 **"I've obtained new documents"** Ibid.

55 **"And [the trainer] told Treasury"** "Critical Race Theory Has Infiltrated the Federal Government."

55 **"the President has directed me"** Russell Vought, "Memorandum for the Heads of Executive Departments and Agencies," Office of Management and Budget, Sept. 4, 2020, www.whitehouse.gov/wp-content/uploads/2020/09/ M-20-34.pdf.

56 **The next morning, Trump** Donald J. Trump (@realDonaldTrump), Twitter, Sept. 5, 2020, 5:52 A.M., twitter.com/realDonaldTrump/status/1302212909 808971776.

56 **A couple weeks later** Donald J. Trump, "Executive Order on Combating Race and Sex Stereotyping," White House, Sept. 22, 2020, trumpwhitehouse.archives .gov/presidential-actions/executive-order-combating-race-sex-stereotyping/.

56 **As I told the neo-fascist** "Charlie Kirk vs. CRT Advocate Rachel Bitecofer," YouTube video, posted by Turning Point USA, Mar. 17, 2022, www.youtube .com/watch?v=r4G4ks7_7JY.

57 *The New Yorker* **wrote** Wallace-Wells, "How a Conservative Activist Invented the Conflict over Critical Race Theory."

57 **The right-wing Heritage Foundation** Jonathan Butcher and Mike Gonzalez, "Critical Race Theory, the New Intolerance, and Its Grip on America," Heritage Foundation, Dec. 7, 2020, www.heritage.org/civil-rights/report/critical -race-theory-the-new-intolerance-and-its-grip-america.

57 **The Republican National Committee** "Research: Americans Reject Critical Race Theory," Republican National Committee, Jun. 24, 2021, gop.com/ research/americans-reject-critical-race-theory/.

57 **According to an analysis** Jeremy Barr, "Critical Race Theory Is the Hottest Topic on Fox News. And It's Only Getting Hotter," *The Washington Post,* Jun. 24, 2021, www.washingtonpost.com/media/2021/06/24/critical-race -theory-fox-news/.

57 **By then, Republican legislatures** Rashawn Ray and Alexandra Gibbons, "Why Are States Banning Critical Race Theory?," Brookings Institution, Nov. 2021, www.brookings.edu/blog/fixgov/2021/07/02/why-are-states -banning-critical-race-theory/.

58 **According to publicly available** "Virginia: Governor: 2021 Polls," FiveThirtyEight .com, accessed Jun. 16, 2023, projects.fivethirtyeight.com/polls/governor/ virginia/.

58 **In August, a survey conducted** Harry L. Wilson, "Roanoke College Poll: McAuliffe Leads Youngkin in Race for Virginia Governor," Institute for Public Opinion Research, Roanoke College, Aug. 20, 2021, www.roanoke.edu/ about/news/rc_poll_politics_aug_2021.

58 **As angry parents crammed** David Weigel (@daveweigel), Twitter, May 3, 2021, 1:21 P.M., twitter.com/daveweigel/status/1389298970602606592.

58 **He bemoaned CRT** "Glenn Youngkin Talks with Tucker Carlson About What's at Stake in Virginia If Democrats Keep Control," YouTube video, posted by Glenn Youngkin, May 4, 2021, www.youtube.com/watch?v=DA7g _U43JxA.

58 **Lo and behold** Hannah Natanson, "No, Virginia Is Not Moving to Eliminate Advanced High School Math Classes," *The Washington Post*, Apr. 26, 2021, www.washingtonpost.com/local/education/virginia-advanced-math-classes -equity/2021/04/26/41f3dbd0-a6a3-11eb-bca5-048b2759a489_story.html.

58 **Through the summer of 2021** Warren Fiske, "Youngkin Offers Little Proof Critical Race Theory Is in 'All' Virginia Schools," PolitiFact, Aug. 10, 2021, www.politifact.com/factchecks/2021/aug/10/glenn-youngkin/youngkin -offers-little-proof-critical-race-theory-/.

59 **"Why are we not paying our teachers?"** Cameron Cawthorne, "Terry McAuliffe Calls Critical Race Theory Concerns a 'Right-Wing Conspiracy,'" Fox News, Jun. 14, 2021, www.foxnews.com/us/mcauliffe-critical-race-theory -right-wing-conspiracy.

59 **Soon after the primary** Robert McCartney, "Republican Glenn Youngkin Has a Surprisingly Good Chance of Winning Virginia Governorship," *The Washington Post*, May 17, 2021, www.washingtonpost.com/local/virginia -governor-youngkin/2021/05/16/cd3fe5c2-b5b1-11eb-ab43-bebddc5a0f65 _story.html.

60 **Throughout 2021, countless Americans** Republican National Committee, "Research."

61 **"When Republicans turned an obscure"** Paul Waldman and Greg Sargent, "Opinion: Why Democrats Must Figure Out Their Message on Schools and Race," *The Washington Post*, Mar. 31, 2022, www.washingtonpost.com/ opinions/2022/03/31/democrats-message-schools-race-crt/.

61 **We responded by acknowledging** "Debate Transcript," Presidential Debate at Case Western Reserve University and Cleveland Clinic in Cleveland, Ohio, Commission on Presidential Debates, Sept. 29, 2020, www .debates.org/voter-education/debate-transcripts/september-29-2020-debate -transcript/.

61 **When the Trump administration** Cory A. Booker, "Letter Requesting Judiciary Committee Hearing on Trump Administration Directive Ending Anti-racial Bias Trainings," U.S. Senate, Sept. 17, 2020, www.booker.senate .gov/imo/media/doc/9.17.20%20CAB%20Letter%20to%20Chairman %20Graham%20on%20Racial%20Sensitivity%20Training%20Directive %20-%20Signed.pdf.

62 **If you say CRT is wrong** Butcher and Gonzalez, "Critical Race Theory, the New Intolerance, and Its Grip on America."

63 **"This legislation lacks flexibility"** Alanna Durkin Richer, "Virginia Governor Vetoes Sexually Explicit Books Bill," Associated Press, Apr. 4, 2016, apnews .com/article/a70abb4d49534501aca471bc663067ea.

63 **"You believe school systems should"** "Terry McAuliffe, Glenn Youngkin Square Off in Final Gubernatorial Debate," YouTube video, posted by WSLS 10, Sept. 28, 2021, youtu.be/z0UC018P9mc?t=1768.

63 **"When my son showed me"** "Youngkin Ad About Parent Involvement in School Omits Key Context," video, *The Washington Post*, Oct. 26, 2021, www .washingtonpost.com/video/politics/youngkin-ad-about-parent-involvement

-in-school-omits-key-context/2021/10/26/becdc789-b6ad-4238-a1de-2343b 5eef2ea_video.html.

64 **Another Youngkin ad featured** "Social Warrior," YouTube video, posted by Glenn Youngkin, Oct. 30, 2021, www.youtube.com/watch?v=7X6rMnu viPg.

64 **"As parents, Dorothy and I have"** Brandon Jarvis (@Jaaavis), Twitter, Oct. 18, 2021, 2:37 P.M., twitter.com/Jaaavis/status/1450199344863399939.

65 **"Now, in the final days"** "Our Voice Matters | Terry McAuliffe for Virginia Governor 2021," YouTube video, posted by Terry McAuliffe, Oct. 29, 2021, www.youtube.com/watch?v=c9Vv8GOzvM0.

65 **"[Youngkin] wants to ban"** "McAuliffe: Youngkin Is 'Ending His Campaign on a Racist Dog Whistle,'" *Meet the Press*, NBC News, Oct. 31, 2021, www.nbcnews.com/meet-the-press/video/mcauliffe-youngkin-is-ending -his-campaign-on-a-racist-dog-whistle-125032005514.

66 **Charles Siler, a self-described** "The Right-Wing Furore over Critical Race Theory Is Manufactured, Says Charles Siler," *Economist*, Jul. 14, 2022, www .economist.com/by-invitation/2022/07/14/the-right-wing-furore-over-critical -race-theory-is-manufactured-says-charles-siler.

67 **We weren't even talking about** "Trends in Number of COVID-19 Cases and Deaths in the US Reported to CDC, by State/Territory," Virginia: Nov. 3, 2020–Nov. 2, 2021 (10,375 deaths), COVID Data Tracker, U.S. Centers for Disease Control and Prevention, accessed Jun. 16, 2023, covid.cdc.gov/ covid-data-tracker/#trends_totaldeaths.

67 **Glenn Youngkin beat Terry McAuliffe** "Virginia Governor General Election: November 2, 2021," Virginia Department of Elections, accessed Jun. 16, 2023, historical.elections.virginia.gov/elections/view/147466/.

67 **The next day Fox News** Andrew Mark Miller, "Critical Race Theory Top Factor for 25% of Virginia Voters, While 72% Called It Important: Fox Analysis," Fox News, Nov. 3, 2021, www.foxnews.com/politics/critical-race-theory -virginia-top-factor-important-fox-analysis.

67 **PEN America examined twenty-four** "Educational Gag Orders: Legislative Restrictions on the Freedom to Read, Learn, and Teach," PEN America, 2021, pen.org/wp-content/uploads/2022/02/PEN_EducationalGagOrders _01-18-22-compressed.pdf.

68 **Chris Rufo admitted on Twitter** Christopher F. Rufo (@realchrisrufo), Twitter, March 15, 2021, 1:17 P.M., twitter.com/realchrisrufo/status/13715410445 92996352.

68 **Chris Rufo had also just claimed** Graham Colton, "Disney Injecting Queerness into Children's Programming: Chris Rufo," Fox News, Mar. 30, 2022, www .foxnews.com/media/disney-injecting-queerness-childrens-programming -chris-rufo.

68 **"Marketing sneakers or those goofy mouse"** "Ingraham: They're Going After the Kids," YouTube video, posted by Fox News, Apr. 7, 2022, www .youtube.com/watch?v=w5I3xXKJrFc.

69 **A few months earlier** "California Teachers Recruit Students to Gay Club

Behind Parents' Backs," YouTube video, posted by Fox News, Dec. 2, 2021, www.youtube.com/watch?v=egA2kEaBw9I.

69 **"The Democrat Party has wholly embraced"** Jim Banks, "Memo: Lean into the Culture War," Republican Study Committee, via *Politico*, Jun. 24, 2021, www.politico.com/f/?id=0000017a-3f65-d283-a3fb-bf6f99470000.

Chapter 5: This or That?

74 **Achieving that also required** Judicial Watch, "Judicial Watch Statement on Supreme Court Ruling Protecting Obama 'DACA' Amnesty Program," press release, Jun. 18, 2020, www.judicialwatch.org/daca-ruling/; Judicial Watch, "Judicial Activist Nominated to High Court," press release, Feb. 25, 2022, www.judicialwatch.org/judicial-activist-nominated-to-high-court/.

76 **In 2022, the Pew Research Center** "As Partisan Hostility Grows, Signs of Frustration with the Two-Party System," Pew Research Center, Aug. 9, 2022, 31, www.pewresearch.org/politics/wp-content/uploads/sites/4/2022/08/PP_2022.09.08_partisan-hostility_REPORT.pdf.

77 **In 1992, the independent presidential candidate** 1992 Presidential Election Results, American Presidency Project, University of California, Santa Barbara, accessed Jun. 16, 2023, www.presidency.ucsb.edu/statistics/elections/1992.

77 **More than 97,000 of those votes** 2000 Presidential Election Results, American Presidency Project, University of California, Santa Barbara, accessed Jun. 16, 2023, www.presidency.ucsb.edu/statistics/elections/2000.

78 **No Labels is a secretly funded** "No Labels Secures Ballot Access in Oregon for 'Unity Ticket,'" Associated Press, March 10, 2023, apnews.com/article/no-labels-party-oregon-ballot-access-2d71418a75277277e7e21526b8335a5e.

78 **No Labels says it wants** "Insurance Policy 2024," No Labels, accessed Jun. 16, 2023, 2024.nolabels.org/.

78 **"No Labels is committed to fielding"** "The No Labels Third-Party Bid: A Plan That Will Re-elect Trump," Third Way, Mar. 7, 2023, www.thirdway.org/memo/the-no-labels-third-party-bid-a-plan-that-will-re-elect-trump.

80 **the Servicemen's Readjustment Act** "75 Years of the GI Bill: How Transformative It's Been," U.S. Department of Defense, Jan. 9, 2019, www.defense.gov/News/Feature-Stories/story/Article/1727086/75-years-of-the-gi-bill-how-transformative-its-been/.

81 **While some of these accomplishments** Josie Rodberg, "America Used to Agree on Public Funding for Family Planning. What Happened?," *Slate*, Feb. 22, 2011, slate.com/human-interest/2011/02/america-used-to-agree-on-public-funding-for-family-planning-what-happened.html.

82 **A conservative historian** Kevin Roberts, "Commentary: Tomorrow's Heritage," Heritage Foundation, Dec. 3, 2021, www.heritage.org/conservatism/commentary/tomorrows-heritage.

82 **The mission of Heritage** Heritage Foundation, "About Heritage," accessed Jun. 16, 2023, www.heritage.org/about-heritage/mission.

83 **When *The New York Times* wrote** Philip M. Boffey, "Heritage Foundation:

Success in Obscurity," *The New York Times,* Nov. 17, 1985, www.nytimes .com/1985/11/17/us/heritage-foundation-success-in-obscurity.html.

83 **In 1980, just ten days** Kathy Sawyer, "Heritage Foundation Gives Reagan Passing Grade," *The Washington Post,* Nov. 22, 1981, www.washingtonpost .com/archive/politics/1981/11/22/heritage-foundation-gives-reagan-passing -grade/6ddd166c-ef59-4f2d-b669-372f19bc4d6b/.

83 **Heritage estimates it got most** Kai Ryssdal, "From Reagan to Trump: How the Heritage Foundation Has Influenced Policy," *Marketplace,* May 3, 2017, www.marketplace.org/2017/05/03/economy/from-reagan-to-trump-how -heritage-foundation-influenced-policy/.

83 **After Reagan's first year** Phil Gailey, "Heritage Foundation Disappointed by Reagan," *The New York Times,* Nov. 22, 1981, www.nytimes.com/1981/11/ 22/us/heritage-foundation-disappointed-by-reagan.html.

84 **Public records indicate Heritage** Heritage Foundation, 2021 IRS Form 990 Financial Disclosure Statement, accessed Jun. 16, 2023, pdf.guidestar.org/ PDF_Images/2021/237/327/2021-237327730-202231649349300228-9.pdf.

84 **It has published multiple editions** Heritage Foundation, "Mandate 2020," accessed Jun. 16, 2023, www.heritage.org/mandate-2020.

84 **The project, Roberts added** Kevin Roberts, "Letter from the President," in 2022 Annual Report, Heritage Foundation, 6, thf_media.s3.amazonaws .com/2022/Annual_Report.pdf.

85 **ALEC describes itself** American Legislative Exchange Council, "About ALEC," accessed Jun. 16, 2023, alec.org/about/.

85 **The progressive Center for Media** Center for Media and Democracy, "What Is ALEC?," ALECexposed.org, accessed Jun. 16, 2023, www.alecexposed .org/wiki/What_is_ALEC%3F.

86 **ALEC, which counts the NRA** Center for Media and Democracy, "ALEC Castle Doctrine," ALECexposed.org, accessed Jun. 16, 2023, www.alecexposed .org/wiki/ALEC_Castle_Doctrine.

86 **The language matched almost word** Center for Media and Democracy, Side-by-side comparison of Wisconsin's 2015 "Right to Work" bill and ALEC's model bill, ALECexposed.org, accessed Jun. 16, 2023, www.prwatch.org/ files/wi_rtw.pdf.

86 **Almost all of ALEC's revenue** American Legislative Exchange Council, 2021 IRS Form 990 Financial Disclosure Statement, accessed Jun. 16, 2023, pdf .guidestar.org/PDF_Images/2021/520/140/2021-520140979-202213159349 9302316-9.pdf; American Legislative Exchange Council, "Legislative Membership," accessed Jun. 16, 2023, alec.org/membership-type/legislative -membership/.

86 **No, 98 percent of its funding** Brendan Greeley and Alison Fitzgerald, "Psst . . . Wanna Buy a Law?," Bloomberg, Dec. 1, 2011, www.bloomberg .com/news/articles/2011-12-01/pssst-dot-wanna-buy-a-law; American Legislative Exchange Council, "Private Sector Membership," accessed Jun. 16, 2023, alec.org/membership-type/private-sector-membership/.

87 **ALEC's Mad Libs–style** American Legislative Exchange Council, "A Public Safety Resolution Calling On the [Insert Jurisdiction] to Define [Insert Juris-

diction] as a Rule of Law Community," Sept. 9, 2017, alec.org/model-policy/
a-public-safety-resolution-calling-on-the-insert-jurisdiction-to-define-insert
-jurisdiction-as-a-rule-of-law-community/.

87 **Nationalizing politics can look like this** Senator Marco Rubio, "Rubio,
Banks Introduce Bill to Regulate Transgender Service in U.S. Military,"
press release, Feb. 16, 2023, www.rubio.senate.gov/public/index.cfm/
2023/2/rubio-banks-introduce-bill-to-regulate-transgender-service-in-u-s
-military.

88 **The idea behind REDMAP** David Daley, "Inside the Republican Plot for
Permanent Minority Rule," *The New Republic,* Oct. 15, 2020, newrepublic
.com/article/159755/republican-voter-suppression-2020-election.

89 **The Democrats, by the way** Dave Daley, "How Democrats Gerrymandered
Their Way to Victory in Maryland," *The Atlantic,* Jun. 25, 2017, www
.theatlantic.com/politics/archive/2017/06/how-deep-blue-maryland-shows
-redistricting-is-broken/531492/.

89 **In fact, as *The New Republic*** Daley, "Inside the Republican Plot for Permanent Minority Rule."

90 **At least one data firm** Jon Keegan, "How Political Campaigns Use Your
Phone's Location to Target You," Markup, Nov. 8, 2022, themarkup.org/
privacy/2022/11/08/how-political-campaigns-use-your-phones-location-to
-target-you.

90 **Several years later, as chairman** Steve Friess, "The GOP's Digital Deficit,"
Politico, Jan. 27, 2013, www.politico.com/story/2013/01/gop-digital-divide
-may-take-years-to-bridge-086761.

90 **In 2010, VAN merged** NGP VAN, "Voter Activation Network and NGP Software to Merge," press release, Nov. 4, 2010, www.prnewswire.com/news
-releases/voter-activation-network-and-ngp-software-to-merge-106718013
.html.

90 **The end product** Mike Allen and Kenneth P. Vogel, "Inside the Koch Data
Mine," *Politico,* Dec. 8, 2014, www.politico.com/story/2014/12/koch-brothers
-rnc-113359; "Cambridge Analytica Is Not Alone: i360 and Data Trust Disastrous for Democracy," YouTube video, posted by Real News Network,
Mar. 29, 2018, www.youtube.com/watch?v=aoouFIuF_HQ.

91 **i360 boasts that it offers** "The Database: Individual-Centric Data Ware-
house," i360, accessed Jun. 16, 2023, Wayback Machine, web.archive.org/
web/20220901050219/https://www.i-360.com/the-database/.

91 **As *Politico* reported in 2014** Allen and Vogel, "Inside the Koch Data Mine."

91 **Today i360 assigns scores** Natasha Singer, "Why Am I Seeing That Political
Ad? Check Your Trump Resistance Score," *The New York Times,* Oct. 23,
2022, www.nytimes.com/2022/10/23/technology/voter-targeting-trump-score
.html.

91 **It also scores voters** "Model Definitions," i360, accessed Jun. 16, 2023, Wayback Machine, web.archive.org/web/20220707020401/https://www.i-360
.com/i360-models/.

91 **According to *The Washington Post*** Matea Gold, "Koch Network Strikes New
Deal to Share Voter Data with RNC-Aligned Firm," *The Washington Post,*

July 29, 2015, www.washingtonpost.com/news/post-politics/wp/2015/07/ 29/koch-network-strikes-new-deal-to-share-voter-data-with-rnc-aligned -firm/.

92 **In 2016 the Republicans' superior** David Jackson, "Trump Outsources Voter Turnout Operation to Republican Party," *USA Today*, Sept. 21, 2016, www.usatoday.com/story/news/politics/elections/2016/2016/09/21/trump -outsources-voter-turnout-operation-republican-party/90772710/.

93 **Their funding goes toward** Heritage Foundation, 2021 IRS Form 990 Financial Disclosure Statement.

Chapter 6: All Politics Are National

95 **"If they can do it"** House Judiciary GOP (@JudiciaryGOP), Twitter, Aug. 8, 2022, 5:55 P.M., twitter.com/JudiciaryGOP/status/1556791214875328515.

95 **"The real target of this investigation"** "Laura Ingraham: The Real Target of This Investigation Is You," YouTube video, posted by Fox News, Aug. 8, 2022, youtu.be/TaIr-dSPCjo?t=55.

96 **"If they can target a former"** "Mark Levin Audio Rewind—8/8/22," *The Mark Levin Show*, Aug. 8, 2022, interview with Senator Tim Scott, podcast, 1:30:58, open.spotify.com/episode/5g4ke4tOkwuyD2xp33UVMs.

96 **"It was Trump today"** Lauren Boebert (@laurenboebert), Twitter, Aug. 8, 2022, 9:32 P.M., twitter.com/laurenboebert/status/1556845893332205569.

96 **"If they think they can treat"** Heritage Foundation, "Heritage President on Mar-a-Lago Raid: 'Imagine What They Think They Can Do to the Average American,'" press release, Aug. 9, 2022, www.heritage.org/press/ heritage-president-mar-lago-raid-imagine-what-they-think-they-can-do-the -average-american.

96 **"If the Democrat establishment"** Ronna McDaniel, "Opinion: Trump Targeted by Biden Administration, and They Can Do It to You, Too," Fox News, Aug. 10, 2022, www.foxnews.com/opinion/trump-targeted-biden-administration-you.

96 **"I know Tennesseeans are"** "Senator Blackburn on FBI Raid of Trump's Home," YouTube video, posted by Fox Business, Aug. 12, 2022, youtube/ AkkfLvdxZxU?t=377.

98 **In March 2023** Donald J. Trump (@realDonaldTrump), Truth Social, March 16, 2023, 4:27 P.M., truthsocial.com/@realDonaldTrump/posts/110 035313831561994.

98 **"It's not even about Donald Trump"** Vivek Ramaswamy (@VivekGRamaswamy), Twitter, March 30, 2023, 6:46 P.M., twitter.com/VivekGRamaswamy/ status/1641602755071471617.

99 **In 2018, researchers from Johns Hopkins** Johns Hopkins University, "Americans Don't Know Much About State Government, Survey Finds," press release, Dec. 14, 2018, hub.jhu.edu/2018/12/14/americans-dont -understand-state-government/.

99 **And Portland State University** Portland State University, "Who Votes for Mayor?," 2016, www.whovotesformayor.org/.

99 **In the fall of 2010** "The List: RNC's 'Fire Pelosi' Bus Tour," *Politico*, Sept. 16,

2010, Wayback Machine, web.archive.org/web/20100921175819/http://
www.politico.com/click/stories/1009/rncs_fire_pelosi_bus_tour.html.

100 **In those midterms, Republicans not only** Tim Storey, "GOP Makes Historic
State Legislative Gains in 2010," Rasmussen Reports, Dec. 10, 2010, www
.rasmussenreports.com/public_content/political_commentary/commentary
_by_tim_storey/gop_makes_historic_state_legislative_gains_in_2010.

100 **Republicans also replaced or unseated** "Governor Map—Election 2010,"
The New York Times, accessed Jun. 16, 2023, www.nytimes.com/elections/
2010/results/governor.html.

102 **"For there to be relief"** George Lakoff, *The All New "Don't Think of an Elephant!"* (White River Junction, Vt.: Chelsea Green Publishing, 2014),
chap. 1, Kindle.

103 **Luntz helped Newt Gingrich** Frank Luntz, *Words That Work: It's Not What
You Say, It's What People Hear* (New York: Hachette, 2007).

103 **Frank Luntz regularly offers** Frank Luntz, "The New American Lexicon,"
Luntz Research Companies, 2005, 132.

103 **His messaging guidance** Luntz, *Words That Work.*

103 **And in a leaked copy** Luntz, "New American Lexicon," 16, 17.

104 **Confirmation bias explains why** CNN, Topline Results of 2024 Presidential
Election Survey of 1,045 Republicans and Republican-Leaning Independent
Voters, Conducted March 8–12, 2023, by SSRS, 12, accessed Jun. 16, 2023,
www.documentcloud.org/documents/23706881-cnn-poll-most-republicans
-care-more-about-picking-a-2024-gop-nominee-who-agrees-with-them-on
-issues-than-one-who-can-beat-biden.

106 **"I will bring back jobs"** "Trump and Clinton Debate Their Economic Policies," YouTube video, posted by *PBS NewsHour,* Sept. 26, 2016, youtube/
EnfJVqSr_wM?t=40.

107 **The *Globe's* analysis** Matt Viser, "For Presidential Hopefuls, Simpler Language
Resonates," *Boston Globe,* Oct. 20, 2015, www.bostonglobe.com/news/politics/
2015/10/20/donald-trump-and-ben-carson-speak-grade-school-level-that
-today-voters-can-quickly-grasp/LUCBY6uwQAxiLvvXbVTSUN/story.html.

107 **In fact, according to data** Emily Schmidt, "Reading the Numbers: 130 Million American Adults Have Low Literacy Skills, but Funding Differs Drasti-
cally by State," APM Research Lab, Mar. 16, 2022, www.apmresearchlab
.org/10x-adult-literacy.

110 **Trump won Texas by more** Texas Secretary of State, "Texas Election Results,
2020," Nov. 3, 2020, results.texas-election.com/races.

110 **In the end, the Republican audit** Texas Secretary of State John B. Scott, "Texas
Secretary of State Releases Phase 1 Progress Report on Full Forensic Audit of
2020 General Election," press release, Dec. 31, 2021, www.sos.state.tx.us/
about/newsreleases/2021/123121.shtml; Alexa Ura and Allyson Waller, "First
Part of Texas' 2020 Election Audit Reveals Few Issues, Echoes Findings from
Review Processes Already in Place," *Texas Tribune,* Dec. 31, 2021, www
.texastribune.org/2021/12/31/secretary-state-texas-election-audit/.

110 **Then, as sore winners** Texas Republican Party, "Report of the Permanent 2022
Platform & Resolutions Committee," 2022, 40, texasgop.org/wp-content/

uploads/2022/06/6-Permanent-Platform-Committee-FINAL-REPORT-6-16 -2022.pdf.

111 **"We do this for opportunity"** "Mandela Barnes for Senate Announcement," YouTube video, posted by Mandela Barnes for Senate, Aug. 4, 2021, youtube/ watch?v=f8lqzF2lAbw.

112 **"Women's lives and women's health"** "Ron Johnson, Mandela Barnes Face Off in Live U.S. Senate Debate," YouTube video, posted by TMJ4 News, Oct. 13, 2022, www.youtube.com/watch?v=6_S9CVLylOo&t=3385s.

112 **Public polling suggested** Eli Yokley, "Ron Johnson Is Unpopular in Wisconsin. Can He Win Anyway?," Morning Consult, Jan. 25, 2022, morningconsult.com/2022/01/25/ron-johnson-unpopular-in-wisconsin-can -he-win-anyway/.

112 **"Mandela Barnes coddles criminals"** "One for the Team," YouTube video, posted by Ron Johnson, Oct. 3, 2022, www.youtube.com/watch?v=qIrJe TmPAeg.

112 **The short ad featured** "SLF: 'Crime' 6s—WI," YouTube video, posted by Senate Leadership Fund, Sept. 6, 2022, www.youtube.com/watch?v=GIF USIuF3yk.

112 **A longer ad** "SLF: 'Feel Safe' 30s—WI," YouTube video, posted by Senate Leadership Fund, Sept. 13, 2022, www.youtube.com/watch?v=laXfcYxeZgE.

113 **"Wisconsin voters ought to be asking"** "Ron Johnson, Mandela Barnes Face Off in Live U.S. Senate Debate."

113 **The Barnes campaign instead tried to paint** "Taxes," YouTube video, posted by Mandela Barnes, Oct. 28, 2022, www.youtube.com/watch?v=_OO JnDYP6bk; "Ron Johnson: Scary Things," YouTube video, posted by Mandela Barnes, Nov. 15, 2022, www.youtube.com/watch?v=EZ1VLPcGNe4.

113 **Ron Johnson won his 2022** Wisconsin Elections Commission, "Canvass Results for 2022 General Election," Nov. 8, 2022, elections.wi.gov/sites/ default/files/documents/Statewide%20Summary%20Results_1.pdf.

114 **As the president of the Minneapolis** Jenna Wortham, "How a New Wave of Black Activists Changed the Conversation," *The New York Times Magazine*, Aug. 25, 2020, www.nytimes.com/2020/08/25/magazine/black-visions -collective.html.

115 **Bullock pioneered a successful** "The Honorable Steve Bullock," Jobs for America's Graduates (biography), accessed Jun. 16, 2023, jag.org/board -member-steve-bullock/.

115 **He repeatedly stated his opposition** "Steve Bullock: 2020 General Election Q&A," Montana Public Radio, Oct. 9, 2020, www.mtpr.org/candidate -questionnaires/2020-10-09/steve-bullock-2020-general-election-q-a.

115 **"Steve Bullock refuses to stand"** "Sheriff Shane," YouTube video, posted by Steve Daines for Montana, Sept. 8, 2020, www.youtube.com/watch?v=0 ECs4ecLIXI.

116 **Daines beat Bullock** Montana Secretary of State, "2020 Statewide General Election Canvass," Nov. 3, 2020, 3, sosmt.gov/wp-content/uploads/State _Canvass_Report.pdf.

116 **In 2022, well after House Speaker** David Winston, "'Defund the Police'

Still Haunts Democrats," *Roll Call*, Apr. 27, 2022, rollcall.com/2022/04/27/ defund-the-police-still-haunts-democrats/.

116 **"Woke leaders blame the police"** "Crime," YouTube video, posted by John Kennedy, Sept. 30, 2022, www.youtube.com/watch?v=Bo7KiU_8WiY.

117 **"We have a messaging problem"** Alex Wagner, "Newsom Knocks Democrats for Poor Messaging on Successes Versus Republicans," *Alex Wagner Tonight*, MSNBC, Sept. 27, 2022, www.msnbc.com/alex-wagner-tonight/ watch/newsom-knocks-democrats-for-poor-messaging-on-successes-versus -republicans-149409861550.

Chapter 7: Controlling the Narrative

118 **With a straight face** "Full Comer: 'We're Going to Have to Have Spending Cuts' in New Congress," YouTube video, posted by NBC News, Jan. 8, 2023, youtu.be/6mSzgoNaoYI?t=374.

119 **Geraghty had halfheartedly opined** Jim Geraghty, "Opinion: Millions Flowed to Biden Family Members. Don't Pretend It Doesn't Matter," *The Washington Post*, May 18, 2023, www.washingtonpost.com/opinions/2023/05/18/ foreign-payments-to-biden-family-members/.

119 **On May 22, 2023** "This Is One of the Most 'Serious Accusations' Against a Politician in History: Comer," YouTube video, posted by Fox News, May 22, 2023, youtu.be/F-ILzGgNCEE?t=441.

119 **"They are admitting through their own"** Katherine Doyle, "White House Memo Says GOP Was Caught 'Telling the Truth' on Motive for Hunter Biden Probe," NBC News, May 24, 2023, www.nbcnews.com/politics/white -house/white-house-memo-says-gop-telling-truth-investigation-motives-rcna 86078.

121 **"10 years ago Islamic"** Ted Cruz (@tedcruz), Twitter, Sept. 11, 2022, 7:01 A.M., twitter.com/tedcruz/status/1568947777371275264.

122 **A month after the attack** Elise Labott, "Clinton: 'I'm Responsible for Diplomats' Security,'" CNN, Oct. 16, 2012, www.cnn.com/2012/10/15/us/clinton -benghazi/index.html.

122 **Instead, it found that** Joseph I. Lieberman and Susan M. Collins, "Flashing Red: A Special Report on the Terrorist Attack at Benghazi," U.S. Senate Committee on Homeland Security and Governmental Affairs, Dec. 30, 2012, 5, permanent.fdlp.gov/gpo33519/Flashing%20Red-HSGAC%20Special %20Report%20final.pdf.

122 **In the twenty months following** Rob Savillo and Hannah Groch-Begley, "Report: Fox's Benghazi Obsession by the Numbers," Media Matters for America, Sept. 9, 2014, www.mediamatters.org/sean-hannity/report-foxs -benghazi-obsession-numbers.

122 **With control of the House** U.S. House of Representatives, Roll Call Vote No. 209, Resolution Establishing the Select Committee on the Events Surrounding the 2012 Terrorist Attack in Benghazi, May 8, 2014, clerk.house .gov/evs/2014/roll209.xml.

123 **Just a few months after** HuffPost Pollster, "Poll Chart: Hillary Clinton Fa-

vorability Rating," aggregated data compiled by *HuffPost*, Dec. 2, 2012, Way-back Machine, https://web.archive.org/web/20151211231755/http://elections.huffingtonpost.com/pollster/hillary-clinton-favorable-rating.

124 **In December 1998** Mark Gillespie, "Hillary Clinton Remains Polarizing Figure," Gallup News Service, Jun. 6, 2003, news.gallup.com/poll/8572/hillary-clinton-remains-polarizing-figure.aspx.

124 **After First Lady Clinton pitched** Edwin Feulner, "Guest Column: Deciding Just What Will Work," *Germantown News*, Jun. 2, 1994, newspapers.com.

124 **A few days after** HuffPost Pollster, Sept. 22, 2014.

124 **On April 13, 2015** HuffPost Pollster, Apr. 13, 2015.

124 **Shortly after she appeared** HuffPost Pollster, Oct. 25, 2015.

124 **By Election Day 2016** HuffPost Pollster, "Poll Chart: Hillary Clinton Favorability Rating," aggregated data compiled by *HuffPost*, Nov. 8, 2016, Wayback Machine, https://web.archive.org/web/20161108191302/http://elections.huffingtonpost.com/pollster/hillary-clinton-favorable-rating.

125 **After all, the purpose of the Select** Mary Troyan, "House Benghazi Committee Files Final Report and Shuts Down," *USA Today*, Dec. 12, 2016, www.usatoday.com/story/news/politics/2016/12/12/house-benghazi-committee-files-final-report-and-shuts-down/95336692/.

125 **"Everybody thought Hillary Clinton"** "Rep. Kevin McCarthy How He Would Differ from John Boehner," YouTube video, posted by Fox News, Sept. 29, 2015, youtu.be/Qq7nIIvRFAE?t=262.

126 *The Washington Post* **counted** Glenn Kessler, Salvador Rizzo, and Meg Kelly, "Trump's False or Misleading Claims Total 30,573 over 4 Years," *The Washington Post*, Jan. 24, 2021, www.washingtonpost.com/politics/2021/01/24/trumps-false-or-misleading-claims-total-30573-over-four-years.

126 **But when Quinnipiac University** Quinnipiac University, "Biden Runs Better Than Clinton Against Top Republicans, Quinnipiac University National Poll Finds," press release and top-line results, Aug. 27, 2015, 9, poll.qu.edu/images/polling/us/us08272015_Ueg38d.pdf.

128 **ProPublica first reported** Joshua Kaplan, Justin Elliott, and Alex Mierjeski, "Clarence Thomas and the Billionaire," ProPublica, April 6, 2023, www.propublica.org/article/clarence-thomas-scotus-undisclosed-luxury-travel-gifts-crow.

128 **Then came a story** Justin Elliott, Joshua Kaplan, and Alex Mierjeski, "Billionaire Harlan Crow Bought Property from Clarence Thomas. The Justice Didn't Disclose the Deal," ProPublica, Apr. 13, 2023, www.propublica.org/article/clarence-thomas-harlan-crow-real-estate-scotus.

128 **Then CNN reported** Ariane de Vogue, "Clarence Thomas to Amend Financial Disclosure Forms to Reflect Sale to GOP Megadonor," CNN, April 17, 2023, www.cnn.com/2023/04/17/politics/clarence-thomas-amend-disclosure-gop-megadonor/index.html.

128 **Senator Lindsey Graham** U.S. Senate Committee on the Judiciary, "Full Committee Hearing: Supreme Court Ethics Reform," video, 21:55, May 2, 2023, www.senate.gov/isvp/?auto_play=false&comm=judiciary&filename

=judiciary050223&poster=https://www.judiciary.senate.gov/assets/images/ video-poster.png&stt=.

128 **They did nothing to make** Tommy Cummings, "Inside Harlan Crow's 'Garden of Evil' and His Collection from Washington to Monet," *Dallas Morning News*, Apr. 11, 2023, www.dallasnews.com/arts-entertainment/2023/ 04/11/inside-harlan-crows-garden-of-evil-and-his-collection-of-artifacts -and-books/.

128 **And even though they were** *Dobbs v. Jackson Women's Health Organization,* 597 U.S. ___ (2022) (Thomas, C., concurring), www.supremecourt.gov/ opinions/21pdf/19-1392_6j37.pdf.

Chapter 8: Stronger Messaging in Seven Steps

138 **"Freedom? It's under attack"** Newsom for California—Governor 2022, "Gavin Newsom: 'Florida Freedom' | Campaign Ad 2022," video, *The Washington Post*, Jul. 5, 2022, www.washingtonpost.com/video/elections/gavin -newsom-florida-freedom-campaign-ad-2022/2022/07/05/9e52917a-3374 -4090-bcc6-5634fc3aae82_video.html.

139 **"It has frustrated me"** Ronald Brownstein, "The Glaring Contradiction of Republicans' Rhetoric of Freedom," *The Atlantic*, Jul. 8, 2022, www .theatlantic.com/politics/archive/2022/07/democrats-republicans-rhetoric -freedom-rollback/661519/.

140 *Politico* **published a leaked draft** Josh Gerstein and Alexander Ward, "Supreme Court Has Voted to Overturn Abortion Rights, Draft Opinion Shows," *Politico*, May 2, 2022, www.politico.com/news/2022/05/02/ supreme-court-abortion-draft-opinion-00029473.

140 **The** *following day,* **the White House** Joseph R. Biden, "Statement by President Joe Biden," press release, White House, May 3, 2022, www.whitehouse.gov/ briefing-room/statements-releases/2022/05/03/statement-by-president-joe -biden-4/.

140 **The Democratic National Committee** Democratic National Committee, "DNC on Reporting That SCOTUS Plans to Overturn Roe v. Wade," press release, May 3, 2022, democrats.org/news/dnc-on-reporting-that-scotus-plans -to-overturn-roe-v-wade/.

141 **"Where the hell is my party?"** "Gov. Gavin Newsom Discusses California's Commitment to Safeguarding Reproductive Freedom," YouTube video, posted by FOX 11 Los Angeles, May 4, 2022, www.youtube.com/watch?v =rBPWxWE7IAY.

141 **Justices "should reconsider"** *Dobbs v. Jackson Women's Health Organization,* 597 U.S. ___ (2022) (Thomas, J., concurring).

142 **"One hundred percent"** "McConnell: '100 Percent of Our Focus Is on Stopping This New Administration' | NBC News," YouTube video, posted by NBC News, May 6, 2021, www.youtube.com/watch?v=LURV7yqTo3w.

142 **The Senate minority leader's comment** "Mitch McConnell: Top Priority, Make Obama a One Term President," YouTube video, posted by Political-Hay, Dec. 7, 2010, www.youtube.com/watch?v=W-A09a_gHJc.

142 **"I hope for Democrat gridlock"** "Sen. Johnson Rips Democrats for 'Living in a Fantasy World,'" YouTube video, posted by Fox News, Oct. 17, 2021, youtu.be/sCrek-sC38s?t=343.

143 **"If you're on Medicare"** Amy Klobuchar (@amyklobuchar), Twitter, Nov. 28, 2022, 11:41 A.M., twitter.com/amyklobuchar/status/1597299536421998598.

143 **After Congress passed** Governor Jared Polis, "Governor Polis, Legislators Unveil American Rescue Plan State Funds Package to Power Colorado Comeback," press release, May 24, 2021, www.colorado.gov/governor/ news/5286-governor-polis-legislators-unveil-american-rescue-plan-state-funds -package-power-colorado.

144 **Do you know why Congress** Gallup News Service, "Gallup Poll Social Series: Crime," Final Topline Results, Oct. 3–20, 2022, accessed Jun. 16, 2023, news.gallup.com/file/poll/405275/221121Guns.pdf.

145 **On Election Day 2022** Nebraska Secretary of State, "Official Results: General Election—November 8, 2022," Initiative Measure 433, accessed Jun. 16, 2023, electionresults.nebraska.gov/resultsSW.aspx?text=Race&type=PA&map=CTY; Nebraska Secretary of State, "Informational Pamphlet Initiative Measure Nos. 432 & 433, Appearing on the 2022 General Election Ballot," 6, accessed Jun. 16, 2023, sos.nebraska.gov/sites/sos.nebraska.gov/files/doc/elections/ 2022/Pamphlet%20for%20Initiatives%20432%20%26%20433.pdf.

145 **On the same day** Nebraska Secretary of State, "Official Results: General Election—November 8, 2022," for Governor and Lt. Governor, accessed Jun. 16, 2023, electionresults.nebraska.gov/resultsSW.aspx?text=Race&type =SW&map=CTY; Rob McCartney, "Jim Pillen Shares Gubernatorial Plan for Nebraska," KETV-TV, Oct. 25, 2022, www.ketv.com/article/nebraska -republican-jim-pillen-gubernatorial-plans/41771442.

146 **Democrats passed the Elementary** Alia Wong and Jennifer Borresen, "Time-line: A Look at the Progression of Education Policy in US Politics," *USA Today*, Oct. 19, 2022, www.usatoday.com/in-depth/graphics/2022/10/20/ education-policy-timeline-democrats-republicans-election/10475166002/.

146 **So it was no surprise** Gallup News Service, "June Wave 1," Final Topline Results, June 7–11, 2017, 4, accessed Jun. 16, 2023, www.gallup.com/file/ poll/212810/170626PartyIssues.pdf.

146 **Among a little more than** *Washington Post*–ABC News Poll, Topline Results (Abt Associates), Nov. 7–10, 2021, 10, accessed Jun. 16, 2023, context-cdn .washingtonpost.com/notes/prod/default/documents/417a5111-a75e-4efb -b100-f1f10f164fb1/note/6fea9024-8be9-4506-837a-fa425b061393.#page=1.

147 **This survey, from a pro-charter** Democrats for Education Reform, "House Battleground Poll," Topline Results, Education Reform Now Advocacy, Jun. 14–21, 2022, 7, accessed Jun. 16, 2023, dfer.org/wp-content/uploads/ 2022/07/Baseline-Nationwide-BG-Education-Summer-2022-.pdf.

147 **The survey's +/– 3.5 percent** Lauren Camera, "Democrats Cede 'Party of Education' Label to GOP: Poll," *U.S. News & World Report*, Jul. 20, 2022, www.usnews.com/news/education-news/articles/2022-07-20/democrats -cede-party-of-education-label-to-gop-poll.

147 **And from *USA Today*** Alia Wong, "The GOP Is Strengthening Its Grip on

Education. Parents Say Democrats Are to Blame," *USA Today*, Oct. 27, 2022, www.usatoday.com/in-depth/news/education/2022/10/27/gop-strengthens -grip-education-america-democrats-scramble/8136243001/.

147 **One of the organizations** Education Reform Now Advocacy, "New Polling: Reclaiming Education as Democratic Stronghold," Jul. 13, 2022, dfer.org/ wp-content/uploads/2022/07/Polling-Memo-FINAL.pdf.

147 **No, the Republican Party's** Republican National Committee, "Republican Platform 2016," 34, accessed Jun. 16, 2023, prod-cdn-static.gop.com/media/ documents/DRAFT_12_FINAL%5B1%5D-ben_1468872234.pdf.

148 **The National Bureau of Economic** Alan S. Blinder and Mark W. Watson, "Presidents and the U.S. Economy: An Econometric Exploration," National Bureau of Economic Research, Jul. 2014, www.nber.org/system/files/ working_papers/w20324/w20324.pdf.

148 **Nonetheless, the Republicans' pro-business** Zach Schonfeld, "Republicans Hold 14-Point Advantage on Which Party Would Do Better Job on Economy: Poll," *The Hill*, Oct. 23, 2022, thehill.com/homenews/campaign/3700047 -republicans-hold-14-point-advantage-on-which-party-would-do-better-job -on-economy-poll/.

148 **This bonkers idea** David Wessel, "What We Learned from Reagan's Tax Cuts," Brookings Institution, Dec. 8, 2017, www.brookings.edu/blog/up -front/2017/12/08/what-we-learned-from-reagans-tax-cuts/.

148 **Republicans have caused nine** David Kelly, "Every Republican President over the Last 100 Years Has Had a Recession," Medium, March 16, 2020, medium.com/@davidkellyuph/every-republican-president-over-the-last-100 -years-has-had-a-recession-baa20aa7b107.

148 **In March 2022** Nick Buffie, "Debunking Sen. Rick Scott's Claims About Taxpaying Americans," Center for American Progress Action, Mar. 28, 2022, www.americanprogressaction.org/article/debunking-sen-rick-scotts -claims-about-taxpaying-americans/.

148 **Senator Rick Scott** "Rick Scott," estimated net worth of $259,663,681 in 2018, Open Secrets, accessed Jun. 16, 2023, www.opensecrets.org/ personal-finances/rick-scott/net-worth?cid=N00043290&year=2022; Zoë Richards, "Sen. Rick Scott Removes Tax Increase Proposal from Agenda After GOP Backlash," NBC News, Jun. 9, 2022, www.nbcnews.com/ politics/elections/sen-rick-scott-removes-tax-increase-proposal-agenda-gop -backlash-rcna32652.

150 **"If the maniacs"** Ronny Jackson (@RonnyJacksonTX), Twitter, Jan. 10, 2023, 8:51 A.M., twitter.com/ronnyjacksontx/status/1612839703018934274.

150 **"As a nation, we have to ask"** "Remarks by President Biden on the School Shooting in Uvalde, Texas," transcript, White House, May 24, 2022, www .whitehouse.gov/briefing-room/speeches-remarks/2022/05/24/remarks-by -president-biden-on-the-school-shooting-in-uvalde-texas/.

151 **Researchers showed volunteers** Lynn Hasher, David Goldstein, and Thomas Toppino, "Frequency and the Conference of Referential Validity," *Journal of Verbal Learning and Verbal Behavior* 16 (1977): 107–12, Wayback Machine, web.archive.org/web/20160515062305/http://www.psych.utoronto.ca/users/

hasher/PDF/Frequency%20and%20the%20conference%20Hasher%20et
%20al%201977.pdf.

152 **Donald Trump tweeted those two words** Donald Trump, "Witch Hunt,"
Trump Twitter Archive, accessed Jun. 16, 2023, www.thetrumparchive.com/
?searchbox=%22witch+hunt%22.

152 **Even long after Trump** Bradford Betz, "Trump Blasts 'Witch Hunt' FBI
Raid on Mar-a-Lago in Donation Email," Fox News, Aug. 9, 2022, www
.foxnews.com/politics/trump-blasts-witch-hunt-fbi-raid-mar-lago-donation
-email.

152 **A few weeks later** Donald J. Trump (@realDonaldTrump), Truth Social,
Sept. 21, 2022, 10:56 A.M., truthsocial.com/@realDonaldTrump/posts/
109037444657827753.

152 **In 2018, *The Atlantic* cited** Olivia Paschal, "Trump's Tweets and the Creation of 'Illusory Truth,'" *The Atlantic*, Aug. 3, 2018, www.theatlantic.com/
politics/archive/2018/08/how-trumps-witch-hunt-tweets-create-an-illusory
-truth/566693/.

153 **"The receptive powers"** Adolf Hitler, *Mein Kampf*, trans. James Murphy
(London: Hurst and Blackett, 1939), chap. 6.

Chapter 9: How to Land Punches

154 **"When someone is cruel"** "Michelle Obama: 'When They Go Low, We Go
High,'" YouTube video, posted by CNN, Jul. 25, 2016, www.youtube.com/
watch?v=mu_hCThhzWU.

154 **"Going high doesn't mean sitting"** Leila Fadel, "Michelle Obama Opens Up
in Her New Memoir 'The Light We Carry,'" *Morning Edition*, NPR, Nov. 15,
2022, www.npr.org/2022/11/15/1136738650/michelle-obama-opens-up-in
-her-new-memoir-the-light-we-carry.

155 **"I don't care if the scoreboard"** Ro Khanna (@RoKhanna), Twitter, Sept. 29,
2021, 9:12 P.M., twitter.com/RoKhanna/status/1443413313371660289.

156 **Colorado congresswoman Lauren** Sharon Sullivan, "'They Are Putting Litter Boxes in Schools for People Who Identify as Cats,' Says Boebert. 'Not
True,' Responds Durango School District," *Colorado Times Recorder*, Oct. 4,
2022, coloradotimesrecorder.com/2022/10/they-are-putting-litter-boxes
-in-schools-for-people-who-identify-as-cats-says-boebert-not-true-responds
-durango-school-district/49272/.

156 **Unsuccessful Republican gubernatorial** "Scott Jensen Repeats Debunked
Claim About Litter Boxes in Schools," KARE 11, Oct. 4, 2022, www.kare11
.com/article/news/politics/scott-jensen-repeats-false-rumor-about-litter-boxes
-in-schools/89-f3f72174-db76-441b-95a3-9e73f4c239d0.

156 **GOP lawmakers passed** State of Florida, "Text of SB 1438," 2023 Florida
Legislature, April 20, 2023, www.flsenate.gov/Session/Bill/2023/1438/
BillText/er/PDF.

156 **Though the Orlando furry** 2023 Megaplex Convention, "Statement on State
of Florida Legislation," May 24, 2023, megaplexcon.org/node/64.

157 **"The furry thing has nothing"** "Senator: Furry Convention Has 'Nothing to

Do' with Florida Law | On Balance," YouTube video, posted by NewsNation, May 30, 2023, youtu.be/Jn-VPm2f-dA?t=172.

158 **As Florida Republicans nanny-stated** Chris Isidore, "Florida's Homeowner Insurance Rates Are Four Times the National Average. That's Not Getting Better Anytime Soon," CNN, Jun. 1, 2023, www.cnn.com/2023/06/01/business/florida-homeowner-insurance-rates/index.html.

159 **I heard a textbook example** Roger Sollenberger, " 'Pro Life' Herschel Walker Paid for Girlfriend's Abortion," *Daily Beast,* Oct. 3, 2022, www.thedailybeast.com/pro-life-herschel-walker-paid-for-girlfriends-abortion-georgia-senate.

159 **"Why is the Republican Party"** Leila Fadel, "Republicans Continue to Support Herschel Walker Even After Abortion Report," *Morning Edition,* NPR, Oct. 6, 2022, www.npr.org/2022/10/06/1127158931/republicans-continue-to-support-herschel-walker-even-after-abortion-report.

160 **Pence began his response** "Former Vice President Mike Pence on 'Face the Nation with Margaret Brennan' | Full Interview," YouTube video, posted by CBS News, April 23, 2023, youtu.be/VopqYHxa6gY?t=414.

161 **After decades of watching media** Ceekay Tschudi (@beyondabyssal), Twitter, profile, accessed Jun. 16, 2023, twitter.com/beyondabyssal.

162 **That year Abbott** Julia Mueller and Julia Shapero, "Here's Where GOP Governors Have Sent Nearly 13,000 Migrants," *The Hill,* Sept. 19, 2022, thehill.com/homenews/3647988-heres-where-gop-governors-have-sent-nearly-13000-migrants/.

162 **"Let me be clear"** Governor JB Pritzker (@GovPritzker), Twitter, thread, Sept. 14, 2022, 10:09 A.M., twitter.com/GovPritzker/status/1570082242793472000.

163 **A few days earlier** Tina Sfondeles, "Communication Breakdown? Pritzker, Texas Governor Disagree on Who's Ignoring Whom in Immigrant Busing Dispute," *Chicago Sun Times,* Sept. 8, 2022, chicago.suntimes.com/2022/9/8/23343717/pritzker-texas-governor-greg-abbott-lightfoot-immigrant-busing-dispute-border-biden-letter.

165 **"Republican Members of Congress"** Joseph R. Biden, "Statement from President Joe Biden on the Shooting in Allen, Texas," White House, May 7, 2023, www.whitehouse.gov/briefing-room/statements-releases/2023/05/07/statement-from-president-joe-biden-on-the-shooting-in-allen-texas/.

167 *The Republican party now justifies* Jonathan Weisman and Reid J. Epstein, "G.O.P. Declares Jan. 6 Attack 'Legitimate Political Discourse,'" *The New York Times,* Feb. 4, 2022, www.nytimes.com/2022/02/04/us/politics/republicans-jan-6-cheney-censure.html.

Chapter 10: How to Give Wedgies

169 **"All of you at home"** "WATCH: 'We All Apparently Agree' on Saving Medicare and Social Security, Biden Teases at SOTU," YouTube video, posted by *PBS NewsHour,* Feb. 7, 2023, www.youtube.com/watch?v=BKeYcFk3bTQ.

172 **He called his bill** Julie Rovner, " 'Partial-Birth Abortion': Separating Fact

from Spin," NPR, Feb. 21, 2006, www.npr.org/2006/02/21/5168163/partial-birth-abortion-separating-fact-from-spin.

172 **"Partial-birth abortion"** National Right to Life Committee Inc., "The State of Abortion in the United States," Jan. 2022, www.nrlc.org/uploads/communications/stateofabortion2022.pdf.

172 **The Centers for Disease Control** Katherine Kortsmit et al., "Abortion Surveillance—United States, 2020," U.S. Centers for Disease Control and Prevention, Nov. 25, 2022, www.cdc.gov/mmwr/volumes/71/ss/ss7110a1.htm?s_cid=ss7110a1_w.

174 **"The only thing that stops"** "Transcript: Statement by National Rifle Association's Wayne LaPierre, Dec. 21, 2012," Associated Press, Dec. 21, 2012, www.masslive.com/news/2012/12/transcript_statement_by_nation.html.

177 **America has made about** Jennifer Mascia, "How Many Guns Are Circulating in the U.S.?," *The Trace*, Mar. 6, 2023, www.thetrace.org/2023/03/guns-america-data-atf-total/.

178 **But that's exactly what** Republican National Committee, "Republican Platform 2016," 13.

179 **A national survey by the Pew** "2022 Pew Research Center's American Trends Panel," Topline Results of Survey of 6,174 American Adults, Conducted Jun. 27–Jul. 4, 2022, 2, accessed Jun. 16, 2023, www.pewresearch.org/politics/wp-content/uploads/sites/4/2022/07/PP_22.07.05_Roe-v-Wade_TOPLINE.pdf.

179 **According to an April 2023 survey** Fox News Poll, Topline Results of Survey of 1,004 Registered Voters, Conducted Apr. 21–24, 2023, by Beacon Research and Shaw & Company Research, 18, accessed Jun. 16, 2023, static.foxnews.com/foxnews.com/content/uploads/2023/04/Fox_April-21-24-2023_National_Topline_April-27-Release.pdf.

182 **The definitive scientific document** Intergovernmental Panel on Climate Change, *Climate Change 2007: Impacts, Adaptation, and Vulnerability* (New York: Cambridge University Press, 2007), www.ipcc.ch/site/assets/uploads/2018/03/ar4_wg2_full_report.pdf.

182 **"We need cleaner forms of energy"** "Nancy Pelosi and Newt Gingrich Commercial on Climate Change," YouTube video, posted by Nate Allen, Apr. 17, 2008, www.youtube.com/watch?v=qi6n_-wB154.

182 **These corporate-friendly organizations** Catherine Upin and John Hockenberry, "Climate of Doubt," *Frontline*, PBS, video, Oct. 23, 2012, www.pbs.org/wgbh/frontline/documentary/climate-of-doubt/.

182 **"The right response to the non-problem"** U.S. House of Representatives, Committee on Energy and Commerce, "Preparing for Climate Change: Adaptation Policies and Programs," Mar. 25, 2009, 117, 237, www.congress.gov/111/chrg/CHRG-111hhrg67818/CHRG-111hhrg67818.pdf.

183 **Monckton, by the way** Upin and Hockenberry, "Climate of Doubt."

183 **"The explicit goal that was written"** Ibid.

183 **In 2022, more than a full** "The Impact of Extreme Weather on Views About Climate Policy in the United States," T. H. Chan School of Public Health,

Harvard University, Jun. 2022, 15, cdn1.sph.harvard.edu/wp-content/uploads/sites/21/2022/06/Weather_ClimateChangeReport_FINAL.pdf.

185 **George W. Bush made privatizing** William A. Galston, "Why the 2005 Social Security Initiative Failed, and What It Means for the Future," Brookings Institution, Sept. 21, 2007, www.brookings.edu/research/why-the-2005-social-security-initiative-failed-and-what-it-means-for-the-future/.

185 **In 2012, the Wisconsin Republican congressman** Paul N. Van de Water, "Medicare in the Ryan Budget," Center on Budget and Policy Priorities, Mar. 28, 2012, www.cbpp.org/research/medicare-in-the-ryan-budget.

185 **And Republican senator Ron Johnson** Steve Benen, "On Social Security, GOP's Ron Johnson Walks Along the Third Rail," MSNBC, Aug. 22, 2022, www.msnbc.com/rachel-maddow-show/maddowblog/social-security-gops-ron-johnson-walks-third-rail-rcna44177.

187 **According to the Pew Research Center** Kim Parker et al., "Urban, Suburban, and Rural Residents' Views on Key Social and Political Issues," Pew Research Center, May 22, 2018, www.pewresearch.org/social-trends/2018/05/22/urban-suburban-and-rural-residents-views-on-key-social-and-political-issues/.

189 **Turns out Americans love** Ted Van Green, "Americans Overwhelmingly Say Marijuana Should Be Legal for Medical or Recreational Use," Pew Research Center, Nov. 22, 2022, www.pewresearch.org/fact-tank/2022/11/22/americans-overwhelmingly-say-marijuana-should-be-legal-for-medical-or-recreational-use/.

189 **The federal government still** U.S. Drug Enforcement Administration, "Drug Scheduling—Schedule 1," accessed Jun. 16, 2023, www.dea.gov/drug-information/drug-scheduling#.

189 **In a comprehensive survey** Van Green, "Americans Overwhelmingly Say Marijuana Should Be Legal for Medical or Recreational Use."

Chapter 11: The Proof Is in the Pudding

193 **Lake, a former TV personality** Zach Schonfeld, "Kari Lake Calls for Imprisoning Maricopa County Election Officials," *The Hill*, Dec. 8, 2022, thehill.com/homenews/campaign/3780237-kari-lake-calls-for-imprisoning-maricopa-county-election-officials/.

193 **Over the news clips** "Moment of Truth," YouTube video, posted by Katie Hobbs, June 27, 2022.

193 **A few months later** "Katie Hobbs: Kari Lake Is a 'Dangerous' Election Denier," YouTube video, posted by MSNBC, Oct. 12, 2022, www.youtube.com/watch?v=exLtyvrX72w.

194 **"We have a decision to make"** "Democracy Is a Decision," YouTube video, posted by Adrian Fontes, Oct. 12, 2022, www.youtube.com/watch?v=m_FenboRvho.

194 **On Election Day** Arizona Secretary of State, "State of Arizona Official Canvass—2022 General Election," Nov. 8, 2022, azsos.gov/sites/default/files/2022Dec05_General_Election_Canvass_Web.pdf.

194 **If the Court overturned** *Roe* Governor Gretchen Whitmer, "Whitmer Files Lawsuit and Uses Executive Authority to Protect Legal Abortion in Michigan," press release, Apr. 7, 2022, www.michigan.gov/whitmer/news/press -releases/2022/04/07/whitmer-files-lawsuit-and-uses-executive-authority -to-protect-legal-abortion-in-michigan.

195 **She filed motions in court** Governor Gretchen Whitmer, "Whitmer Statement on Michigan Court of Claims Ruling on Abortion," press release, Sept. 7, 2022, www.michigan.gov/whitmer/news/press-releases/2022/09/ 07/whitmer-statement-on-michigan-court-of-claims-ruling-on-abortion.

195 **Whitmer's Republican opponent** Bryan Pietsch, "Top GOP Governor Candidate: Mich. Abortion Ban Should Cover Rape, Incest," *The Washington Post*, Jul. 21, 2022, www.washingtonpost.com/politics/2022/07/21/michigan -republican-tudor-dixon-abortion-ban-rape/.

195 **"Yeah, perfect example"** "Trump's Gal Tudor Dixon Wants to Be Your Gov.—One on One Lunch with Charlie LeDuff Part 1," YouTube video, posted by No BS Newshour, Jul. 18, 2022, youtu.be/wc-xDaKpgXE?t=581.

195 **"Tudor Dixon has now gone"** Michigan Democratic Party, "Breaking: Tudor Dixon Calls Incestual Rape of a Child a 'Perfect Example' of Her Dangerous Plan to Ban Abortion," press release, Jul. 20, 2022, michigandems.com/ breaking-tudor-dixon-calls-incestual-rape-of-a-child-a-perfect-example-of-her -dangerous-plan-to-ban-abortion%EF%BF%BC/.

196 **On Election Day, voters** Michigan Secretary of State Jocelyn Benson, "Michigan Election Results," Nov. 8, 2022, mielections.us/election/results/ 2022GEN_CENR.html.

196 **Despite the Beltway's fawning** Ohio Secretary of State Frank LaRose, "2022 Election Results—Statewide Races Summary," Nov. 8, 2022, www.ohiosos .gov/globalassets/elections/2022/gen/statewide-races-summary.xlsx.

197 **According to Way to Win** Jenifer Fernandez Ancona, "TV Congress: An Analysis of 2022 Midterm Broadcast Media," Way to Win, May 2023, 7.

197 **Ryan's campaign even aired** "Fox News Friends," YouTube video, posted by Tim Ryan for Ohio, Jul. 18, 2022, youtu.be/5vxz2R_VTjA.

197 **"When Obama's trade deal"** "Neighborhood," YouTube video, posted by Tim Ryan for Ohio, Jun. 15, 2022, youtu.be/GuF1ZjpkYZw.

198 **In fact, Democratic House candidates** Ancona, "TV Congress," 5.

198 **GOP candidates running** Ibid.

199 **Demings's campaign did run** Bridget Bowman, "Demings Launches First TV Ad on Abortion in Florida Senate Race," NBC News, Sept. 7, 2022, www .nbcnews.com/meet-the-press/meetthepressblog/demings-launches-first-tv -ad-abortion-florida-senate-race-rcna46576.

199 **"I know something about fighting crime"** "Chief Val Demings | A Crime," YouTube video, posted by Val Demings, Sept. 6, 2022, youtu.be/rBHoxrf ONfo.

199 **And, as Way to Win notes** Ancona, "TV Congress," 4.

199 **Democrats running for Congress** Ibid., 7.

200 **"When talking about jobs"** Ibid., 4.

200 **"You said the economy?"** "Newsom Defends Biden's Presidency: 'Man of

Decency and Character,'" YouTube video, posted by Fox News, June 12, 2023, youtu.be/s5HqxVoKqgU?t=571.

202 **When Oz starred in a poorly** "Dr. Oz Goes Shopping," YouTube video, posted by Lincoln Project, Aug. 16, 2022, www.youtube.com/watch?v=UTR2PVNOGow.

202 **Then, just when it couldn't** Kylie Cheung, "Dr. Oz's Scientific Experiments Killed over 300 Dogs, Entire Litter of Puppies," *Jezebel*, Oct. 3, 2022, jezebel.com/dr-oz-s-scientific-experiments-killed-over-300-dogs-e-1849609272.

202 **Fetterman beat Oz** Pennsylvania Department of State, "2022 General Election Results—Statewide," Nov. 8, 2022, www.electionreturns.pa.gov/General/SummaryResults?ElectionID=94&ElectionType=G&IsActive=0.

202 **Warnock ended up narrowly** Secretary of State Brad Raffensperger, Georgia General Election Runoff Results, Dec. 6, 2022, results.enr.clarityelections.com/GA/116564/web.307039/#/summary.

202 **In a viral speech** "Obama Mocks Herschel Walker's Vampire Remark," YouTube video, posted by CNN, Dec. 2, 2022, www.youtube.com/watch?v=yW3W4J6Sj4A.

203 **More than 1.7 million** Georgia 2022 Runoff Election Results.

203 **"We're in a post-shame world"** Chauncey Devega, "NeverTrumper Rick Wilson on the Midterms: 'Democrats Are About to Pay a Terrible Price,'" *Salon*, Oct. 27, 2022, www.salon.com/2022/10/27/nevertrumper-rick-wilson-on-the-midterms-democrats-are-about-to-pay-a-terrible-price/.

Chapter 12: Voters Are Just Not That into You

209 **No, they won South Florida** Anthony York, "The GOP's Latino Strategy," *Salon*, Jan. 13, 2000, www.salon.com/2000/01/13/latinos/.

213 **Republicans wised up** Andrew Marantz, "The Man Behind Trump's Facebook Juggernaut," *The New Yorker*, Mar. 2, 2020, www.newyorker.com/magazine/2020/03/09/the-man-behind-trumps-facebook-juggernaut.

Conclusion: Democracy, If We Can Keep It

215 **On the evening of October 2** "'Big Trail' Opens at Chinese," *Los Angeles Record*, Oct. 2, 1930, newspapers.com.

215 **According to an account** Rosalind Shaffer, "'The Big Trail' Is a Bit Disappointing," *Commercial Appeal*, Oct. 12, 1930, newspapers.com.

219 **"I think where [Democrats] get into trouble"** "Obama's Advice for Democrats," *Pod Save America*, podcast, Crooked Media, Oct. 15, 2022, crooked.com/podcast/obamas-advice-for-democrats/.

219 **As Benjamin Franklin reportedly said** "To Benjamin Franklin from Thomas Jefferson, [June 21, 1776?]," U.S. National Archives, Founders Online, n1, founders.archives.gov/documents/Franklin/01-22-02-0284.

Index

About the Author

Rachel Bitecofer is a political scientist and election forecaster turned political strategist. Bitecofer's interviews and analyses have been featured by *The New York Times, The Washington Post, Salon, Politico, The New Republic, Real Time with Bill Maher,* CNN, MSNBC, and many other prominent news sources. Bitecofer was recognized for her novel theory that negative partisanship predicted a large "Blue Wave" in the 2018 midterm elections much earlier than other forecasters.

Aaron Murphy is a writer and political strategist who served as chief of staff to U.S. senator Jon Tester (D-Mont.) during the turbulent early years of the Trump administration. A former journalist, he previously served as the senator's communications director and speechwriter. Murphy co-wrote Tester's 2020 memoir, *Grounded: A Senator's Lessons on Winning Back Rural America.*

About the Type

This book was set in Scala, a typeface designed by Martin Majoor in 1991. It was originally designed for a music company in the Netherlands and then was published by the international type house FSI Font-Shop. Its distinctive extended serifs add to the articulation of the letterforms to make it a very readable typeface.